MEN OF MARK

MAKERS OF
EAST MIDLAND ALLIED PRESS

By

DAVID NEWTON
(Joined EMAP 1933)

EAST MIDLAND ALLIED PRESS LIMITED
PETERBOROUGH

First published 1977
© 1977 by EAST MIDLAND ALLIED PRESS
ISBN 0 9505954 0 3

Photoset by West Suffolk Newspapers Ltd
Bury St Edmunds, Suffolk.

Printed and bound by Weatherby Woolnough
Wellingborough, Northamptonshire

FOREWORD

by R. P. WINFREY M.A., LL.B.
Founder in 1947 of East Midland Allied Press
Son of Sir Richard Winfrey (1858-1944)

Publication of this factual record of the development of East Midland Allied Press from one small weekly newspaper in rural Lincolnshire satisfies a long-held personal wish to share the story with my colleagues and friends, especially those of a younger generation. I am particularly glad that opportunity has been taken to recall some of the achievements — both in business and public life — of my father, the late Sir Richard Winfrey, whose example has been a constant spur and without whose early initiatives there would have been no story to tell. For almost a hundred years of newspaper endeavour the Winfrey family have been remarkably fortunate in the support given by those who have shared the work at all levels, and as my own career closes I look back with gratitude for all we have been able to accomplish together.

The Press can play a decisive part in preserving so many of the healthy privileges that our forebears fought to gain for us, and it is my hope that the East Midland Allied Press Group will never cease to bear the torch aloft through whatever clouds may overshadow the path. "Much yet remains to be done," wrote Sir Richard Winfrey towards the end of his busy life. "If you have a clear conscience that what you do is from a deep sense of duty to your fellow creatures — that is enough. In public life a clear conscience and a thick skin will carry you through."

To read this book is to catch something of his meaning and to take note of his example. Should some far-off unhappy event ever write Finis to the EMAP story, we can deserve no better epitaph than this. Meanwhile, his words should remain our motto.

It has been my privilege to watch David Newton, over several years, preparing the manuscript of this book, and I have greatly admired his patient and painstaking researches. He has interviewed many individuals and sifted through a vast amount of material, some of which has not been easy to trace. He has written and presented this material with a sympathetic understanding which is typical of him. The result is an admirable and accurate account for which he deserves our congratulations and our thanks, and to these I add assurances of my own personal gratitude and continuing regard.

CONTENTS

PICTURE PAGES
In three sections

MEN OF MARK
Makers of East Midland Allied Press

"ONE cannot properly realise the real
significance of the present without a proper
knowledge of the past, placed in rational
and intelligent perspective with an
anticipation of the future course of events."

Sir Richard Winfrey

23 November 1913

PART I   LAYING THE FOUNDATIONS —
THE VICTORIAN AGE TO WORLD WAR II

Introduction

THIS book about newspapers and men who ran them describes the origins and growth of the East Midland Allied Press Group of provincial and national publications, one of Britain's most progressive and still independent enterprises in the newspaper field. What brought this Group together? Who were the men of mark whose efforts made its founding possible?

Part I identifies the opportunities and ideals which led to control of a succession of journals in Eastern England by the Winfrey family of Peterborough and their like-minded friends. Dominating the scene is the late Sir Richard Winfrey, father figure whose influence from Victorian times to World War II is inseparable from the record and whose contribution to politics and public affairs — briefly touched on here — is its essential background.

Part II, concerned with those who followed him and built on the foundations he laid, brings the EMAP story up-to-date, with a third Winfrey generation meeting the challenges of today and tomorrow.

SIR RICHARD WINFREY: CHRONOLOGY

1858 Born at Long Sutton, Lincolnshire, August 5th.
1873 Apprenticed to Mr Rees, Stamford chemist.
1877 Assistant to Mr John Newcome, Grantham chemist.
1880 To London to prepare for pharmaceutical examinations.
1881 Joined John Bell & Co, Oxford Street chemists.
1885 Left Bell's to help Halley Stewart in Spalding election.
1887 Purchased *Spalding Guardian*.
1889 Elected vice-chairman of the first Holland County Council.
1890 Started *North Cambs Echo*, Wisbech.
1893 Purchased *Lynn News*.
1894 Death of father, Richard Francis Winfrey, May 23rd.
1895 Elected chairman of Long Sutton's first urban council.
     Lincolnshire Small Holdings Association formed.
     Defeated in South-West Norfolk Parliamentary election.
1896 Appointed managing director, Peterborough Advertiser Co.
1897 Married and moved to Sutton House, Peterborough.
1898 Purchased two London papers, *The Morning* and the *Echo*.
     Started *Peterborough Mid-Weekly Advertiser*, later *The Citizen*.
     Elected to Peterborough City Council.
     Daughter born, Ellen, September 8th.
1899 Norfolk Small Holdings Association formed.
1900 Defeated in South-West Norfolk Parliamentary election.
     Daughter born, Lucy, December 23rd.
1901 Appointed managing director of Northamptonshire Printing and Publishing Co.

1902 Built house, Flaxwell, at Hunstanton.
      Son born, Richard, June 24th.
1903 Appointed managing director of Bury St Edmunds
      Printing and Publishing Co.
1904 Elected to the Soke of Peterborough County Council.
1906 Daughter born, Ruth, September 14th.
      Elected to Parliament for South-West Norfolk.
1910 Re-elected for South-West Norfolk, January.
      Re-elected for South-West Norfolk, November.
1913 Elected Mayor of Peterborough.
1914 Awarded knighthood in New Year Honours.
      Read Riot Act in Peterborough streets.
1916 Appointed Parliamentary Secretary to the President,
      Board of Agriculture, in Lloyd George's war-time
      Government.
1917 Death of mother, October 31st.
1918 Re-elected for South-West Norfolk.
1919 Purchased Castor House.
      Resigned from Soke of Peterborough County Council.
1920 Resigned from Peterborough City Council.
1922 Re-elected for South-West Norfolk.
      Amalgamated *Lynn News* and *Lynn Advertiser*.
      Purchased *Suffolk Free Press*.
1923 Elected to Parliament for Gainsborough, Lincoln-
      shire.
1924 Defeated at Gainsborough.
1925 Purchased *Boston Guardian*.
1929 Son, R. P. Winfrey, married in Ireland, April 2nd.
1931 Grandson born, Richard John Winfrey.
1933 Seventy-fifth birthday: staff garden party at Castor
      House.
1934 Completed Castor memorial homes.
      Grandson born, Francis Charles Winfrey.
1935 Sold *Boston Guardian* and *Spalding Guardian* to
      Westminster Press Group.
1944 Death at Castor House, April 18th.
      Funeral service at Park Road Baptist church, Peter-
      borough, April 21st.

1. THE NEWSPAPER DREAM

THREE generations of Winfreys have helped make East Midland Allied Press what it is today. Independent newspaper companies in Eastern England controlled by Sir Richard Winfrey were formally grouped together after his death during World War II by his son, R. P. Winfrey, chairman till 1973. The latter expanded the Group's activities and paved the way for the third generation to carry on in the person of his sons, Richard John Winfrey and Francis Charles Winfrey. Meanwhile, a fourth generation is growing up to ensure a continuing link. Yet it was an accident, a political accident, which brought Sir Richard into newspapers. Sound and successful though he was as journalist and publisher, it was politics that dominated his life. He learned his politics at grass roots level. They revealed him as one of the remarkable characters of the day, abused by many, admired by more. They led him from the countryside of his forebears to the corridors of power.

When he was born, on 5 August 1858, in the little town of Long Sutton on the Lincolnshire edge of the Wash, Queen Victoria had been on the throne for 21 years. His grandfather Richard, who was 85 when he died in 1873, was regarded over the whole district as "a man of mark" and so described in newspaper reports of his death. His second son, Richard Francis (father of Sir Richard Winfrey) turned from his father's Toryism and Church to Liberalism and Dissent, influenced no doubt by the quiet piety of his Baptist mother. RFW was among county growers who discovered a good market for Fenland potatoes in London and was working hard for Liberalism long before Long Sutton formed its own Liberal Association in the 1880's with him as president. Richard Francis made no secret of his views and had little time for Liberals of the weak-kneed and covert sort. He was a devoted and lifelong Congregationalist, austere but genuine, of striking appearance and marked integrity. When men raised their caps as he rode round the parish they were paying unconscious tribute to the Victorian virtues — Sunday observance, a Bible-based moral code, a political faith aimed at helping the underdog, strenuous self-exertion, honest business success, and discreet benevolence.

As a boy of ten young Richard helped Liberalism in the 1868 general election by riding his father's mare Kitty round Long Sutton with a placard on his back: "Vote for Packe." He went with his father to the Corn Exchange to vote — it was the last election before the secret ballot was introduced — and the poll book shows that whilst Richard Francis voted Liberal his father and brother voted Tory. Sir Richard had moral courage of a high order. Right to the end he never hesitated to swim against the tide when necessary and to the last it was his father's loyalty to conviction which helped to inspire him.

While studying in London — he passed the Pharmaceutical Society's Minor examination in December 1879 and the Major in April 1880 at the earliest times possible — Richard could be found every Sunday listening to the great preachers, such men as C. H. Spurgeon at the original Spurgeon's Tabernacle, Dr Parker at the City Temple, Guinness Rogers at Clapham Park, and Henry Simon at Westminster Chapel, who had stayed in his father's home. To this kindly man Richard owed many a Sunday meal and many a searching talk about the Christian faith which left a permanent mark. He was uncle to the young lawyer who became Sir John Simon, leader of the Liberal National Party in the 1930s and later Viscount Simon, Lord Chancellor during World War II. He also had his share of fun in the 1880 general election. Gripped by hero worship of Gladstone, Prime Minister for the second time and at the height of his fame, Richard offered his youthful help to Lawrence and

McArthur, City Aldermen who won both Liberal seats at Lambeth. Using a ticket for the Strangers' Gallery from McArthur, Richard paid his first visit to the House of Commons and sat through a four-hour display of Gladstone's oratory.

As an outstanding student, Richard Winfrey was quickly invited to join the staff of John Bell & Company, the historic and exclusive pharmacy founded in Oxford Street in 1798 and a leader in the pharmaceutical profession. This kept him in London, with spare time given to visiting the House of Commons and to speaking in the Parliamentary Debating Society which met over the St James's Restaurant in Piccadilly. With his father as chairman, he made his first public political speech in Long Sutton in the summer of 1885. It was the day when Richard the Pharmacist died and Richard the Politician was born, for he soon left Bell's to become honorary election agent working for the return of Halley Stewart, Spalding Division Liberal candidate in that year's general election.

In Stewart — Congregational pastor and Liberal apostle who went on to make fortunes in milling and in bricks, founded the Sir Halley Stewart Trust[1] and died in his 100th year in 1937 — three generations of the Winfrey family were to find a loyal and generous friend. In 1885 he missed victory by only 78 votes. He was defeated again in July 1886, by which time young Winfrey had already acquired a reputation as a campaign organiser. His reply to a Liberal presentation to honour his "energetic and intelligent efforts to educate politically the inhabitants of the division" expresses his approach in those tough times. Abuse, vituperation, misrepresentation? He took them as compliments from his opponents. Wealth, title, the influence of squires, parsons and lawyers flowing full-tide against him? He knew their tricks. Organisation? He challenged the division to make full use of the Party machinery he had perfected. Political equality? A man earning his daily bread honestly, even though living in the humblest cottage, must be as politically

[1] *Sir Halley Stewart, Preacher, Politician, Businessman, Benefactor*, published for the Trust by Allen & Unwin in 1968, has many references to the Winfreys.

3

important — as man and Englishman — as the greatest nobleman living on the industry of others. Voting? His creed called for one man one vote; for elections everywhere on the same day; for reliable electoral lists; for cutting costs so that the calibre of candidates could be based on worth, not wealth, on men, not money.

With the 1886 election over Richard knew his days as full-time unsalaried servant of the Liberal Party must soon end. He was 28, with excellent prospects in his profession, yet in the end he horrified his father by throwing them over for what seemed a wild dream. Richard, the Pharmacist-turned-Politician became Richard the Newspaper Owner. Gladstone had a soft spot for provincial papers. He believed there could be no political maturity for the working classes without a cheap Press, and new journals had been taking the field since he abolished the duty on paper in 1861, completing the freedom gained in 1853 from the advertisement tax and in 1855 from stamp duty. In his election campaigns Richard had seen at close quarters the power of the local Press to encourage one side or frighten the other.

At Boston, where Joseph Cooke ran the *Guardian*, they called him the "Newspaper King". Richard knew him not only as editor to whom he sent reports but as a Liberal who spoke on the same platforms. He had started from scratch as impecunious apprentice and seven years later was successfully operating as newspaper owner. Cooke bought the *Boston Guardian* in 1880, having trained on the paper and returned to it as manager. He started other editions — the *Spalding Guardian* 1882, the *Grantham Times* 1884 to support Sir Arthur Priestley and the *Louth Times* for Sir Robert Perks, both Liberal M.P.s. He was concerned in the *Retford Herald* and bigger ventures lay ahead. A glutton for work, he made it all pay handsomely enough to retire in comfort at 50. He offered to train Richard in newspaper management at the *Boston Guardian* office, to sell him the copyright of the *Spalding Guardian* (which had its own office in Spalding) and to continue printing it at Boston on contract. But so miserable was the revenue from advertising and printing that Halley Stewart warned Richard against paying £250

4

and it finally changed hands at a nominal figure nearer £100.

Richard went into lodgings at Spalding and began life as a newspaper proprietor in April 1887. The *Guardian's* eight pages came out on Saturday for a penny. With only one senior and an office boy to help him, Richard tore round fixing up extra agents and influencing advertising; he sat up into the night writing reports and notes; he kept the books; he sometimes swept out the office in disgust at the way other people did it; to through pages put in at Boston carrying a London Letter, serial story, home hints, farm notes and funny anecdotes he added his own personal column. He attacked the opposition *Spalding Free Press* (out on Mondays) for unbalanced reporting and castigated his political opponents.

Printing staff at Boston sometimes annoyed him on press days by setting Boston type before his own. He saw the papers off the press, helped pack agents' parcels, lent a hand loading them into hampers, and often bore the indignity of wild last-minute rushes with barrows through the streets to catch the Spalding train. Many a time he was pushed through the carriage door to sprawl on top of the hampers as the train moved off. Gallantly, his father saddled up and personally helped in distribution beyond Long Sutton by horse. On April 16th, his second issue, he promised to start a series of competitions — the first Lincolnshire editor to do so [1]. They would fill in a lazy hour after work and defeat Satan looking for idle hands, he announced, and the first invited readers to name the best preachers and orators in the district. Another was to identify literary quotations; another, to predict the attendance at the agricultural show; yet another, to forecast the voting figures and size of majority in the Spalding by-election.

For by-election there was! Instead of quiet years in which to build up his new business, Richard found himself, three months after settling at Spalding, plunged into campaign work as divisional agent. He had at once gone up to London to persuade Arnold Morley M.P., Liberal Whip, and Francis

[1] The *Spalding Free Press* soon copied the idea, starting a series of guessing competitions in June.

5

Schnadhorst, secretary of the National Liberal Party Federation and chief organiser of the party, that Spalding Liberals intended to have Stewart as their candidate rather than any ex-Cabinet Ministers and VIP Liberals unseated at the previous election. He won his point and the organisation he had perfected, better understanding of Gladstone's Home Rule policy for Ireland, and promises to fight for land for the labourer, combined to win the seat for Stewart by 747 votes.

For the first time Lincolnshire had returned a Liberal M.P. in a contested election. It was the beginning of a run of victories, "the pivot on which all England would turn" as John O'Connor M.P. put it. *The Times*, surprised by the result, gave some credit to the "separatist Press" in the division (the *Spalding Guardian* came out twice weekly during the campaign). Gladstone took fresh heart. Ireland's hopes rose once more. Lincolnshire's landed gentry, having expected a walkover for Rear Admiral Sir George Tryon of Bulwick Park, were aghast. So was the editor of the *Spalding Free Press*, who had already set up a "triumphant Tryon" edition. To Lord Randolph Churchill the lesson of Spalding was clear and Richard had taught him it — the Tories must realise their own need of "energetic organisation and untiring labour among the masses." For 50 years onwards from 1887 the name of Winfrey was to be familiar in the records of the Liberal Party. As for Morley and Schnadhorst, they invited Richard's help in nearly every by-election that followed till he stood for Parliament himself in 1894.

2. A CHAMPION EMERGES

WHILE Stewart was being cheered and welcomed in the House of Commons after the poll on 1 July 1887, Richard was busy clearing up after a fantastic month. Apart from his swift, compressed campaign as agent, the *Guardian* itself entailed double work, complicated by Queen Victoria's Golden Jubilee on June 21st sparking off a round of celebrations — including a salvo fired over the Wash by duck guns! Ridlington, his one senior assistant — he had previously run the *Guardian* for Cooke — was a tower of strength, among the wonders he performed being a series of mock elections at village meetings to teach the labourers how the ballot worked.

The *Guardian* began to be a paying concern — within two years the circulation doubled — and Richard's father conceded that the newspaper dream was perhaps not so wild after all. To Richard himself there was nothing dreamy about the dream. He knew by now that he was born a fighter. There was nothing soft about wringing a living out of a little country newspaper, yet he would not only do this but make it razor-sharp to cut through sham and expose vested interest. He would work for the underdog, fight the folk who blocked the path to progress and, because he was a fighter, he would make fighting his life. He was hard-headed, far-sighted, ardent, ambitious, capable, sincere. He saw beyond wounds to victory. He knew that honeyed speech and soft manners were no weapons against the privileged Haves. To help the Have-nots he would attack them in the daylight, challenge them in fair fight, make fun of their foolishness, battle against them for his beliefs, shoot them down with brusque broadsides of hard fact, confront them with cussed refusals to be browbeaten.

How could such a character avoid collisions in public life? As occasion demanded he could be winningly frank or abrasively curt. Life was to see him best his critics by being always a jump ahead — and take puckish delight in their dismay. In family life he would be sometimes more than difficult to live with. In the newspaper offices he was to rule he would be second only to God. His manner could be withering, his look a sword-thrust. But he was no sour and bitter struggler in a joyless class campaign. He was straightforward and open. His course was clear. Men knew where they stood with him. Between him and his staffs trifling was unthinkable, yet many proved him to be solicitous, confiding, endearing. If he revelled in the rough and tumble of politics he also loved the healthy pleasures of any other country gentleman. He was to be one of the father figures of the Eastern Counties and to be rich in the unbought loyalty and respect of the people whose champion he had become.

At Spalding, Richard was the first to get about on one of the new safety bicycles which had two wheels the same size instead of one large and one small. He cycled well over 700 miles in 1887 and again in 1888, when he won first prize in the Bank Holiday sports cycle race against other competitors on old machines with 52-inch wheels. In the clapping crowd, over for the day from Ruskington, were Harry Millhouse, an old pal from London chemist days, and Harry's friends the Pattinson girls — a merry party for Richard to entertain in his lodgings.

To a farm worker earning twelve shillings a week or less, a plot of land for his spare time or a holding where he could work for himself was as good as winning the pools today. He could rarely afford meat, he sent his children to bed supperless unless he found a stray swede, and in illness and old age had to rely on parish relief. When county councils were first formed in 1888/89, Richard won for the Liberals 22 out of Holland's 42 seats with "Land for the People" as his campaign motto, and as chairman of the county allotments committee put Holland's progress far ahead of other counties. "With a newspaper behind me I was able to make things hum," he said, but the movement to put men full-time on smallholdings was yet to get under way.

Before 1889 ended, Richard Winfrey was invited to be election agent to the Hon Arthur Brand in the adjoining Isle of Ely Division of Wisbech but felt lost without a newspaper of his own. So he and Brand started one, produced at King's Lynn as an edition of the *Lynn News* then controlled by Jeremiah James Colman of Norwich. At sixty, Colman had become almost a legend, not as mustard maker to the world but for political work. Six times Norwich sent him to Westminster and he sat for 24 years without a break as city Member. To the moneyed and easy-going 1970's, with privilege so common that it loses meaning, the efforts and ideals of men like Colman and Richard Francis Winfrey may seem almost quaint. But from them flowed what history calls the Nonconformist conscience which swept the Liberal Party — and Richard with it — to the peak of power.

When Richard Francis was born, births could be registered only on baptism in the parish church. Men had to take Communion regularly as members of the Church of England to qualify for any office under the Crown or a municipal corporation. Whether they liked it or not they could marry only in parish churches and be buried only according to the Anglican prayer book. They could attend and pay for a Nonconformist chapel but were still compelled to pay a rate to repair the parish church. As Dissenters they were kept off many boards of governors and their sons out of the universities. For the record, Gladstone won Parliamentary battles to end the compulsory church rate from 1868, to abolish religious tests in the universities from 1871, and to allow Nonconformist ministers to officiate in parish graveyards from 1880. But it was the mood of men like Richard's father, whose goods were seized and sold on Spalding market place because he refused to pay church rates — which made these freedoms possible.

Colman had needed a newspaper to back his work in Norwich for these and other reforms and in 1845 joined with J. H. Tillett and John Copeman in bringing out the *Norfolk*

News as a weekly devoted to "civic, religious and commercial freedom". He was behind the *Eastern Daily Press* when it started in 1870 and in 1887 took over the *Lynn News*. It was natural that in 1890 he should welcome Winfrey and Brand as young comrades-in-arms.

Richard, however, fretted at trying to edit a paper in another man's printing works. To start it he had taken the *Wisbech Chronicle,* an existing companion to the *Lynn News,* and from February 1890 pushed it throughout the Wisbech Division as Mr Brand's Liberal organ under a new title, the *North Cambridgeshire Echo.* It helped get him into Parliament in July 1891 with 260 votes in hand compared with the previous Tory majority of more than a thousand. In the fight Richard found a new kind of help in Mrs Brand, whose singing at political meetings in the Fens that summer was the most talked-of angle of the campaign. Mr and Mrs John Clarke, staunch Conservatives farming between Wisbech and Long Sutton, even named their new baby Edith after her. Years later, Edith Clarke joined the Winfrey household at Castor and remained as parlourmaid for fourteen years, surviving both Sir Richard and his lady and staying on in one of the Winfrey retirement homes. On her death in April 1973 she left the bulk of her £17,000 estate to medical and other charities.

To solve the King's Lynn problem Richard and Arthur Brand asked Colman if he would sell out. Colman agreed and in 1893 a new company was formed with Alfred Jermyn, one of Lynn's most energetic Liberal businessmen, as chairman and Cooke of Boston as first managing director. They survived the defection of Achilles Sylvester Page, editor of the *Lynn News,* to the chair of the strongly-entrenched Tory *Lynn Advertiser,* shut down an unprofitable stationery sideline, and streamlined production in premises built to their own design hard by the picturesque 17th century Customs House on the tidal Ouse. Here the company operated until moving to other premises in 1975.

To help supply the *North Cambs Echo* and the *Spalding Guardian* with a constant stream of leading articles, notes and political news, Richard made great use of an admirable person named John Derry. A schoolmaster who moved from London to Bourne, near Spalding, he had confided his longing to be a journalist to Cooke when they met at an election meeting in 1880 and Cooke started him off on the *Boston Guardian*, then moved him to the *Grantham Times* as editor. Richard was so drawn to him that John and his talented wife left Grantham to share Richard's house in Spalding but the Derrys left when John was invited — probably through Arthur Brand's instigation — to edit the *Nottingham Daily Express* controlled by Arnold Morley, Liberal Chief Whip. At Nottingham, Richard one day met Derry's latest protege, a poor pale lad who went on to achieve fame as Arthur Mee of the *Children's Newspaper*, the *Children's Encyclopaedia* and 37 county volumes in The King's England series.

When Derry moved to the *Sheffield Independent* in 1895 he found Frank Ridlington already there. After nursing the *Spalding Guardian* from infancy he had turned to city life and in 1891 Richard found a new editor in John Harber Diggle, son of a nearby farmer. Reporting his chief's activities on Holland County Council (he was chairman of its first Small Holdings committee in 1893) Diggle found that Richard had pushed his committee to a standstill — they declined to vote for any more land for labourers! Richard's answer was to form a syndicate of helpful Liberals including Halley Stewart to acquire land privately and John Diggle was given an extra job as part-time steward of the holdings they began to let. By 1895, Diggle was full-time steward of the South Lincolnshire Small Holdings Association, and teaching his teenage brother Tom, barely out of school, to hold the ropes at the *Spalding Guardian* office. Niggles over production of the paper in the Boston works were ended by printing it in the new office at Lynn.

Just before this Richard made particular use of the *Guardian* in fighting legal battles over a footpath. When Sutton Bridge labourers were told to stop crossing farmland which saved them a three-mile tramp to work, he backed their claim but the local Bench declined to adjudicate. The *Guardian* ran an appeal fund and with this behind him he carried the case to the High Court. In June 1891 he took twenty witnesses to the London hearing to prove that the footpath had been a boon to working men for more than fifty years, only to be floored by a legal technicality. To his chagrin the labourers were therefore forced to go on plodding home by the wearier way but determination deepened to take their part.

Richard came back from his 1893 trip to Chicago and the Rockies to find a surprise invitation to stand for Parliament in the South-West division of Norfolk. Behind it was Henry Lee Warner, member of an old county family and brother of Sir William Lee Warner of the India office. Lee Warner, who had retired from Rugby School to live at Swaffham, had a regular visitor there in Joseph Chamberlain's elder son Austen, an old pupil. He had been defeated as Liberal candidate in the division, which adjoined the Wisbech division, and the two men had met at election meetings. Lee Warner saw that Richard had something more vital than the moneybags of wealthier aspirants — a grip of principle and guts to push it. He gave Richard the run of his home and backed him all the time all the way through seven successive elections.[1]

So at 35, with the blessing of Halley Stewart and Arthur Brand, the new candidate borrowed a young mare from his father and for a month that autumn rode round his vast rural constituency from stables in Thetford. His literature included leaflets headed "What a thousand Lincolnshire men say of Alderman Winfrey". The original manuscript, exhibited in Swaffham, carried 1,008 signatures of men who knew that because of Richard, more land had been freed in their area for the working man than anywhere else in the country. If returned, he could do the same for Norfolk.

Meanwhile Richard was behind moves in Holland Standing Joint committee to make the Tory-Liberal balance more even among county magistrates and in April 1894 saw his father's name in the list of new justices. However, Richard Francis sat on the Bench only twice, for in May his health worsened and he died on May 23rd after a three-day illness,

---

[1] Lee Warner was 83 when he died in November 1925, the year after Sir Richard Winfrey retired from Parliament.

in his 69th year. The chestnut mare Kitty, favourite mount for a quarter-century, drew the coffin to the churchyard where men from the Winfrey farm bore it to the grave. Although it was a Saturday afternoon, Long Sutton people closed all their shops and crowded overflowingly into the chapel to which in life he had always given first place.

Richard lived with his mother for a time while he looked after the farm and his father's affairs and this meant cutting down his Norfolk activities. In his first election battle in South-West Norfolk in 1895 he was nearer victory than either Stewart or Brand at Spalding and Wisbech, attracting 3,762 votes against 3,968 for Sir Thomas Hare, who had earlier defeated Lee Warner. He had the artillery of the *Lynn News* to counter the big guns of the *Lynn Advertiser* but the contest was so unexpected that he had gone off early in June to Italy on one of the first educational tours organised by Dr (later Sir) Henry Lunn, an ex-missionary and son of a Liberal-Methodist chemist known to Richard in Horncastle. He became a lifelong friend and patron of Sir Henry Lunn, whose early idea of the organised tour has evolved into the immense package-holiday industry today. But as Lunn started them, trips were either boldly educational or linked with religious conferences.

Two troublesome libel actions were further election year diversions. Harry Pollock, who beat Halley Stewart at Spalding, was a City financier and solicitor involved in certain transactions which Halley and Richard exposed. Pollock's writ for libel and threats of others failed to silence them but on winning the seat he did not proceed with it. For four months Richard baited him with barbed paragraphs in the *Guardian* and on 23 November 1895 wrote: "If you and your election agents could have ruined me you would have done so. You have dropped your writs because I have been more than a match for you and your legal advisers . . . Directly I got the writ I investigated the matter and I snapped my fingers in your face and challenged you to go before a jury . . ." Failing to rouse a response, in December he obtained an order against Pollock in the Queen's Bench Division for all his costs.

13

Pollock had been in the Queen's Bench courtroom when Richard's other action reached its climax in August. It was not only a complicated affair but a glaring example of the way political opponents tried to squash this seemingly unconquerable Winfrey. It started with the Liberal Acts of Parliament of 1894 which set up urban, rural and parish councils to operate from January 1895. In the autumn of 1894 Richard went to a London conference on the working of the Parish Councils Act and started a series of articles in the *Guardian* on election procedure, parish powers and the conduct of parish meetings.

At Long Sutton, Richard headed the poll and became chairman when the first urban council was elected, six of its nine members being Liberals. He ran into difficulty, however, over elections for other councils after volunteering to act in place of a returning officer who had rejected revised fees for the duty. Attempts by a defeated candidate to fault Richard's conduct in this unusual situation eventually led to the July Assizes at Lincoln where the judge wearied of two days of "a wretched business at best" before adjourning for legal argument in chambers. "Whether it will have the effect of driving Mr Winfrey from public life in his district for a season remains to be seen but the object of all these actions and threatened actions can only be too obvious" was the *Spalding Guardian* comment. At the Queen's Bench finale the judge ruled that he had not exceeded the ordinary rights of citizenship and allowed the matter to drop, each party paying their own costs. Richard had pressed the case right to the end and now that all suggestion of any sort of corruption had been withdrawn he was satisfied. Expenses were heavy, but every penny was met for him from a public subscription got up by friends in the Spalding division.

3. MARRIAGE AND A MOVE

HARRY MILLHOUSE, Richard Winfrey's pharmacy friend who had taken a partnership in Kingsford & Company, Piccadilly chemists, hailed from Heckington, near Sleaford. Richard's acquaintance with the Pattinsons — in the same area at Ruskington — started when he spent a holiday from Bell's at Harry's home, and the friends vied with one another in honouring Annie Lucy Pattinson as queen among several daughters. Before long they realised they both wanted her, a dilemma settled by spinning a coin. The toss went against Richard but he maintained friendship with both and was best man when Millhouse and Annie Lucy were married at Ruskington in September 1890. This marriage ended with Harry's death in January 1896. There were no children and she was left with independent means, setting up her own home at Sleaford. Richard continued the association and they became engaged in the autumn of 1896, when he took a stable locally and spent the weekends hunting and courting.

Richard was now 38, and at 30 Annie Lucy was a gay and gifted woman. There were ten children in the Pattinson home at Ruskington — three sons and seven daughters, of whom she was the third — with William Pattinson at its head. His family were connected with the Pattinsons who for 400 years have been building in Lakeland slate and stone and who developed Windermere as a resort in late Victorian times. By virtue of their ownership of land in the village, the Ruskington Pattinsons had for several generations been lay chancellors of the parish church where the chancel screen commemorates William Pattinson's death in 1906. William

15

and his brother Samuel had made their mark as railway and general contractors and a string of stations kept them busy as railway networks were laid down. At Liverpool they built the world's largest grain warehouse. In London, the Grafton Galleries and parts of the great Gothic railway terminus at St Pancras were theirs, and at Wisbech the elegant and lofty memorial to William Clarkson, slave emancipator. William was a leading Lincolnshire Liberal and in time two of his sons, Robert (later knighted) and Samuel, contested Liberal seats in the county, in the Grantham-Sleaford and the Horncastle divisions. In 1923 they were both returned and so shared Richard's final session in the Commons.

Annie was no shrinking violet but a figure in her own right and certainly not abashed by Richard's demanding ways. Many were to bless her for pouring oil on waters troubled by Winfrey winds, and well Richard knew it. Years later he put it this way: "She has stuck to me through thick and thin on all necessary occasions. I recognise that she is vastly more popular than I am, and my advice to young men going into public life is to get hold of the right sort of wife." [1] And this is what Annie herself said in 1912: "I say without fear of contradiction by men that no man can put a case so well as a fully prepared educated woman." These two forthright folk were married in Ruskington village church on Tuesday 23 March 1897, with Anthony Mundella, Lobby writer for the *Manchester Guardian*, as best man. Four hundred and sixty-six allotment holders in the Spalding area chose the occasion to present Alderman Winfrey with a silver salver to mark "the great services rendered by him to the working classes of South Lincolnshire." For a month the couple honeymooned along the Riviera and into Italy before re-entering the fray — but the fight was now to be in a fresh field.

At the time he became engaged Richard added two cathedral cities to his newspaper sphere, Lincoln and Peterborough. Conservatives ran all the journals in Lincoln and had just bought the only one that leaned towards Radicalism. Five Liberals in the city, including Thomas Wal-

[1] Speech at end of year as Mayor of Peterborough, November 1914.

lis the current Mayor, agreed to form the Lincolnshire Press company and launch a new paper, helped by Joseph Cooke, then doing well with extra interests in Sheffield and Doncaster, and by Richard as director in charge. The *Lincoln Leader & County Advertiser* (eight pages for a penny) came out for the first time on 31 October 1896.

Cooke printed it and brought W. E. Dowding from the *Boston Guardian* to edit it, which he did from a room in the Liberal Club until new premises were opened in St Benedict Square. Said the Leader: "Our tone will be that of a bold outspoken thorough Radicalism. The men who own the paper have succeeded elsewhere in building up journals not only commercially prosperous but fulfilling the higher aims of energising public life and securing the political and moral advancement of the masses . . ." Readers took shares in the new company towards its £15,000 capital but financially the venture proved an uphill job. Ten years were to pass before it paid a dividend and in 1910 Richard, with irons in other fires, sold out his interest. Though he and his friends had turned it into a paying concern they never realised their goal of starting an evening paper.[1]

Far different was the Peterborough story. Here the *Advertiser,* doing as well for the Liberal cause as for its founder Joseph Slatterie Clarke, was in the market. After 42 years and with a retirement home in the Isle of Wight, Clarke disposed of this valuable weekly not to his staff (as fully expected) but to George and Arthur Keeble, local Liberals and company directors who asked Richard to help them float a new *Peterborough Advertiser* company. George Keeble came in with Jesse Adnitt as chairman and John T. Miller, two leading Peterborough Liberal businessmen; Richard brought in William M. Boulton, a Wisbech Liberal stalwart, and William H. Lead, a printer friend from Leicester. H. B. Hartley, rising young lawyer and Liberal firebrand who had helped in the Wisbech division, was secretary; and John Diggle did the auditing till Smart and then his young partner Joseph Stephenson took over. The Keebles

[1] The *Leader* ran to December 1929 and merged with the *Lincolnshire Chronicle* in January 1930. After World War II it became a Westminster Press newspaper and is now in the *Lincolnshire Standard* Group.

were paid out to the tune of £10,000 cash and £3,000 shares. There would, however, be only one boss and there would be no repetition of the friction that had irked Richard in other offices. Alexander Peckover, Liberal banker at Wisbech, helped put him in the controlling position by enabling him to subscribe more than half the capital of the new company. He knew Richard's situation. He knew Richard's indispensable help to Arthur Brand. He knew Richard's father. "I know," he said, "that a Winfrey will not let me down."

Richard decided to live in Peterborough, then a place of 25,000 people. The *Advertiser* was a fine paper, solidly founded, loyally staffed and devotedly read. The company became his pet, its management his pride. He kept its dividends modest, its equipment up-to-date. His private papers were found to include a simple personally-maintained analysis of its financial condition for every year from 1900 to 1942, all crowded on to three cards covered with his own bold handwriting. He began to exploit its potential on settling in Peterborough in May 1897. From John Lound, leading Congregationalist, he took lease of a roomy house with grounds close to where the hospital now stands and at once called it Sutton House. Lound added stables for Richard's hunter from Sleaford and also for Kitty III, a mare of his father's breeding. This was used in the dog cart, a Winfrey family present which *Advertiser* staff used on press days for distributing papers and which also went in the light landau bought for Mrs Winfrey.

Richard was to become one of the most constant followers of the Fitzwilliam Hounds, proud to claim that he was never without a horse for hunting bred from the line started at Long Sutton by his father with Kitty I, the old mare which Richard first rode when he was eight. At Peterborough he rode and drove Kitty III till she was 23, and from her bred Jack, Jill and Kitty IV, the latter producing Peter as the fifth generation in direct descent for him to ride. Of them all no horse was so perfect a hunter, so coveted in the field and so loved by its master as Jack, a three-year-old in 1903 and hunted for another nineteen seasons. He served, too, in the political arena for canvassing by horseback in South-West

Norfolk. "Nothing gave me so much pleasure as riding Jack," wrote Richard. "I forgot all my troubles and worries and my grief is that by losing Kitty IV to the war in 1915, Peter must be the last of the breed," for pneumonia had earlier robbed him of Jill.

By the end of 1897 the *Peterborough Advertiser* company had acquired the *Hunts County News* [1] on being offered it and bought the *Spalding Guardian* from Richard, production being moved from King's Lynn. He had ordered his first rotary printing press, an Annand costing £1,950 from the Northern Press and Engineering Company of South Shields, and altered the premises in Cumbergate to take it. With extra composing room equipment he was ready for larger and better-printed papers.

Politically the big event of 1897 for Richard was the kick-off of the Eastern Counties Liberal Federation. The Liberal Chief Whip, Tom Ellis, suggested he should launch this body to co-ordinate work throughout the region and at the inaugural meeting at Peterborough in July, Richard was elected its executive chairman. He challenged them at once. They had nineteen seats to win in Lincolnshire, Norfolk, Cambridgeshire and Huntingdonshire: seats which had been lost through unpreparedness and would be lost again if they merely trusted in providence or in headquarters. Neither did he spare the city Liberals, pushing them into holding six public meetings that winter.

A chance to have a finger in the Fleet Street pie cropped up in September 1898 when John Derry persuaded Richard to join Joseph Cooke in buying a London paper called *The Morning*. Cooke asked Richard to influence his well-to-do Liberal friends to take shares and brought in as chairman his friend Sir William Ingram, Member for Boston and proprietor of the *Illustrated London News*. Ingram's father Herbert was born in Boston and at the time of the Crimean War was its Member and also owner of the *Boston Guardian*. The immense success of Ingram management of the *Illustrated* was a good omen. Associating the *Echo* with it was

---

[1] An edition of the *Hunts County News* called the *Ramsey Herald* was discontinued in 1908.

19

another. It was one of London's first evening papers to sell at a ha'penny and its bright approach earned a circulation of 300,000 and £8,000 a year for its owner, Passmore Edwards. This philanthropic businessman had been his own editor, with lofty ideals as to what was good for readers, and tips from the racecourse were not among them. Strangely, after selling a two-thirds interest in the *Echo* he bought it back at an advanced figure when management disagreements threatened progress.

Edwards had only recently sold out again to a small group including Sir John Barker M.P. of the great London store, when the Cooke-Ingram-Winfrey trio came on stage. They agreed to take over the *Echo* and by April 1899 their company, Consolidated Newspapers Ltd, was publishing their evening *Echo* and their daily (re-named the *Morning Herald*) at a ha'penny each. On the board with Cooke and Richard were Thomas Lough M.P. and Sir Hugh Gilzean Read. They added to their twenty Linotype machines and had three rotary presses. A man trained under Derry came to edit the *Morning Herald*, with David Christie Murray, well-known from the old *Morning,* as special writer, and the exclusive sporting memories of W. G. Grace to tempt new readers. Biggest controversy in Fleet Street just then was over an idea the *Daily Telegraph* and other papers had of publishing seven days a week. Newsagents joined with Sabbatarians in protest and the *Herald*'s rejection of the idea reacted in its favour. It aimed instead at giving a "really good substantial halfpennyworth of reading on six days of the week and six days only."

For Cooke, director on the spot, this London operation was his toughest-ever test. Often he worked a double shift, having only four hours sleep in Anderton's Hotel between finishing with the *Echo* and starting night work on the *Herald.* His health suffered but it was not his fault that the money-making *Echo* suffered also. Trouble in South Africa split the Liberal Party into pro-war and pro-Boer factions, young David Lloyd George first making a name for himself among the latter. Board room quarrels over editorial policy followed loss of sales and advertisement revenue and by

20

July 1900 the practical newspapermen forced Lough to buy them out — at 10s in the £! The *Echo* continued to appear from St Bride Street for another five years before its doors finally closed but its sister daily survived as the *Daily Express & Morning Herald*, being taken over by C. A. Pearson and merged with the front-page-news *Express* he launched with such flair earlier in 1900. Four hundred and twenty-six issues of these papers had burned Richard's fingers quite enough and neither he nor Cooke ever again touched a Fleet Street enterprise.

Nine years as vice-chairman of Holland County Council, chairmanship of Long Sutton Urban Council and membership of Spalding School Board was fair preparation for Richard's contribution to local government in the City and the then Soke of Peterborough. Slatterie Clarke had successfully campaigned in the *Advertiser* for a charter of incorporation for Peterborough but did not join the new council when formed in May 1874. Richard was city councillor 1898 to 1920 and served on the Soke County Council 1901 to 1919. He lived to be last survivor of that first Holland County Council as well as of Peterborough City Council members he joined round the horseshoe table in the old Restoration period Guildhall.

After his election in the North Ward, which included the New England working class district with a high proportion of railwaymen ("New England" because railway development brought a new era to Peterborough in the 1850's), Richard was carried shoulder high to his committee room. "I came as a stranger and ye took me in," he said. Less than a month before the election he launched a ha'penny eight-page Wednesday edition of the *Advertiser*, which was then selling nearly 15,000 copies at a penny on Saturdays and had to cry Hold to advertisers and correspondents.

Richard brought Tom Diggle over from Spalding to edit the *Mid-Weekly Advertiser* (re-named *The Citizen* in 1903) and ran it out of revenue, charging nothing to capital. There were small losses on the paper up to 1910 and the *Hunts County News* was also a liability, with the result that at board meetings in 1899 Richard came under fire and in his

21

absence the directors even appointed a small committee to investigate expenditure. However, they were only just learning that his views were broader than theirs. Far from yielding he rightly forecast that the mid-weekly would become a "valued asset, a source of profit and a power for usefulness in the city". It gave special coverage to the regular Friday night City Council meetings, to news and notes on the important railway yards and brickworks, and to religious matters.

Richard's Radical thrustfulness made him a natural leader of the railwaymen and their friends. He could rely on their Liberalism but wanted to see them catered for in social and other ways. Ten years earlier the idea of a Workmen's Hall had been dropped. He picked it up and in 1902 a non-political non-sectarian hall was opened with smoke room, reading room, concert hall and slipper baths — a £3,000 project in which workmen as well as Richard and other leaders had shares. He started the New England Pleasant Sunday Afternoon (P.S.A.) in this hall in 1903. Leaflets calling men to the first meeting were printed in the *Advertiser* office and distributed by the apprentice Ernie Searle, and several men from the staff joined. Most notable of these was an uninhibited Yorkshireman named Oliver ("Ollie") Halcrow, self-taught leader of the orchestra and choir. Since coming from South Shields to install the Annand rotary press he had stayed on as engineer and stereotyper, and Richard relied on his genius to keep everything in good mechanical trim.

It was a great record. Richard was founder and first president of the P.S.A. and on every Sunday afternoon when he was not abroad or detained on official business he was there as chairman and frequently as speaker till resigning in 1919. Men who tackled his kind of week with his newspaper, political, Parliamentary, local government, agricultural and hunting interests and found time for church on Sundays could be excused if they spent Sunday afternoons in deck chair or armchair. But Richard cycled along after lunch, often with a child on the crossbar and another cycling beside him, to what his youngsters called the "Please Stay Away."

22

He disliked the way the Workmen's Hall was run and the committee's preference for drink instead of social and educational programmes and eventually the P.S.A. withdrew to meet in a school. The hall was closed down and was used as a cinema for a time till the Peter Brotherhood engineering firm took it over as a club in 1920. The P.S.A. still continues in its own modest building which the members worked for and opened in 1927.

Norfolk learned that Richard's interest in smallholdings was not all talk. In 1899 he formed a Norfolk Small Holdings Association with three M.P.s — Sir Fred Wilson of Mid-Norfolk, Sir George White of Norwich, and Felix Cobbold of Ipswich, starting with a farm at Swaffham. Backed by Earl Carrington, Lord John Hervey and others, Richard — with Alfred Jermyn and J. A. Parsons, fellow directors from the *Lynn News* — made up a sub-committee charged with looking for other estates. The idea was not simply to bring back men driven from the land or to keep others from leaving, but to create a ladder for them to rise in life and reach comfortable old age without going cap in hand to the Poor Law guardians.

Richard took a house at Swaffham for the 1900 Khaki Election and Charles Hughes, a reporter from the *Peterborough Advertiser*, helped in organisation. Hare's majority was reduced to a mere 66 votes. Elsewhere, Halley Stewart was defeated by 160 votes after a quick fight at Peterborough, where he operated from Richard's house, and Spalding made atonement by rejecting Pollock by 57 votes in favour of Horace Mansfield. This exuberant Methodist businessman, who ran a P.S.A. at Coalville with 1,300 members, held Spalding till 1910 and contributed a weekly Parliamentary letter to the *Guardian*. He was also chairman of the *Peterborough Advertiser* board from 1909 till ill-health closed his public career in 1911, when Richard succeeded to this company post.

Hughes was rewarded by going with Richard for a week to the Paris Exhibition. Though only nineteen, Hughes had taken to political organisation and to Winfrey ways like a duck to water and was to be a lifelong servant. Richard found him in the *Hunts County News* office where he was completing an all-round printing apprenticeship. The boy's background appealed to the new boss: Grandfather Hughes had been a prominent Dissenter and led the revolt in Huntingdon against the church rate, whilst his father's tailoring workshop was a nightly haunt of old and young Radicals and teetotal Rechabites.

At seventeen Hughes was teaching shorthand to boys of Huntingdon Grammar School in the old Norman classroom where Oliver Cromwell learned his lessons. For six months he lived at Sutton House till he found digs in Peterborough and divided his time between secretarial work for Richard and newspaper work, to the frequent and highly vocal annoyance of Frank Loomes, *Advertiser* editor. Deskwork for the new Eastern Counties Liberal Federation at once fell to him and he went on to give 30 years service to the Liberal Party in this office as well as being steward of the Small Holdings Association for nearly 25 years from 1911.

Happy note at the end of election year 1900 was the arrival at Sutton House on December 23rd of Lucy, joining Ellen who was born two years earlier on September 8th. Two more years passed before another Richard Winfrey was added to the line on 24 June 1902, and finally the birth of Ruth on 14 September 1906 completed the family of four. All had Pattinson as their second name and R. P. Winfrey has been commonly known as Pat from his earliest days.

4. CALLED TO CONTROL

EARLY in 1901 Richard was called in to save an enterprise going sick in Northamptonshire. Midway between Peterborough and Northampton, where Kettering, Wellingborough, Rushden and Thrapston make a foursome of shoe manufacturing towns, were newspapers backed by a group of county Liberals centred in Wellingborough and Kettering. They had a double headache: the bank was restive about their growing overdraft, and their chief executive, Thomas Collings, had been less than open with them about the business. He had done well since taking over the *Wellingborough News* in 1881, working for Liberalism and helping local Baptist chapels till asked to be minister at Burton Latimer. In 1887 Liberals included him as managing director when they formed the Northamptonshire Printing and Publishing Company which now operated weekly journals and stationery shops in the four towns as well as an evening paper in Kettering. There was a fifth shop in Northampton. In November 1900 the directors learned from an auditor's probe that Collings had misled them over the accounts. They suspended him, gave further personal guarantees to the bank, and tried to economise.

They faced several opposition newspapers; they had backed Collings in 1894 in starting a mid-weekly called *The Citizen* — it became the Saturday football paper in 1897 — and in launching the *Evening Telegraph* as a daily the same year; they had installed their first Linotype machines, and the Boer War demand for news spurred them to buy their first rotary press (a year after Richard had put in the Annand at Peterborough); they had been obliged to extend

25

their premises; and they had had to raise more capital. Some of these Liberal directors had built up sound businesses of their own but they were not practical newspapermen. They needed the journals to carry the Liberal message and their chairman, John Turner Stockburn, born in the same year (1825) as Richard Francis Winfrey, sought John Morley[1] for top-level Liberal Party advice. It was simple: "Ask Winfrey." With the company's shop at Thrapston as rendezvous, Richard met Stockburn and Thomas Bird, another director. Christine, youngest of the Stockburn girls, drove over with them in the trap. She was the last of Stockburn's seventeen children and seventy years later clearly recalled this secret meeting. It led to Richard being appointed managing director in April 1901. Forty-three years later he was still there, only survivor of the board which consulted him in their need.

Time for Kettering was limited. He took a mere £150 a year as salary plus £26 expenses — little more than one of his editors would be paid. By 1905 the shops were disposed of, bank indebtedness reduced by £8,000 and expenditure cut from £21,300 to £10,900, with profits pegged. An unrelenting grip on spending was typical of Richard's method. Waste was wicked. Replacements had to be pleaded for. Looking back fifty years later, David Goodman, commercial printing manager, wrote of the new chief as a "noted physician and surgeon, called in for all such complaints as affected his Kettering patient, and his canny ability to diagnose their origin was often very disconcerting to the delinquent responsible."

When Richard took the reins there was no doubt as to the driver. Present or absent, what he said went. If not, then staff knew there were piercing brown eyes to face and sharp boardroom cross-examinations with staccato questions direct and unnervingly on-target. There were no automatic wage rises. Each had to be thoroughly earned and personally approved. In the year he took over the Master Printers asked for an increase for union men in the Dryland Street

[1] John Morley, created Viscount 1908, Liberal Minister, author, entered Parliament after a career in London journalism.

newspaper works but Richard, backed by the board, could not agree to this because of the parlous state of company finance. There were times when advertisement accounts had to be specially collected before wages could be paid. Unless Richard had applied the squeeze so thoroughly at Kettering, EMAP might not now include its substantial Northamptonshire sector. In 1905 the directors were asked by W. T. Martin, writing from a London hotel, if they would sell out the whole concern. Richard tackled Martin when they met at the National Liberal Club and found he was touting for someone else. There was no deal. Why should there be? The company had turned the corner and its papers were from that time to maintain steady returns and solid support for the progressive ideals which had brought Richard and the rest of the board together.

Liberal trail-blazers were already in full possession when Richard moved into Northamptonshire and father figures in the boardroom included John Stockburn, a political giant who could remember the first election after the great Reform Bill of 1832. Rugged, progressive, high-principled, courteous and courageous in controversy, he was one of the first two Radical middleclass Nonconformists to be appointed Justices of the Peace for Northamptonshire. Counties were then run by magistrates in Quarter Sessions and his entry in 1882 into a circle of justices drawn wholly from the landed class was bitterly resented. A leading Congregationalist, he ran a clothing factory, established the hospital, was an amateur farmer and rode to hounds, and lived in the big old Mission House where in October 1792 William Carey persuaded fellow Baptists to form the Baptist Missionary Society and send him out to evangelise India. They called him Honest John throughout the county. Stockburn was 96 when he died in 1922 and for 20 years presided over Richard's board meetings, reviewing balance sheets without any notes and never getting a figure wrong.

Another senior director was Thomas Bird, born in 1840 and father of T. N. Bird, first chairman in 1947 of East Midland Allied Press Ltd. Statesman of the national footwear industry and son of a Kettering Chartist enthusiast,

Thomas chaired the company for five years after Stockburn died, to be followed by J. Alfred Gotch, chairman till 1942. Distinguished as architect and author, he was the first president of the R.I.B.A. to be elected from outside London. Other directors who met Richard at his first board meetings were Richard Winship Stockburn, John's son and secretary of the company, and representatives of Liberalism and business in the area: George Smith of Thrapston, George Denton of Rushden, William Meadows and A. G. Jones of Kettering. James Heygate, Liberal Association secretary, was solicitor. Heygate had seen to the launching of the company in 1887 when its first secretary was F. C. Marriott, his managing clerk. A week after World War I Armistice Day, Marriott's nephew, Frederick Arthur Cooper, started as an office boy in the Wellingborough office. By the end of World War II he was the company's general manager, secretary and accountant, and thereafter became director and secretary of East Midland Allied Press and its subsidiaries. Even his retirement in 1969 following fifty years service to two Winfrey generations did not sever links with the Northamptonshire company's earliest days for he continues to sit on its board.

The company's story started in 1887 with one title, the quarter-century-old *Wellingborough News,* founded in 1861. The directors launched the *Kettering Leader* in 1888 soon after young Frank Hutchen had become apprenticed to its printer. He graduated from the printing shop to the editorial side, worked under Collings — who was editor as well as managing director — and before long was himself editor and chief executive. He was Sir Richard's first lieutenant at Kettering till 1942 when, on a war-time St Valentine's Day, he died after collapsing in the office. He gave 54 years to building up the company and perfecting its newspapers and equipment, and for 41 of these had Sir Richard as leader. He was a Congregationalist, his going-to-church dress up to World War I being the top hat and frock coat then in vogue. He was vegetarian, non-smoker, teetotaller, lover of sport with Saturday's football *Pink 'Un* his special pet, explorer of Northamptonshire past and present by book, bicycle or car,

Liberal though no politician, and all through and all the time a dedicated newspaperman. So far as possible Richard backed him not merely in keeping mechanically up-to-date but in pioneering new machines and methods.

In 1904 Richard pressed for company reconstruction on the grounds that long-overdue depreciation of machinery added to loss figures in the balance sheet would preclude dividends for many years unless subscribed capital was written down by half, from £16,310 to £8,155. Shareholders thus found their sickly £10 shares trimmed to more healthy £5 shares. It was a drastic operation and almost up to World War I these could be bought for £3 15s, debentures being issued to meet special needs. However, before World War II steady growth and bonus issues had converted a £5 share into a holding of 21 £1 shares. When EMAP Ltd was formed in 1947, company shares were exchanged for parent company holdings at the rate of three for one (divided equally between preference and ordinary shares), 21 £1 Kettering shares thus becoming 63 EMAP shares. A risk of £3 15s in the bad old days therefore equalled £63 forty years later.

Sparing of praise, Richard knew that the Kettering company and particularly the *Evening Telegraph* might not have made the progress they did without Hutchen's flair and daily devotion. Richard never realised his ambition to run an evening paper on a permanent basis at Peterborough and at the staff dinner to mark the Advertiser's 70th birthday he wondered if anyone there would live to see one. But though he said it took years to set it on its feet it had, in fact, been done. It had been done at Kettering — by Mr Hutchen.

Changes in the *North Cambs Echo* sprang from the fact that Arthur Brand, defeated in the Wisbech Division in 1895, successfully re-took the seat in 1900 and sat in Parliament till retiring in 1906. Richard, no longer agent to Brand, was working away in Norfolk and Brand's new agent in 1900 was Joseph Collingwood of March, one of several Liberals who wanted a paper of their own. Richard and William Boulton, his Wisbech friend and fellow *Advertiser* director, joined them in floating the Isle of Ely Printing and Publishing Company, selling them for £400 plant made idle at Huntingdon by the decision to produce the *Hunts County News* in the Peterborough works[1]. Richard ceased printing the *North Cambs Echo* at the Lynn News office and sold the copyright to Collingwood's company, which produced it from 17 April 1903 under its previous title of *Wisbech Chronicle*. On 22 April 1903 the company's new *March Advertiser* appeared as another penny eight-pager, Joseph Collingwood's sons Stanley and Hughes helping with it.

Chief item in their Station Road premises at March apart from the flatbed press and folder was a Linotype machine. Collingwood was lyrical in telling readers about the set-up in his first issue. "We have stocked our office with abundant machinery of the latest patterns that inventive skill has been able to devise. For the first time in the history of this territory there is now working in the Isle of Ely, in the production of this journal, a Linotype composing machine. With this complicated piece of mechanism the old tedious method by which a printer picked up and arranged each letter separately has been surpassed . . ." The opposition *Cambs Times* twitted the new March arrival on the fact that half its pages were filled with matter already seen in the Peterborough paper. "We paid for it," retorted Collingwood. He was hurt by the opposition's "almost prehistoric mental attitude towards our new machinery. What do *Times* men feel," he demanded, "about importing columns of stereotype readymade from London at about a shilling a column . . . ?" Though due off the presses at midday on Wednesday, the *March Advertiser* waited for Wednesday morning news, was frequently late, never achieved an adequate sale, and succumbed to wartime conditions in February 1915. The gap in Liberal coverage of the March and the Isle of Ely was filled by an Isle edition of the *Peterborough Advertiser* with Hughes Collingwood in charge.

With the *North Cambs Echo* finished, decks at the *Lynn News* office were clearer for Tom Diggle to go into action. Well-read, self-taught, given to leg-pulling, his way with the *Mid-Weekly Advertiser* had pushed its sales in Peter-

[1] *The Hunts County News*, started in March 1886, was issued as an edition of the *Peterborough Advertiser* from January 1927 to August 1947.

borough. He could be, and liked to be, pungent and pointed. Joseph Cooke's scanty attention to Lynn ended when Richard succeeded him as managing director, and Diggle came over in January 1903 as editor-manager. He was 24: full of the fire and fun which made him Lynn's leading journalist for 40 years. Richard soon entrusted the managing-directorship to him and when the Tory *Lynn Advertiser* came to terms in a company amalgamation in 1922, Diggle edited both newspapers as partners instead of rivals.

Hunstanton was already a charming little resort when Richard went into Norfolk and he and his sister Mrs Coupland built houses there as summer retreats. Within six months of moving to Lynn, Diggle brought out the *Hunstanton News*, an edition confined to the holiday season till World War I stopped it. On October 10th an edition called the *Downham Market News* — a "businesslike paper for businessmen" — started a twelve-year run which took it to 1915, and on 23 April 1904 the *Swaffham News* appeared, also in Richard's division, only to last 75 weeks. At the same time an *Ely Chronicle* edition started in Colman's time was dropped. The *Lynn Football Star* was bright spot of club, pub and home on Saturday nights. This also dated from October of Diggle's first year but in 1915 was another casualty of war. Its pink pages included national football results personally telephoned from Kettering in the early days by Frank Hutchen, and also "Saturday Night's Tittle Tattle" — mirthful to most, outrageous to some, first to be read and quoted by everyone.

While Diggle was feeling his feet at King's Lynn in the spring of 1903, Richard extended his newspaper grip by moving into Suffolk journalism at Bury St Edmunds. Again, it was an unsought opportunity and again it came through a political friend, this time Felix Cobbold, Liberal Member for Ipswich and involved with him in settling men on the land in Norfolk. At Bury, then home of 17,000 people, Conservatives read the *Bury & Norwich Post*, launched 1782, and Liberals took the *Bury Free Press*, started when Gladstone ended the stamp tax in 1855. Its eight pages cost a penny and a circulation of 8,000 was claimed. A young compositor from the *Bury Post*, Thomas Francis Lucia, had started it as an opposition paper, achieving success while echoing the familiar battle cries of progress, reform, civil and religious liberty, and free and fair reporting. Since his death in 1886 executors had run the *Free Press* till Henry Bankes Ashton, prominent townsman, solicitor, sportsman and leader of the Liberals, was left in control. Richard agreed to buy the newspaper and with Thomas Ridley, wholesale grocer and Liberal stalwart, and Bankes Ashton as co-directors, formed the Bury St Edmunds Printing and Publishing Company to acquire it from him, Cobbold coming in as a substantial shareholder.

No sweeping changes were made. In 1874 Lucia had built the King's Road works and editorial offices still in use today (site and premises both extended since), and Bankes Ashton continued to keep the commercial department in his own Abbeygate premises (built by Lucia but quickly outgrown). Ashton was for some years the real power behind the *Free Press* in spite of all his other commitments, holding editorial sway and also amusing himself and entertaining other people with his "Behind the Scenes" column of witticisms, criticisms and comments. When he died in May 1931 his son, Thomas Mason Ashton, became secretary and director, and John N. B. Ashton, younger brother and member of the family legal firm, joined the board in November 1947. Tom Ashton relinquished the secretaryship in 1948 when F. A. Cooper became secretary of the newly-formed EMAP company and of its subsidiaries. Mr Ashton then took the position of deputy chairman of the parent company.

Richard's Grantham friend Harry Escritt introduced him to motoring in the summer of 1903 when together they toured South-West Norfolk in a series of pre-harvest political meetings. The car gave many villagers their first chance to look over such a marvel and Richard acquired one of his own in the spring of 1904 — a Beaufort four-seater open car with hood bought from John Lound, owner of Sutton House. Its behaviour defeated Richard's attempts to be its master and Arthur Naylor, a *Peterborough Advertiser* Linotype operator, was called on to have days off to drive it — much to the annoyance of staff left to set his copy. Naylor was useful too as a kind of personal bodyguard, standing by Richard in all sorts of tight corners during election rowdyism. The Beaufort's index number was FL20, linking it with Peterborough's first registrations under the Roads Act in December 1903. Even in 1909 there were only 34 cars in the county. When its days on the road were ended and its number passed to another car in 1921, the Beaufort was used on the farm at Long Sutton which Richard's nephew Dick was then running.

A good pal and professional adviser as valuer, Harry Escritt had another link with Richard — his father had passed on to him the proprietorship of the *Grantham Journal*. When Harry died in 1910, Richard and the other trustees met the widow's needs by selling the paper back to Escritt senior for £10,000 and investing the capital.

For Richard Winfrey, running newspaper companies was only part of a life increasingly devoted to public affairs. Whether in city or county matters, in Liberal Party campaigning, or in national developments and protests, he pulled no punches and deserted no cause. In the first flush of work for Halley Stewart in 1885 he found many a village meeting repeating what his father had said, that there must be a show-down with the House of Lords over its veto and with the National Church over its exclusive privileges. The picture was burningly clear, and in 1886 Richard painted the general background from the Toleration Act of 1689 onwards in articles for the *Boston Guardian*, repeated by Jo Cooke in the *Grantham Times*.

In 1889 he became one of the earliest executive members of the National Education Association, formed that year to push the case for an educational set-up which was unsectarian and under the people's control. Many of the country's leading Liberals belonged to it and its secretary was his old friend and best man Anthony Mundella, who did this work and served on the London School Board as well as carrying on as *Guardian* Lobby correspondent. Liberals and Free Churchmen were indignant when Balfour's 1902 Act not only put board schools under the new county and borough education committees but also the non-provided (church) schools, while permitting the latter to teach denominational religion and to recommend the choice of teachers (i.e., those acceptable on religious grounds). The Act meant that Free Church ratepayers were paying for the upkeep of schools teaching doctrines and practices they would not tolerate and a wave of passive resistance to paying the new education rate swept the country.[1]

Richard used Press, platform, pulpit, public authority and private position as ratepayer in attacking the Act, and from spring to autumn of 1903 the *Peterborough Advertiser* carried nearly twenty articles by Mundella which pointed the way to protest. Richard helped form the Citizens' League to oppose the Act in Peterborough, explaining it all to his men at a P.S.A. meeting: how he wanted every child to have equal opportunity to climb the ladder of education, how he joined both county and city education committees to make the best of the Act, and how his compromise proposals had been rejected. "It has been a difficult week for me," he said. "I will tell you what has weighed most with me in coming to a decision — it has been my father's memory. I remember hearing of the part he took in the abolition of the church rate and how he fought that our universities should open to the sons of Nonconformists. I asked myself what he would have said to religious tests for teacherships in schools wholly supported by the State. He would not have willingly submitted to it, for forcing any particular form of Christian religion upon any living creature is a violation of Christianity itself . . ."

Non-payment of the Education portion of the rate brought crowds of Free Churchmen into courtrooms at Peterborough and elsewhere and unless enthusiasts preferred prison, magistrates issued warrants to distrain upon goods. A silver inkstand presented by Thetford Liberals was regularly taken from Sutton House and just as regularly Mrs Winfrey sent someone into the city to buy it back. Richard's Hunstanton house gave him another chance to keep pay-

[1] Lloyd George's resolution against teaching sectarian dogmas at the public expense was adopted by the Free Church Council's national conference at Brighton in March 1903.

34

ment back in Norfolk so he was summoned there too, suffering along with Sir Alfred Jermyn, his *Lynn News* director colleague. Jermyn, who was knighted in 1919 and had the Royal family from Sandringham as personal shoppers at his fine store in King's Lynn, was chairman of the local Bench which made orders against passive resisters. As a resister himself he would leave the Bench for his own case and shut himself in the dock to make his periodic protest.

Richard had extra chance to denounce the Act in 1905 when he was in and out of pulpits all over Lincolnshire as president of the county Free Church Council. Some steam went out of the resistance movement when the Liberals got back into power but to the end of his life Richard never swerved from his ideal of a thoroughly national system of education, paid for by the people, controlled by the people, and having no other object but the educational well-being of the people — and that without distinction of class or creed. For 70 years the National Education Association worked as a pressure group to achieve this ideal. For 55 years Richard backed its work and in his eighties its regular executive meetings were among the few things which took him up to London. In 1929 he became treasurer and in 1931 chairman, giving this up because of deafness only three months before his death in 1944. Its secretaries were acknowledged in Whitehall as educational experts and worked to influence legislation until 1959, when N.E.A. affairs were taken over by Free Church national headquarters.

5.   AN UNFORGETTABLE MAYORALTY

BOTH in 1907 and 1912 there was Peterborough City Council talk about Richard and the Mayoralty but there was to be no plain sailing into the mayoral chair. How the chain was finally fastened round Richard's neck in November 1913 is part of Peterborough history. By then he was senior Liberal councillor and agreed to be Mayor provided the Tories supported his claim to the aldermanic bench. This was not accepted so he declined office and preferred a fresh air outing with the Fitzwilliam Hounds to Guildhall squabbling on Mayor-making morning. In the afternoon he met the ex-Mayor out riding and learned that Tory votes, with Liberals abstaining, had put him in the chair in his absence — a procedure never before heard of. Richard at once ordered his solicitor, H. B. Hartley, "to get me out of this" whilst the Editor of The Citizen, walking round to Sutton House to get his chief's views, found him relaxing in the study — "hunting boots replaced by slippers, and his pipe and dachshund dreaming on the hearthrug" — and amused by the Tories trying to play "Hamlet" without the Prince of Denmark on stage. After a night's sleep and a warning from Hartley that there was no escape, Richard accepted the situation, but said he would confine himself to strictly municipal engagements — no social ones and none outside — because of the claims of Parliament and South-West Norfolk. (His election as Member is described later.) People were mostly understanding. They remembered Mrs Winfrey rebuking some of Richard's critics in 1908 when she bluntly said an M.P.'s duty "is in Parliament, and he mustn't be expected to turn up at every little dog hanging."

It was no ordinary mayoralty. Within three months Tories who had intrigued to bind the Samson of the council with the trappings of Mayor found themselves in the Guildhall, with flag flying above it, passing congratulations to him on figuring in the 1914 New Year Honours List as a knight bachelor. Lady Winfrey too, congratulated at her next Board of Guardians meeting, said she was all the more proud because she knew the honour had been earned and not bought. She served on church and charitable bodies, bringing an unconventional touch to proceedings which was usually delightful and occasionally disconcerting, and was as ready to fight for a principle as Sir Richard. One of her chief offices in Peterborough was presidency of the Liberal Women's Association, which studied current issues and was, for instance, among early supporters of the Anti-Sweating League formed just before World War I. Wage earners of the 1970's can scarcely credit details of the sweated labour which Lady Winfrey wanted this league to expose. Women glove makers were an example. If their wages went up by 50 per cent, gloves would even then cost only one farthing more per pair. There were young tailoresses earning only tu'pence-ha'penny for making a coat, and taking home five shillings after a week at eighteen hours a day. There were women producing a dozen shirts for sixpence, or doing 84 buttonholes for fivepence, or making a gross of strawberry baskets for three shillings and sixpence.[1]

On 4 August 1914 Sir Richard had been in the Commons to hear Sir Edward Grey speak on his ultimatum to Germany to keep out of Belgium, and as he travelled home on the midnight train and reached Peterborough in the early hours of his 56th birthday he knew Britain was at war. During Friday evening, August 7th, the Chief Constable telephoned to say war excitement and anti-German fever had so turned the heads of some people that, with crowds swelling and swarming round them, they were smashing shop windows and flinging about the streets food belonging to Frederick Frank and Frederick Metz, both German-born pork butchers who were old residents and deserved no such shameful treat-

[1] *The Citizen*, 6 March 1912.

ment. Would the Mayor come and read the Riot Act so that the police could if necessary call on Northamptonshire Yeomanry (billeted at that time in the city and camping in nearby Milton Park) to help disperse the people? Sir Richard cycled into town and stood on a box to face the shouting, swaying crowd and plead with them to go home but their response was to shower him with stones. So he declaimed the Act as fast as he could and felt lucky to cycle back without a broken head. It was an uncomfortable, scarcely credible experience but police and special constables, backed by a squadron of troopers, stood their ground and made several arrests. On Monday, Sir Richard swore in 100 more specials and issued a proclamation asking citizens to be indoors by nine o'clock. So calm was restored, but it is believed that this was the last time the Riot Act was read in this country.

At the end of that worrying week he was presiding in the Guildhall at a conference to organise Red Cross work in the City and Soke, his auditor, Joseph Stephenson, becoming secretary. He was kept at it as Red Cross chairman for Peterborough throughout the war and raised £29,590 for relief work as well as providing 579,395 articles of clothing. A hostel near the station for Servicemen in transit catered for 270,238, hundreds of food parcels went to our men in German prison camps, and 15,816 hospital articles for the Allied armies. At another public meeting within a week of war starting he launched local support for the Prince of Wales Fund, with Charles Hughes as honorary secretary, and a few days later sent £2,000 to London. Further gifts brought this to £3,910. Recruiting started the day after war was declared and Sir Richard found himself addressing batches of men as they were drafted away under the Derby Recruiting Scheme, with Charles Hughes again helping as honorary organiser.

In October 1914 he brought Henry Fielding Dickens K.C., son of the great Charles, to give readings in Peterborough from his father's books in aid of Red Cross funds. Elaine Dickens was also there with her violin. Charles Hughes did the organising and H. B. Hartley, as literary as he was legal

38

and father of L. P. Hartley the novelist,[1] told the audience that as a boy he pumped a tank full of water each day, spending the twenty minutes pumping with one hand and holding a book by Dickens in the other, reading most of them that way. Young Mr Malcolm Sargent of Stamford — he had been a pupil of Dr Keeton at Peterborough Cathedral and had just got his Mus.Bac. and been appointed organist at Melton Mowbray — was another Peterborough visitor in November. This young man who became the great Sir Malcolm gave an organ recital in the cathedral but this was in support of yet another of Sir Richard's wartime cares, the Belgian refugees. As the Germans poured into Belgium to turn the flank of the French Army, the people fled before them and were offered hospitality in Britain. Sir Richard was among provincial Mayors asked to find homes for some of them and on September 14th brought the first batch to Peterborough by train. Further batches brought the number to 160.

The Belgians soon became self-supporting and when they left at the end of the war took with them far more in cash and kind than they had brought. Sir Richard was chairman of the Refugee Committee throughout and the Belgians presented him with a portrait of their King at a farewell party. To Charles Hughes, who for four years as honorary secretary had borne with their troubles from day to day, they gave a present of table silver. Hughes was honoured with the Medaille du Roi Albert, only 60 of which were struck, and for his voluntary war work generally received the M.B.E. As a guest later of the refugees he was able to tour the Flanders battlefields. Sir Richard's own visit to Belgium in July 1919 was as a member of the Anglo-Belgian Friendship Committee which Herbert (later Lord) Samuel asked him to join at the end of war.

After his term as Mayor Sir Richard gave six more years to the City as Councillor and during his mayoralty was also vice-chairman of the Soke of Peterborough County Council, sitting under the Marquess of Exeter. When the first post-

---

[1] L. P. Hartley died in December 1972, a year after the film of his novel "The Go-Between" won chief award at the Cannes Festival.

war elections came round in March 1919 he resigned after serving since 1901, and left the City Council a year later. He had moved away from Peterborough to Castor and felt that 22 years service to the City could now appropriately end, especially as war, with its heavy duties in the Board of Agriculture Office, had severely taxed him.

6. GLORIOUS EXPERIMENT

SIR RICHARD had done far more at Spalding in 1887 than organise a Liberal by-election victory for Halley Stewart. He had proved to the country that tides were flowing the Winfrey way all through rural England. For too long the labourer had been the poverty-stricken slave of the farming scene. Though we had beaten Napoleon the aftermath forced thousands of small independent farmers out of business, while landowners created large farming units and forced the pace of enclosure: three in the Lincolnshire fens alone accounted for more than 53,000 acres. Richard Winfrey knew all this and history puts him firmly among those practical social reformers who proved in action what others argued on platform and in pamphlet: Give labourer and land lost through enclosure to each other again and the issue of the marriage will be a new deal for the farm worker, a revival of life in the countryside, a more balanced agriculture, and a nation sounder at heart.

But he could not have gone far without the help of Lord Carrington, who in 1887 freed some of his land near Spalding for the Spalding Allotments Club. In 1894 he offered Welby's Farm of 85 acres near Spalding where Richard established Holland County Council's first smallholdings — 30 holdings with 90 applicants for them! These were also the first obtained in England under the Tory 1892 Act but by 1897, when Holland County Council had bought 47 acres at Freiston and another 47 at Tydd St Mary, they would take on no more and turned down an offer by Lord Carrington to release the Willow Tree Farm of 212 acres in Deeping Fen. This was too much for Richard. He persuaded His Lordship to allow him to rent the farm and let it as smallholdings, and then called on political friends to join him in a syndicate to control it with him as chairman. It was soon registered as the South Lincolnshire Small Holdings Association and by 1902 Lord Carrington also leased Cowbit House Farm and Hop Pole Farm, bringing the Association's acreage almost to a thousand.

As noted earlier, Richard had founded the Norfolk Small Holdings Association in 1899 and purchased a farm at Swaffham, the first of three. Before long the two associations amalgamated as the Lincolnshire and Norfolk Small Holdings Association, with John Diggle continuing as steward. Some of their Norfolk tenants were at Nordelph, where Richard personally bought 60 acres and built two cottages. It was in his constituency, deep in the desolate black fens west of the Ouse near Downham Market. The *Norfolk People's Journal* (quoted in the *Peterborough Citizen*, 27 November 1907) pictured the long low-roofed upper room of the village inn on the night of their annual supper, where nearly 30 men sat at one table and their wives at another. "At the head of the men's table sat Mr Richard Winfrey, at ease in a light Norfolk jacket, his keen businesslike face lightened by ready smiles and exchanging banter and chaff. At the other table was his youthful and energetic agent, and both are practical pioneers of a great economic movement, the ultimate object of which is the regeneracy of modern agricultural England . . . Since he came on the scene, poverty has begun to yield to modest comfort, shacks are being replaced by new cottages, uncultured labourers are proving that the land is safe in their hands and that capital invested in it has a sure return."

He was not only their landlord and benefactor. He was their Member, romping home in January 1906 at his third attempt and beating his old opponent Hare by 903 votes (4,416 to 3,513). It was a double triumph: he was the first Liberal ever chosen to represent South-West Norfolk in the Commons; and the Eastern Counties Liberal Federation, with him as chairman and Charles Hughes as secretary, had steam-rollered the region, taking 26 of the 32 seats in Norfolk, Suffolk, Cambridgeshire, Lincolnshire, Huntingdon-shire and the Soke of Peterborough. Richard had brought Sir Edward Grey, David Lloyd George and Sir Henry Campbell-Bannerman to speak at successive annual meetings of the Federation, and the election was a tremendous triumph for the Liberal Party as a whole and for Campbell-Bannerman, who found himself with the largest government majority then known — 86 over all the rest of the Members together and (with Labour and Irish Nationalist support) 356 over the Conservatives. Under him and later Asquith, the Liberals gave Britain her greatest peace-time administration, their crusading ideals and practical reforms halted only by the outbreak of the First World War.

Frank Loomes took the *Advertiser* and *Citizen* staffs to Sutton House to pay their respects to the new Member and handed Richard an address (still extant) which named the 26 members and gave their years of service, from old John Dyson in the works (50 years) to William Ewart Gladstone Rippon, a reporter in his first year — a record, Loomes said, of a united, contented and thoroughly loyal staff. A big man, independent in spirit and masterful in phrase, Loomes told his chief that his political success, like his newspaper success, sprang from a skilful generalship, rare powers of organisation, indomitable energy and discriminative ability. He had made two blades of grass grow where only one had done, and he had made two or three papers flourish where only one had flourished before. Richard replied that his victory meant giving even more time to public work and with engaging simplicity added: "I am trusting you to look after our united interests."

Any man would be proud to sit in that great pre-war Edwardian Parliament, but Richard was lucky too. Lord Carrington asked him to be his unpaid Parliamentary Private Secretary, watching things for him in the Commons while he sat in the Lords as President of Campbell-Bannerman's Board of Agriculture. It meant that Richard started his career as M.P. with an official standing in the House, a room at the Agriculture Office and close acquaintance with its procedure. It also sealed the friendship between the two men. Carrington, who was Governor and Commander-in-Chief of New South Wales 1885 to 1890, had not only helped Richard in his fight for the land but became president of his Eastern Counties Liberal Federation. His father was Member for Buckinghamshire divisions 1818 to 1838 and left him an estate at High Wycombe, and his mother (a second wife) was a daughter of the 22nd Baron Willoughby D'Eresby, with estates in Lincolnshire. By hereditary right through her family (which still retains it) he was Joint Lord Great Chamberlain. The Prince of Wales, later Edward VII, thought the world of him and George V continued his father's trust in the breezy Earl's common-sense. Victoria honoured him with an earldom in 1895 and George elevated him as Marquess of Lincolnshire in 1912 but at his death the marquesate and earldom became extinct as his only son, Viscount Wendover, died of wounds soon after going to the Front in 1915. Carrington's brother succeeded him in the barony, the present Lord Carrington, living near Aylesbury, being appointed Minister of Defence in Edward Heath's first Cabinet after the General Election of 1970. Richard kept in touch till the Marquess died in 1928 and at a simple funeral service in the village churchyard at Wycombe he and his son Pat watched four Lincolnshire smallholders carry the coffin to the grave.

In Parliament, Richard became part of a team dedicated to do on a national scale what he had attempted in his own locality. In Campbell-Bannerman's phrase, the land which had been the pleasure ground of the rich was to become a treasure house for the nation, and Richard's flair for settling men on the land had made the experiment a classic.[1] Their work led to the Small Holdings and Allotments Acts of 1907 and 1908 under which, if the counties did not provide small-holdings, they would be provided over their heads — and six Commissioners were appointed to press the work forward. When extra Commissioners were needed, John Diggle was among those appointed in 1911. When Charles Hughes, keen to marry, asked for a salary rise, Richard's reply was to

[1] Quoted in Government Blue Book: *Departmental Committee of Inquiry into Statutory Smallholdings*, First Report, 1966, pages 6 and 10.

appoint him steward in place of Diggle, and Hughes left the *Advertiser* team for a room in the Trinity Congregational Church buildings at Peterborough from which he ran the Association and the Eastern Counties Liberal Federation and anything else that Richard dropped on his table.

The latter was with a Henry Lunn party in Germany when the 1907 Small Holdings Bill came up for debate and was summoned home from Nuremburg by the Prime Minister to tell the House about his own 20-year struggle to meet hunger for land. When he sat down, Campbell-Bannerman turned round with a warm "Well done." An invitation to dinner at Downing Street followed the next night and the Party printed the speech as a pamphlet. It was not Richard's maiden speech: this had been given on the spur of the moment on March 5th. After a Monday run with the Fitzwilliam he took an evening train and reached Westminster at about 10 p.m. to find the House in committee on the Estimates. Someone was criticising the Department of Woods and Forests and Richard added some shots of his own about mishandling Crown Lands. It was an old sore with him that Crown Lands were let to big landowners and the landed classes whilst requests for smallholdings were refused, so it was not difficult to rattle on for ten minutes. He attacked Norfolk squires when the Land Tenure Bill came up four days later. Was game preserving more important than agriculture? He claimed that in South-West Norfolk acres and acres were given over to the sway of King Pheasant whilst too many cottages were tenanted by men in velveteens.

The "Peasant or Pheasant" crusade was, in fact, started by Richard long before Lloyd George took it up. He made hares equally notorious, with piquancy added because Hare was his opponent. Stories of pheasants and hares appeared in papers and were exchanged over tables in Norfolk mansions including, no doubt, Sandringham House. His Majesty may, in fact, have read this versified leg-pull in the Tory *Lynn Advertiser:*

We are very much delighted
That Richard Winfrey's knighted

For his industry and zeal in our affairs;
But it's much to be regretted
That, not being Baronetted,
The distinction does not follow to his "Hares" . . .

Although Sir Richard claimed to be a fairly silent Member in the Commons, there was plenty of speaking to do outside for he was number one choice for official conferences to explain the Small Holdings Bill. In April, some time before the Bill was finalised, fellow Liberals arranged a dinner in his honour at the National Liberal Club where Sir Walter Foster, chairman of the Land Law Reform Association and another national champion of the rural underdog, presided.

When Lord Carrington persuaded Campbell-Bannerman to add the President of the Board of Agriculture to Commissioners for Crown Lands, Richard had an opening he had long wanted — to take over Crown Land in his home country bordering the Wash, in an area known as Wingland. The name came from Tycho Wing, agent (as his father and brother had been) to the Duke of Bedford, the great Fen landowner, who reclaimed a vast area of washland and created some of Britain's richest farmland for the Crown to control. Of this, 1,000 acres were let to Mr Eastland, whose farmhouse still stands alongside the main King's Lynn road near Walpole Cross Keys. In 1907 the Commissioners let half this area to the Lincolnshire and Norfolk Small Holdings Association and the whole of it after Eastland's death two years later. Holdings were laid out and cottages built — all painted white and giving Wingland the local name of The White City. Richard was chairman of the Co-Partnership Farms Society which he and others formed in 1906, and in 1908 he established Syndicate Farm on 150 of the Wingland acres near Sutton Bridge as the first attempt in Britain to apply co-partnership principles to ordinary farming. In the rush of fruit harvest he drew on his *Peterborough Advertiser* staff for clerical help in booking fruit away from the farm. Usual choice was Basil Riley, a member of the Riley car family who had run away to sea as a boy. Richard, coming across the lad by accident, had helped him out of a difficulty, and Riley went on to give him a lifetime of service, in his later years as advertisement manager at Peterborough. Friction between the profit-sharing workers and disagreements with their farm manager soured the experiment, however, and Richard would not continue it after 1923 when Syndicate Farm reverted to individual holdings.

George Pitcher, ninety when he died in 1970, was a typically successful product of the Winfrey revolution. Eastland employed him as a lad of eleven at sevenpence a day. Then he followed the plough for another farmer for one shilling a day. He was nearly 30 and had scraped together £110 when Richard converted Eastland's farm into holdings and let him have one. Sixteen years later he left it to take his own farm a few miles away. Smallholders had to agree to work the land to keep it in good heart and to cooperate over roads, fences, ditches and hedges. For the rest, every tenant was free "to vote as he likes, to pray where he likes, to shoot what he likes and to farm as he likes, and no notice to quit shall be given on account of difference of political or religious opinions." This paragraph was dropped from agreements after World War I. Except on the best soils, holdings are now considered too small to yield a proper livelihood and are amalgamating into bigger units.

Sir Halley Stewart and Sir Richard Winfrey were the last survivors of the syndicate which started the Lincolnshire and Norfolk Small Holdings Association. In 1936, when they were 99 and 77 respectively, the association gave up control of the smallholdings they held from the Carrington estate, and since then they have come under Carter Jonas and Sons, agents to the estate. A few months before the lease of the Crown holdings at Wingland was due to expire, the association relinquished these also in 1936, and the Commissioners of Crown Lands arranged for their supervision again by Carter Jonas. Forty or more years of Sir Richard's personal smallholdings experiment came to an end with a garden party for tenants at Castor House, where they presented him with a silver salver. He had a great respect for these hard-working men. They had repaid his trust, proved his ideals, and given him their loyalty and confidence whether harvests were good or bad. "Taking it all together it has been a glorious experiment," was how he summed it up.

Part of that experiment was the success of the Marshland and Wingland Trading Association, whose tall mill and spreading warehouses are a landmark on the Wingland side of Terrington St Clement. Richard started it for bulk-buying of feeding stuffs, fertilisers, fuel and seeds as soon as Wingland was converted to smallholdings, tenants having a chance to take shares. The Trading Association also ground their corn and marketed their produce, with Richard as president and a manager and committee of practical men. Before the Second War, however, Sir Richard, having wound up the Small Holdings Association, also gave up control of the Marshland and Wingland Trading Association. Without any outside grants, it had survived nearly all the government-sponsored associations of the same kind and by May 1940 its transfer as a going concern to a new company was complete. The men who took it over were H. A. Cole, a clerk at the mill, and his brother-in-law Harold Featherstone, who had driven its first lorry, a model T Ford. Today the company continues to flourish in serving smallholders and other farming folk over a wide area.

6. Historic picture at party given by Algernon Peckover at Sibalds Holme, Wisbech, to celebrate Arthur Brand's victory as Liberal M.P. in 1891.

Balcony (L to R): Elizabeth Josephine, daughter of Alexander Peckover, later Mrs J. D. Penrose; Alexander, Quaker and banker (later Baron), son of Algernon; Alexandrina, daughter of Alexander and last Peckover to live in Peckover House, Wisbech (then known as Bank House). Below: Richard Winfrey aged 33, agent to the Hon Arthur Brand; Wilhelmina Jane Peckover, daughter of Algernon; Viscount Hampden of Glynde, Sussex, formerly Mr Speaker Brand; Viscountess Hampden; Anna Jane, daughter of Alexander; Arthur Brand; Algernon Peckover, aged nearly 90; Henry Lee Warner of Swaffham, former Liberal candidate, South West Norfolk; Mrs Arthur Brand; Algerina Peckover, daughter of Algernon.

7. Cathedral gateway at Peterborough showing printing office where Slatterie Clarke produced the first *Peterborough Advertiser* in 1854. See picture 56.

8. Sir Richard Winfrey in 1908 caressing his beloved Kitty III with her three offspring looking on (L to R): Kitty IV aged two years; Gill aged four, and Jack aged nine.

9. Offices and works built in Cumbergate for the *Peterborough Advertiser* by Slatterie Clarke in 1874 and used until the 1950 move to Broadway. This 1902 sketch shows crowds hailing news of peace after the Boer War.

10. Outside Flaxwell, their Hunstanton house, Sir Richard and Lady Winfrey in their first car, the four-seater Beaufort acquired in 1904.

(Circulation] # THE LYNN **[6500**

ADVERTISER

And Wisbech Constitutional Gazette.

SIXTY-FOUR LONG COLUMNS. SATURDAY, JUNE 21, 1890.

A FAT STOCK EXHIBITION FOR LYNN.

Mr. Brooks in Trouble Again. Board of Guardians.

SAD END OF A LYNN TRADESMAN.

Drowned in the Loke. TOWN COUNCIL MEETING: The Police Force.

ELY DIOCESAN CONFERENCE.

West Norfolk Highways Committee.

THE FATAL LARKING CASE at BIRCHAM

THE GOVERNMENT AND THE SESSION.

The CIRCULAR SAW CASE at BRANDON

PROPOSED LOCAL BOARD FOR HUNSTANTON.

WISBECH: Town Council. Suicide. Walsoken School Board. End of Strike.

THETFORD: Board of Guardians. Rifle Competition.

COUNTY COURTS: Ely, Thetford, Watton, Lynn, Dereham.

PETTY SESSIONS: Lynn, Wisbech, Downham, Dereham, Terrington, Grimston, March, Ely, &c.

Local Notes. Topics of the Day.

PARLIAMENT. AGRICULTURAL NOTES. CRICKET MATCHES.

Our Ladies' Column. London Letter. Eastern Counties Items. Home and Foreign News.

PRICE TWOPENCE. Thew and Son, Lynn; and all News Agents.

11 and 12. Until company amalgamation in 1923 the *Advertiser* (2d.) and the *News* (1d.) were at each other's throats in the King's Lynn area. These contents bills relate to competing issues published on a Saturday in 1890.

LYNN NEWS

The Best and Largest Penny Weekly Paper in Norfolk.

SATURDAY, JUNE 21st, 1890.

THE HOUSE IN A MUDDLE.   LOCAL TOPICS.

LYNN TOWN COUNCIL:
DISCUSSION ON THE POLICE FORCE.

ROBERT BROOKS BEFORE THE MAGISTRATES:
FULL REPORT.

Sad Death of Mr. James Ducker, Lynn.

WEST NORFOLK HIGHWAYS COMMITTEE.

THE COUNTY COURTS. LYNN BOARD of GUARDIANS.

PROPOSED FAT STOCK SHOW FOR LYNN.

THE FATAL PRACTICAL JOKE AT BIRCHAM.

Petty Sessional Reports: Lynn, Wisbech, March, Terrington, Downham, Grimston, Dereham, &c.

Case of Drowning at Lynn.   Two Norfolk Wills.

THE DUCHESS OF FIFE'S ACCOUCHEMENT.

QUIPS AND CRANKS BY "QUIZ."

LYNN AND WISBECH DISTRICT NEWS.

LIBERAL MEETING at SOUTHERY
ODDFELLOWSHIP AT BURNHAM.

THE LATEST MARKETS AND GENERAL NEWS OF THE WEEK.

13. Jo Cooke II, manager of the *Peterborough Advertiser* company, stands between Sir Richard and Lady Winfrey at a complimentary staff banquet held on 14 February 1914, two days after Sir Richard was knighted by George V. This photograph was published in the *Advertiser* of Saturday February 21st and the original caption is here reproduced in facsimile.

...borough Adver-
...mes, Editor. On
...seen Mr. H. B.
... Secretary to the
L. Getnin, the
...ding Guardian,''
...h-looking gentle-

man seated at the top of the side table to
the right is Mr. E. W. Hall, the Editor of
the "Hunts. County News," and in a cor-
responding position at the other table will
be seen the earnest face of Mr. J. T. S.
Flynn, the Editor of the "Football Citizen."
All the others are celebrities in their various

departments. The veteran in the vice-chair
to the left is Mr. John Dyson, who saw to
press the first "Peterborough Advertiser"
in 1854 and every issue since (still hearty
and a vigorous worker), while in the other
vice-chair is Mr. A. Blake, the good-tem-
pered chief of the Composing Rooms.

(Flashlight Photo, J. B. Etches and Hall.)

14. Entire staff of the *Peterborough Advertiser* in 1886, ten years before Slatterie Clarke sold the newspaper. Standing (L to R): Joseph Parsons, machineman; A. A. Blake, J. Yates, John Dyson, Walter Blake, Thomas Cooper, Walter Farrow, typesetters from the case. Sitting: Edward George, manager; John Lamb Blake, overseer; Edward Newton, editor; W. H. B. Saunders, sub-editor; Frank Loomes, reporter. In front: Ebenezer Holloway and Nathaniel Ball, apprentices.

15. To celebrate his 90th birthday in January 1928 Sir Halley Stewart (president) gave a lunch for tenants of the Small Holdings Association at which this group was photographed (L to R): Charles Hughes, steward; Mrs Coupland, Sir Richard's sister; Sir Richard and Lady Winfrey; Sir Halley Stewart; Mrs S. O. G. Willson, Sir Richard's eldest daughter; and Sir Malcolm Stewart, Sir Halley's son.

16. Sir Richard as Mayor bidding farewell in October 1914 to Peterborough recruits volunteering for service in the early stages of World War I.

17. Dryland Street head office of the Group's Kettering-based newspapers from 1888 to 1976. Painted titles fading on the wall tell their own historical tale.

18. Frank Hutchen directed these newspapers with distinction from 1888 to his death in harness in 1942, aged 71.

19. The *Pink 'Un* (below), published seasonally 1897-1974, was his pride. He used pet names for every team, represented by cartoon faces printed cheerful if winning and miserable if not, as in this specimen of the *Pink 'Un* parade.

1. The *Guardian* office at Spalding when Sir Richard Winfrey's proprietorship started in 1887.

2. *Boston Guardian* offices built by Jo Cooke l in 1887 with living quarters above for himself.

3. Sir Richard Winfrey's father, Richard Francis Winfrey J.P. of Long Sutton (1825-1894).

4. Right. Sir Richard Winfrey (1858-1944). Active in newspapers for 57 years.

5. Below. Offices built in Purfleet Street, King's Lynn, by Sir Richard's company in 1893 after purchasing the *Lynn News.* Occupied until 1975.

20. George Cragg, EMAP's first full-time photographer and block-maker, seen (right) operating the original process camera at Kettering where he opened the Group's first engraving department in 1920.

21. Page from 1897 wages book listing Northamptonshire Newspapers staff based in Wellingborough, where some printing continued till 1908. Minney was chief local editorial man whilst Charles Wilson dealt with accounts and James Wharmby advertisements at company level.

1897

	Nov 27			Dec 4			Dec 11			Dec 18			Dec 25		
Minney	2	5	-	2	5	-	2	5	-	2	5	-	2	5	-
Morris		10	-		10	-		10	-		10	-		10	-
Cato F		5	-		8	-		5	-		5	-		8	-
Wilson	2	5	-	2	5	-	2	5	-	2	5	-	2	5	-
Wharmby	2	7	6	2	7	6	2	7	6	2	7	6	2	7	6
Sear	1	1	-	1	1	-	1	1	-	1	1	-	1	1	-
Smith Mis		12	4		16	3		15	-		16	-		19	4
Hyde		4	-		4	-		4	-		4	-		5	-
Flood		4	6		4	6		4	6		4	6		4	6
Pentelow		4	6		4	6		4	6		4	6		4	6
Jarritt	1	9	9	1	8	1	1	10	-	1	10	-	1	10	-
Rixon	1	6	6	1	6	-	1	7	-	1	7	-	1	7	-
Payton	1	14	5	1	15	7	1	18	6	1	18	10	1	15	7
Coles	1	8	-	1	8	-	1	9	2	1	10	7	1	9	2
Cato		16	-		16	5		16	4		16	5		16	8
Atkins		4	-		4	-		4	-		4	-		4	-
	17	-	6	17	3	10	17	9	6	17	12	4	17	12	3

22. Flashback to 1923: Wilfred Elmore, still communications chief at Kettering, reading news transmitted by the Press Association by private wire and received as punched tape. In 1921 Kettering was one of the first newspaper offices to be equipped with Frederick Creed's newly-invented high-speed morse receivers and the Creed translators which converted morse tape into printed messages.

23. Holding a handful of telephones, Kettering office sports editors in the 1930s received horse racing results and simultaneously passed them on to branch offices. Junior reporters typed them on small stencils for stamping by hand in the *Evening Telegraph* Stop Press column, using inked pads as shown. Street sellers had Stop Press results up-dated each half hour.

24. The Fultograph, an experimental machine which received photographs radioed on 1500 metres by the BBC in 1928 and 1929. At Kettering it enabled the *Evening Telegraph* of 23 March 1929 to print its first same-day picture of the Boat Race finish. Machine seen as preserved at Kettering.

25. First annual report of Sir Richard Winfrey's company formed in 1903 to acquire the *Bury Free Press*. The 1905 report referred to the paper's help towards Liberal Party successes at the polls.

THE

Bury St. Edmund's Printing and Publishing Company,

LIMITED

DIRECTORS' REPORT,

FOR THE YEAR ENDING DECEMBER 31st, 1903.

The Directors have pleasure in presenting the Statement of Accounts for the year ending December 31st, 1903.

There has been a substantial increase of revenue from both the Newspaper and the General Printing, and the Directors consider the profit from the Trading Account is very satisfactory.

They recommend that a Dividend of 6 per cent. be paid to the shareholders which will absorb £144 leaving a balance to be carried forward of £273.

The works in Cemetery Road have been greatly improved, Electric Lighting introduced, and an Electric Motor installed for driving the Linotype Machines. The "Bury Free Press" is to be further enlarged at an early date and there is every prospect of continued prosperity for the Company.

The Directors are of opinion that it would be of great advantage to the Company if the Share Capital could be increased by about £500 to enable the purchase of further up-to-date jobbing plant.

Signed on behalf of the Directors,

R. WINFREY,

Managing Director.

26. *Bury Free Press* staff in 1911. Mark Clarke, oldest-serving employee, sits in shirt sleeves between Sir Richard Winfrey and Henry Bankes Ashton, director and company secretary. Standing behind Sir Richard is R. E. Taylor, works manager, between Fred Patrick, office manager, and the fierce but diminutive W. T. Cox, editor. A staff outing to Lowestoft was arranged by the company that year.

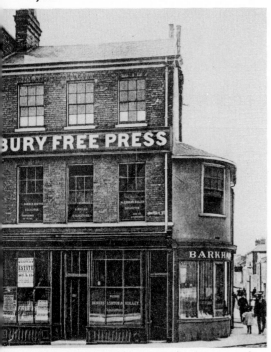

27. Bury St Edmunds premises built in Abbeygate Street by T. F. Lucia for his *Bury Free Press* and used for production till 1874 when he opened works still operating in King's Road. The commercial department remained for some years in part of these premises, H. Bankes Ashton using the rest for his legal practice.

7. WINNING A WAR

FOR seventeen years from 1906 to 1923, South-West Norfolk kept Sir Richard as its Member, sitting under Campbell-Bannerman, Asquith and Lloyd George as Liberal Prime Ministers until the Conservatives took power in 1922. There was no general election between 1910 and 1918 because of the Great War but in 1915 Asquith agreed to head a wartime coalition and in 1916 Lloyd George, succeeding as Prime Minister, gave Britain the war leadership it needed. He was a man more after Sir Richard's own heart than the intellectual Asquith despite his integrity and character. Moreover, Lloyd George had a good opinion of Sir Richard. He had several times stayed with him at Sutton House, Peterborough, starting soon after Richard settled there and was beginning to organise Liberal Party work in the Eastern Counties. When L.G. bought his property in the Surrey countryside at Churt after the war, Richard visited him there more than once, on one occasion advising him on adjacent farmland before he added it to his estate.

"When I formed my administration in December 1916," wrote Lloyd George in chapter 44 of his war memoirs, "I was convinced that if this country should endure to victory, it was essential that both branches of the food problem — production and distribution — should be tackled vigorously and without delay. I therefore regarded the food problem as one of our most important concerns. Food production was entrusted to Mr Prothero, the Minister of Agriculture, and Sir Richard Winfrey, his Parliamentary Secretary. They were both men who had a thorough practical knowledge of agriculture in all its aspects."

49

Sir Richard found Rowland Prothero (later Lord Ernle) a delightful colleague. One-time chief land agent for the Duke of Bedford, he was both practical and scholarly, applying scientific methods to farming and also remembered for his "Psalms in Human Life" in which he showed a rare understanding of the lives of leading Christians throughout history. The two became key figures in the team which converted a sleepy agriculture into a munition of war but their biggest worries were those they kept to themselves — sinkings by German submarines of shipping bringing vital supplies, including a cargo of Ford tractors needed for the ploughing-up programme.

Living at the National Liberal Club, Sir Richard seldom got home till Saturday evening. To cut travelling he moved the family to a furnished house in Hampstead in 1917, remembered because one of London's anti-aircraft guns was close by. If there were alerts at the House of Commons he retreated to his private room at a lower level where he and Stanley Baldwin, who had the next room as Financial Secretary to the Treasury, sheltered together. He little thought to see Baldwin emerge as Prime Minister after the war. Another help was to have Charles Hughes at hand. During Sir Richard's term at the Agriculture Office, Hughes was one of his Private Secretaries (unpaid), going up from Peterborough several days a week, at the same time keeping in touch with Liberal Party headquarters. But for his attachment to Sir Richard he could, in fact, have wholly concentrated on Party work but declined an offer by the Hon Neil Primrose, Chief Liberal Whip in Lloyd George's government.

Two particular matters of lasting credit to Sir Richard marked his years at the Board. One was the Corn Production Act of 1917 and the other was settlement of ex-Servicemen on the land. By 1918 the Act had added nearly three million acres to the national total of wheat and oat land. Corn prices were guaranteed to farmers, War Agricultural Committees set up to achieve county targets, and Agricultural Wages Boards inaugurated to ensure minimum wages for the first time. It was Sir Richard's lot to deal with these latter clauses when drafted. No-one knew the poverty of the labourer better than he did. Both Charles Hughes and Tom Diggle had interviewed scores of them to get the economic facts of their existence, and extracts from these case histories are preserved in his books. [1] It was due mainly to him that labourers' wages rose by 160 per cent between 1914 and 1921. In the latter year, to his disgust, the Act was replaced by less generous peace-time support for the farmer but the principle of the minimum wage survived.

Prothero handed the problem of post-war land settlement to Sir Richard in 1917. Already there was demand for land from men discharged from the Forces and to help them he piloted the Small Holding Colonies Bill through the Commons in August. It was a typical Winfrey effort. The idea of founding colonies where inexperienced men could be trained and marketing services shared had cropped up in 1915: it was Sir Richard who turned theory into practice. Private offers of estates made the work easier and 1,000 acres at Holbeach, in his old haunts, were among areas released by the Crown. He personally selected 100 applicants to take over ten-acre holdings on this splendid soil.

Sir Richard's pioneer Act of 1916 promised 8,000 acres for discharged soldiers and in the summer of 1918 he pushed through the Small Holding Colonies (Amendment) Act, increasing this tenfold to 80,000 acres. In 1919 the Colonies Act was used to acquire another area near his old home — Guy's Hospital estate at Sutton Bridge, across the River Nene from Sir Richard's own Wingland holdings. The estate exceeds 6,000 acres and secures income for the London hospital founded in 1720 by Thomas Guy. But all this was but a preliminary. A survey of troops ordered by Sir Douglas Haig at the request of the Board of Agriculture showed that fifteen per cent of the Army — three-quarters of a million — wanted to settle on the land.

Lloyd George gathered Junior members of his Government around him for weekly breakfasts at Downing Street. Sir Richard usually sat next to Lord Rothermere, Minister

[1] *Leaves from my life* , pages 154-169 and *Great Men and others I have met* , pages 151-154.

for Air, at these meal discussions, and was called from the table on 30 October 1917 to learn that news of his mother's illness had been telephoned to the House of Commons. She died on October 31st. Cruel news followed next day. Lady Winfrey's sister-in-law Kitty (Catherine Lucy), wife of Sir Robert Pattinson, was trying to rescue her dogs from the railway line at Ruskington when she was killed by a train. Her funeral followed the day after Mrs Winfrey was buried at Long Sutton, where Sir Richard expressed family feelings towards their mother at a simple thanksgiving service in the old home. Up to two days before death she retained her wonderful memory and was knitting items to send to her eldest grandson, Richard Finch Winfrey, who was serving as an officer in France. The loss of his mother ended Christmas visits to Long Sutton and the break was spent quietly at Peterborough. "So ended the most anxious and difficult year of my life."

With war and the 1918 election over, Tories pressed for more places when Lloyd George formed his new Coalition Government in January 1919. So Sir Richard was denied the chance to go back and complete his big land settlement schemes. He was sixty, less agile, had lost his light brown hair and all his teeth, and sometimes had touches of lumbago. The dynamo had slowed down. Family and business affairs called and during 1919 he was glad to put in only occasional attendance at the House. Then in 1920 he had his longest-ever holiday — four months from April to July in Canada with Pat before he went to university. Half of the time was spent helping a World Brotherhood fund-raising mission for European relief and the other half checking on the Canadian Government's scheme for settling its own ex-Servicemen on the land.

Back in the House, it was gratifying to hear his successor, Sir Arthur Griffith-Boscawen, say that we were a nation of smallholders; that 65 per cent of farming occupiers in the country had less than 50 acres; that 14,000 of these holdings were created under the 1908 Act and that losses on them had been infinitesimal. By 1924, 16,000 ex-Servicemen were settled on holdings, bringing the number of statutory smallholdings to 30,000. Thus did war highlight the worth of Sir Richard's vision. So did the Great Depression when Ramsey MacDonald brought in the Conservatives and a few Liberals to form his National Government in 1931. Although there was a 1931 Act to provide smallholdings for unemployed it was not till voluntary bodies gingered up the Government in 1933 that action started.

Sir Richard was in this deputation, another being Sir Halley Stewart's eldest son Percy Malcolm, powerful as the enlightened figure reigning over both brick and cement industries. He offered a personal gift of £25,000 on condition the Government contributed a like sum, and within twelve months the Land Settlement Association began to transfer workless men from industry to life on the land. About the same time, Malcolm Stewart was appointed Commissioner for the Special areas where depression was most acute, and he and the Association co-operated in smallholdings experiments. Stewart resigned as Special Commissioner after two years, a baronetcy in 1937 marking his efforts. Meanwhile the Land Settlement Association pressed on and by the Second War had gone far towards the agreed target of 2,000 holdings.

Sir Richard was an early member of the Association and lived to see its tenants playing their part in feeding Britain in World War II. In March 1944 he asked the Editor of the *Peterborough Advertiser* to publish compliments paid in Parliament on the success of the L.S.A. and wrote a commentary to add to them. In it he deftly covered the whole smallholdings story from the early days of his Lincolnshire Association to the day he wrote, with holdings accepted as an integral part of agriculture in every county and tenants achieving comfortable retirement. It was the last thing he wrote for print. It was also his final look around the most notable area of his life's work, for a month later death brought his service to an end. But Britain's smallholdings remain as his permanent national memorial.

Prothero hoped there would be a Privy Councillorship or some other honour for Sir Richard Winfrey when their partnership at the Board of Agriculture ended in 1918 but in the cross-currents of coalition nothing materialised. His knighthood had appeared in the New Year list of 1914 through the recommendation of Lord Carrington, Lewis Harcourt, M.P., and the Chief Whip, after Carrington had reminded Asquith of Richard's long service to Liberalism and agriculture. Richard was at the Palace on 12 February 1914 to receive the accolade and his account of these proceedings was the hilarious highlight of the staff dinner organised in his honour by *Peterborough Advertiser* staff two days later. [1] What impressed him most was the way the great French photographer Lafayette "took" him in six different positions in two minutes when he went to him from the Palace!

Master and man relationships were steadier and surer in those pre-war days and something. of the old intimate atmosphere survives in the report of the dinner. Frank Loomes, who regularly scattered his editorial thunderbolts over five counties, did not spare the master. True, he had been a voice in the wilderness as he championed the land-worker and he had founded a policy to which the Government had set their seal. But Sir Richard had his limitations and his critics were not always wrong. "We are not always convinced of the profoundly angelic qualities of even a knight of the realm," he said. "We have known barometrical changes: times when business overtures were like the gentle zephyrs which stir the strings of the aeolian harp with the sweetest and most inspiriting music; and others when those zephyrs are replaced by tempestuous gales calculated to uproot the very monarchs of the forest were they not so firmly rooted. It only shows that a knight is human after all . . ."

These two had an unusual relationship. Sometimes they had open quarrels. Often they avoided speaking to each other, communicating by means of barbed little notes. Loomes, like his friend Saunders, was a devout Catholic. Winfrey was an ardent Protestant. They were both indispensable to the Advertiser — and knew it. Like most strong-minded individualists called on to work together,

1 *Peterborough Citizen* 18 February 1914 and *Advertiser* 21 February 1914.

54

they looked on each other with mingled respect and contempt, while quieter men like Jo Cooke II, Saunders and Hughes oiled the wheels where they could. Soft leadership would never have satisfied Loomes. Nor did he give it to his staff. Lady Winfrey summed it up. "What would you do without Mr Loomes?" she asked them. "Though he is sometimes stormy like the Chief, he will not allow anyone to say a word against any of you. He says: 'They are all very good boys'."

8. CARRYING THE TORCH

LADY WINFREY shared with Richard in the official and social life of a leading Parliamentarian. The Liberal Party was wealthy and powerful; its functions gay and splendid; its membership glittering with titles[1]. Even the Boer War had not sent up Income Tax beyond 1s 3d in the £, and when the *Peterborough Advertiser* had a demand for £71 in 1905, it was considered so excessive that the company secretary nagged at the Surveyor of Taxes till he reduced it by £10.

Horace Mansfield, elected Liberal Member for Spalding in 1900 and 1906, sent a Parliamentary letter to the *Spalding Guardian* and in February 1906 Richard began weekly notes for his own and the *Norwich Mercury* series. For nineteen years — its title "Beneath Big Ben" changed early on to "Observations from the House of Commons" — he maintained a running commentary on the affairs of Parliament except for the two years of his Parliamentary Secretaryship. He pasted the cuttings into scrap books (not now extant) and drew on them for his memoirs, "but I fear it is all ancient history and will not see the light of day again."

Helping to draft the Small Holdings Bill and see it through in 1907 was monumental task for a new Member but Sir Richard distinguished himself in other Parliamentary moves in those early years. Steps to avenge his 1891 defeat over preservation of a footpath at Sutton Bridge were taken in May 1908 when he brought forward a Public Rights of Way Bill. Other business delayed its passage and eight similar Bills were put forward by others before legislation he

[1] For the record, Sir Richard Winfrey attended five garden parties and two State balls at Buckingham Palace between 1919 and 1934, and was among guests invited to Windsor for garden parties given by Edward VII in 1906 and 1907.

wanted was passed in 1932. He secured strengthening amendments to the 1908 Local Authorities (Admission of the Press to Meetings) Act, which was the journalist's safeguard till superseded in 1960 by the Public Bodies (Admission to Meetings) Act. Introduction of his Pharmacy Bill on behalf of the Pharmaceutical Society (he retained membership of this until 1934) led to the Government's own Poisons and Pharmacy Act of 1908 — and incidentally to clashes with Jesse Boot of Nottingham, then chairman of the Drug Companies' Association, who came daily in his wheeled chair to the Commons to lobby Members against it.[1]

Lloyd George's post-war Coalition Government ended in October 1922 when the Tories withdrew and he resigned as Prime Minister in favour of Bonar Law. A general election followed in November when Sir Richard was returned for the seventh time in South-West Norfolk. With him on the Liberal opposition benches in the new Parliament were Samuel and Robert Pattinson, his wife's brothers, Samuel sitting as the first Liberal ever returned for Horncastle and Robert for Grantham. In recognition of his standing as Parliamentarian and agriculturist, Sir Richard was asked to propose an amendment to the speech from the Throne and to call on the Tory Government to inquire into the unhappy state of agriculture and of men on the land. Lloyd George himself seconded and Bonar Law promised an inquiry but before progress could be made, sickness led Bonar Law to resign in May 1923. Stanley Baldwin found himself Prime Minister and in November went to the country.

Now aged 64, Sir Richard had told his friends in South-West Norfolk that the 1922 election would be the last he would fight for them. Although Parliament had sat for less than twelve months he did not alter his intention and this time Tories regained the seat lost to them 17 years before. Meanwhile the Liberal Party, anxious to keep him, persuaded him to stand at Gainsborough, where he expected to be beaten and so start honourable retirement. He surprised

[1] Sir Richard's part in this Parliamentary campaign is acknowledged in chapter five of *Jesse Boot of Boots the Chemists*, the biography by Dr Stanley Chapman published in 1973.

himself, however, by turning a Tory majority of 1,799 into a Liberal majority of 1,853 after a two-week campaign, while Robert and Samuel Pattinson were similarly successful. Ramsey MacDonald came in as Britain's first Labour Prime Minister, dependent on Liberal support, but when this uneasy partnership ended in October 1924, a fresh election allowed Baldwin to romp home with 419 Tory seats and the Liberals were reduced from 159 to a derisory 40. Sam and Bob Pattinson were out and at Gainsborough Sir Richard suffered his first defeat since 1900.

In the Holland-with-Boston division where Richard and Halley Stewart had toiled and tasted victory so many years earlier, Pat Winfrey — fourth member of the two families to be in the fray at the same time — also fought and lost, though polling more votes than his father. He had gone into the division three months before to fight the by-election following the death of W. S. Royce of Pinchbeck Hall, a Tory turned Labour who had settled near Spalding, his birthplace, after making a fortune in South Africa as a contractor. Pat Winfrey reached his 21st birthday on 24 June 1923. On his next birthday Cambridge conferred on him the B.A. and LL.B. degrees and within hours the question faced him as to whether he should take the plunge and try to fill the gap left by Royce. Within a week he was adopted and started a month's campaign. Nineteen M.P.s and four millionaires were among his Liberal speakers and Halley Stewart, though 86, also turned out.

Pat's by-election opponents were the Tory Arthur Dean, a Grantham gentleman farmer, and Dr Hugh Dalton, future Socialist Chancellor. Dalton had already lost elections in three other divisions — one of them in 1922 in Cambridge where Pat as an undergraduate had worked for the Liberal — and had been told there would be no Liberal candidate in Holland. According to Sir Richard, the Winfrey intervention was gall and wormwood to Dalton and he supposed Labour attributed their defeat largely to this. For though Pat polled only 7,596 votes he reduced the Labour vote by 3,600 to 12,101, while Dean got in by 12,907. For long afterwards Dalton remained unforgiving as far as Pat was concerned

58

though Dean said his fight was one of which any fellow of 22 could be proud. In the October general election Dalton was finally successful at Peckham and Dean retained his seat in Holland. Pat, who battled manfully against an anti-Liberal tide and past neglect of the constituency, won 6,413 of the votes compared with his father's 5,590 at Gainsborough.

Nothing would have pleased Sir Richard more than to see Pat established as a Parliamentarian, carrying the torch for Liberalism as his family on both sides had done. Glorious failures though they were, these two defeats in the division which had been Sir Richard's own training ground, and the overwhelming defeat of the Party in the country, were heavy blows. But he never lost interest in political work nor ceased to be engaged in this and allied causes. Through the Eastern Counties Liberal Federation in particular he became a political father figure whose word carried weight throughout the region. From its inception in 1897 till his death in 1944 he was visiting constituencies and checking organisation. There were national Party conferences to attend — the last he went to was in London in 1942 — and he pulled his weight at by-elections up to 1944 when he spoke for Mrs Corbett Ashby at Bury St Edmunds in February. He was 85 and life was to end for him two months later, but he made the trip and received a great welcome from Clement Davies, then Liberal leader and one who 50 years before had ridden with him horseback to meetings in South-West Norfolk.

In the 1929 general election Pat's earlier efforts in Holland bore fruit in James Blindell's Liberal victory by 13,000 votes to Labour's 9,000. "You did the donkey work and made it all the easier," said Blindell. Lloyd George helped here too: at a Boston open air rally, 15,000 people heard him — the largest meeting Charles Hughes ever handled — with speeches relayed to Spalding market place. Pat himself had nursed the Wellingborough division for two years and in this 1929 election drove the Tory into third place, coming second to George Dallas, a trade union organiser. He drew more support than any other Liberal in Northamptonshire and the division quickly invited him to remain their champion. He withdrew shortly afterwards, however, to concentrate on his career at the Bar. Two things made his campaign unusual. He was the first candidate to use a public address system (this new-fangled equipment was stored in the Market Place offices of the *Wellingborough News*), and he took an Irish bride a few weeks before the campaign began. To a heckler's "You haven't got over your honeymoon yet," Pat retorted: "We had only four days and we spent them in Lanarkshire studying the conditions of the unemployed miners there."

After 30 years splendid service, Charles Hughes found the Eastern Counties Liberal Federation could no longer pay his salary and returned to newspapering in 1930 as general manager of the *Peterborough Advertiser*. He gave voluntary help but it was all hard work and only twenty Liberals survived the 1935 election. E.C.L.F. delegates heard the Winfrey swansong at Cambridge in June 1943 when, aged 84, he presented his last report as treasurer and traced the Federation's history. Conference warmed to the occasion and Wilfred Roberts, national Party organiser, brought fervent congratulations from Lloyd George.

Tributes to Sir Richard's untiring and determined Liberalism flowed when death came ten months later. Herbert Samuel, by then a peer, spoke of his vigorous energy and power of initiative enduring for a full half-century till he became in Eastern England almost a legendary figure. With Liberalism on the decline, there were those who had lost enthusiasm for the fight, wrote H. B. Hartley, comrade-in-arms as solicitor, *Peterborough Advertiser* secretary and election campaigner, "but Sir Richard never put off his armour and died sword in hand."

From Lloyd George, who himself would pass on eleven months later, came a tribute to a "full life of active service in a great cause." He saw clearly why politics and newspapering were for Winfrey so closely combined. "Through his Press he devoted a lifetime to the education of a part of England in the principles and practice of Liberalism. His death is a real loss to the Liberal cause at a time when it stands in need of such men."

Some have said that Sir Richard was a supporter of lost causes. It is truer to say that he believed in and worked for causes long after others allowed difficulties to sap their zeal. While many lost faith in the League of Nations, born out of World War I, he was still working for it during World War II. He originated the Peterborough branch and helped form the Northamptonshire Federal Council in 1928, remaining on its executive throughout. Through his newspapers he helped fan enthusiasm by regular notes on League affairs. Fred Skinner, editor of the Kettering-based weeklies, ran an essay competition in 1929 for school children on "Why I should like to go to Geneva." Grace Thornton, who won the travel scholarship to Geneva to see the League at work, was then a 16-year-old at Kettering High School. Subsequently she made a name for herself in the Foreign Service, particularly during the Indonesian troubles of 1963[1].

Lesser-known aspect was support in earlier days for trade unionism, following Sir Halley Stewart in this. In 1906 George Edwards, a Norfolk campaigner who helped Sir Richard into Parliament and was knighted in Ramsey MacDonald's time, persuaded him and George Nicholls of Peterborough, another ex-labourer, to join in re-starting Joseph Arch's original Agricultural Labourers' Union. The aim was not only to improve working conditions but to help labourers to seats on local councils and in Parliament, and to protect them from political persecution. Though both Nicholls and Winfrey broke with the union over the six-month strike in 1911 at St Faith's, near Norwich — the episode is part of trade union history — the labourers' needs were never out of his thoughts and Sir Richard's work in Parliament revealed him as their special friend at court. It was the Liberals, moreover, who gave the whole working population their first schemes of unemployment and health insurance and also old age pensions.

In his churchmanship Sir Richard maintained Nonconformist loyalties to the last, latterly attaching himself to the Park Road Baptist Church in Peterborough. He and Lady Winfrey were often presiding or speaking at chapel rallies

[1] *Reader's Digest*, August 1969.

or bazaars and were also warm friends of the Salvation Army. They had been so since its founder, General William Booth, had been their guest when he opened the Peterborough Citadel in 1898. Earlier in life the General had been a junior Methodist minister and spent some time in the Spalding Circuit. Sir Richard's own vision, described in 1941, was of one strong united Nonconformist church able to shut down churches and open new ones according to need. Looking back over a full life and many interests, he felt he had drifted from the uncomplicated faith and quiet contentment that marked his parents' home. Yet more than once in his diary he records a simple thankfulness to God for so much happiness and so much success. There was no drying of the springs of his belief.

Part of that happiness, especially between the wars, was greater opportunity to travel, and a list of trips abroad concludes this chapter. Twenty of them were written up for the weekly newspapers as Sir Richard undertook them, these articles being re-published in 1941 as *Days I Remember* , an illustrated 335-page book offered at six shillings. It gives an insight into travel before it became commonplace and shows him making the most of his periods abroad, taking in zestful stride antiquities and modern marvels, agriculture and land settlement, newspaper offices and industrial works; speaking too for England, for Liberal philosophy and for World Brotherhood ideals in private and public. Companionship was essential, whether official or personal, and often Lucy Winfrey, who acted as secretary before her marriage, helped her father compile descriptions as they went along. A later co-writer was Philip Schwabe of the editorial staff at King's Lynn.[1] Seven weeks before a trip to Morocco in 1937 he was alerted to joining the party and told to learn Arabic, which he did by going to an ex-military interpreter.

[1] Schwabe came from the *Yorkshire Gazette* in 1927 to work in the Rushden office of the *Northamptonshire Evening Telegraph*, transferring to King's Lynn in March 1928. In December 1939 he was spared to assist R. P. Winfrey in his appointment as Regional Officer under the Ministry of Information and remained at Cambridge throughout the war as regional Press Officer with William A. Appel, later editor of the *Bury Free Press*, as his assistant. At his wedding in 1943, Pat Winfrey was his best man. After the war, when the Ministry of Information became the Central Office of Information, Schwabe stayed on as head of the Cambridge regional office till retirement in 1973.

On visits to South Africa in 1929 and 1936 Sir Richard treasured opportunities to spend time with General Smuts, whom he first met in London during the 1919 Versailles peace conference. They exchanged acorns from their respective oaks and in 1969, when Pat Winfrey visited the Smuts farmhouse at Irene, Pretoria, he found the Winfrey scorn had flourished better than the Irene acorn planted at Castor. Sleeping in the mahogany four-poster bed at Falmouth used by William Knibb was a feature of tours of Jamaica. This was in the Baptist Mission House, headquarters of this anti-slavery campaigner who was one of Kettering's most famous sons and lived to see all slaves declared free in 1838. Sir Richard preached to congregations of blacks at Falmouth both in 1933 and 1939. Between these visits Kettering was granted borough status in 1938, just 100 years after emancipation, and honoured William Knibb by including in its coat of arms the figure of a liberated Jamaican slave. On behalf of Kettering, Sir Richard presented a large copy of the arms to hang in the Falmouth church.

Sir Richard wrote his own notes on this 1939 West Indian trip. "Once again — and it may be for the last time — I publish the notes of my diary, scribbled from day to day as we journeyed along." Pre-war ferment had obliged Sir Henry Lunn to avoid the Mediterranean and to sail West. It was 40 years since he first travelled with Lunn on his educational tours and this was the last voyage for both of them. Before the year was out Hitler would strike at Poland and cruising days would be over. Lunn himself was a sick man, worsening as the days went by, but invited Richard to his cabin for a last long chat on old times and old friends. On the return journey he was taken off at Toulon for a dash by train and ambulance to a London hospital, but died soon after admission. From Caribbean sunshine Sir Richard arrived home in snow. Truly, in more ways than one, he had come back to a colder world.

SIR RICHARD WINFREY'S VISITS ABROAD

1889	June	Norway
1890	June	Norway
1891	August	Switzerland
1892	June	Germany with Mr and Mrs Brand
*1893	June	Chicago World's Fair and the Rockies
*1895	June	Italy
1896	August	Switzerland
1897	March	Riviera and Italy: honeymoon
*1899	March	Greece, Palestine and Egypt
1901	June	Norway
*1905	June	Germany: Municipal visit
1907	May	Germany
*1910	September	Camping tour of Syria and Palestine
1911	September	Ireland: Eighty Club visit
1912	June	Switzerland
1913	April	Belgium
1914	May	Cologne Exhibition: Municipal party
*1920	April	Canada from East to West
1921	April	Italy
*1921	August	Germany, Czecho-Slovakia, and World Brotherhood Conference, Prague
1922	June	Strasbourg and Brussels: Brotherhood mission
1922	August	Oberammergau Passion Play and Inter-Parliamentary Conference, Vienna
1923	February	Algeria and West Indies
1924	January	Switzerland
1924	August	Switzerland: Conference
*1925	February	Spain
*1926	January	U.S.A.: a Brotherhood mission
1926	September	Prague: Brotherhood conference; Vienna; Italy
1927	January	Switzerland
*1927	August	Canada East to West: Newspapermen's tour
1927	September	Belgium: Brotherhood mission and battlefields
1928	March	Riviera and Corsica
*1928	November	East and South Africa
*1930	January	New Zealand: Farmers' party
1930	April	Canada
1930	August	Oberammergau Passion Play
*1931	March	Egypt, Turkey and Syria
*1932	April	Greece: Hellenic cruise
*1933	February	West Africa and West Indies
*1933	October	Germany: the Hitler regime
*1934	February	Palestine and Syria
1934	June	Sweden
*1936	February	South Africa
*1937	March	Morocco
*1939	February	West Indies

*described in *Days I Remember*

9. THE WINFREY PRESS I
King's Lynn, Spalding, Peterborough

INCORPORATION in May 1947 of East Midland Allied Press Limited formalised the natural grouping of the four Winfrey newspaper companies based on Bury St Edmunds, Kettering, King's Lynn and Peterborough. During the ten-year period up to Sir Richard's death these companies published thirteen papers, owning a dozen and printing the *Newmarket Journal* on contract for Mr F. Simpson. Some of the advantages of grouping — bulk ordering of newsprint for example — were practised between the wars and sharing of Fleet Street advertisement agencies developed. During and after World War I, Fred Paul at No. 151 serviced the Peterborough company for which his author son Leslie reviewed books. He also represented Kettering, and his neighbour George Rogers at No. 150 took over both companies in the late 1920's. Lynn and Bury interests were in the hands of George Jackson, operating as a freelance though a London advertisement staffman for a Yorkshire paper at 145 Fleet Street. While still at No. 145 he opened an office at No. 180 for his own connections, and by the early 'Thirties was there full-time with Len Prichard joining him as a youngster, also from No. 145.

Jackson settled at Cliffords Inn in 1938 and represented (among others) all the Winfrey newspapers with their combined sale of 96,000 per week. This was under a scheme proposed to Sir Richard by Pat Winfrey by which national advertisers placed announcements in all the papers on a one-rate, one-order, one-account basis. One of Fleet Street's rugged characters and a formidable golfer despite losing an arm in World War I, Jackson began to use notepaper headed

"East Midlands Allied Press", a title hit on by himself and Pat. Accounting for this development was handled by the East Midland Amalgamated Paper Company, whose formation was also inspired by Pat. This company dealt, too, with supplies of newsprint but war-time rationing limited its role. Edward Smedley kept the books of this company at Peterborough, where he was office manager. For nearly ten years, therefore, before East Midland Allied Press Ltd was launched, the initials EMAP were familiar in the newspaper world.[1] A co-operative effort conducted each spring and summer from the Cumbergate office at Peterborough was the Holiday Bureau. Starting in 1927, seaside hotels and boarding houses were canvassed on behalf of all the newspapers with Frank Ball (later advertisement manager for the *Cambridge News)* as organiser. Millicent Clements, a teenager who was engaged for three weeks to help him, stayed on to give a life-time's service, continuing to work for EMAP national publications after a 50-year presentation in 1976.

Alternative printing arrangements, sharing of news reports and reporters and transfers of staff were other inter-company advantages. Sir Richard picked his men thoughtfully and gave them rein within well-understood limits. He was nothing if not a master man, with a grasp of affairs, breadth of outlook and sureness of decision which lieutenants were bound to respect and could rarely question. They might have confessions to make and errors to atone for but he freed himself for all his public work by relying on them to carry the Winfrey Press.

Although Sir Richard described himself as editor on purchasing the *Spalding Guardian* in 1887, his editorial mainstay was Ridlington, followed by John Diggle and then his younger brother Tom, the latter being moved to Peterborough to edit *The Citizen* when this was launched as a mid-weekly in October 1898. At 24, Tom Diggle settled at King's Lynn in 1903 to manage the Lynn News and County

[1] George Jackson died in 1963 and Len Prichard, who had been with him for 33 years and succeeded as chairman of his company, sold out and joined Press Alliance Ltd as a director. The company meanwhile had lost EMAP representation when the Group opened a London office and appointed its own team.

Press company and to edit its newspapers. Revenue went up at once, Linotype machines were installed, the uneconomic *North Cambs Echo* was sold to the new Liberal Isle of Ely Printing and Publishing company, and by 1905 turnover and profits had increased considerably. Sir Richard could later say that during Diggle's 40-year association, company progress had been astonishing.[1] Diggle never allowed respect of persons to blunt his pen. One Mayor publicly promised to horsewhip him, whilst to be threatened with everything except decent burial became nothing new as he walked the town. His brother John was on the Lynn board of directors from the time Tom moved from Peterborough until 1913. He rejoined later, contributed regular agricultural articles and was on the board when Tom died in 1943.

On a Saturday in July 1914, just before the start of World War I, Thomas Cossar proudly showed off his original rotary flat-bed printing press to Diggle, up in Otley to see it. He ordered the machine for the *Lynn News* and during the winter Cossar himself erected it — first of his famous rotary flatbed presses to be sold. "Looking back to those midnight hours of February 1915 I can see him now, in a bottomless pit, like an amiable devil in overalls," recalled Diggle.[2] The Cossar did duty till superseded in 1930 by a double-unit version costing £5,000. This was sold when printing was centralised under EMAP arrangements after World War II. On entering the Government in 1916 Sir Richard resigned as managing director[3] and in a war-time promotion, Tom Diggle took the position. After the war shareholders enjoyed ten-per-cent dividends plus bonuses of fifteen-per-cent in place of pre-war returns varying from five to eight-per-cent. It was the pay-off to Sir Richard's policy of steady pegging away in competition with the *Lynn Advertiser*, which was always a bit ahead with sales. The *Advertiser* and the *News* were both weekend papers with 1841 and 1860 as their starting dates, and the *Advertiser* had all along had on-the-spot supervision from the Thew family.

[1] *Lynn News*, 6 April 1943.

[2] *Lynn Advertiser*, 14 February 1930.

[3] Sir Richard became chairman of the board in 1921 on the death of Sir Alfred Jermyn, Lynn's "premier townsman."

Schoolmaster-turned-bookseller and correspondent for other newspapers, John Thew was 42 when he launched a modest sheet from his home at the corner of High Street. From the age of thirteen his son John Dyker Thew (his grandmother's maiden name was Dyker) shared the grind of the printing shop, working thirteen or fourteen hours a day. Often as he sweated under the merciless eye of old Gribble the printer and rolled at the hand press, ceaseless pressure made blood ooze from his hands. Sales grew from 1,000 after the first ten years to the 6,500 which faced Sir Richard at his Lynn debut 40 years later. During that time John Dyker had become part of the local scene — magistrate, three times Mayor, gas company chairman and involved in shipping and the docks. After his death in 1891 Frank Sherwood Thew, second of four sons, carried on the business. He joined the Town Council while his father was still an alderman and followed him on the Bench, having also a reputation as golfer and one of Norfolk's finest shots.

It was the pride of the Thews that the Royal family read the *Advertiser* as their local paper when at Sandringham House — as indeed they still do. Printing work for them included shooting books and invitations to balls, and a treasured relic is the letter dated 11 April 1893 from General Knollys confirming that "His Royal Highness the Prince of Wales will be happy to become a subscriber to the *Lynn Advertiser*". King Edward VII bought the estate as Prince of Wales in 1863. To satisfy bequests under his father's will, Frank was obliged in 1923 to negotiate the sale of the *Advertiser* with Sir Richard. The latter re-formed the *Lynn News* company as the West Norfolk and King's Lynn Newspaper Company, with Frank Thew on the board and working with Tom Diggle as joint managing director. By now the *Advertiser* sale was 8,500 and the *News* 7,000 but when the Lynn News offices absorbed the *Advertiser*, balanced production was achieved at the expense of a Tuesday publication day — and a drop in sales — for the *News*.

In 1928 Diggle was chief guest at a staff dinner to honour his 25 years of journalism in King's Lynn. Though he promised not to go through the news of the whole quarter-century he managed 5,000 words of racy anecdote that are worthy of the annals of Lynn. There was, for instance, the jolly little Mayor with an interest in the licensed trade. Diggle recalled one of the first public meetings he went to in Lynn when the Mayor attacked the Licensing Bill. Verbatim reporting of this City Father produced this gem:

"Spoliation, robbery, and everything of that sort, either from the House of Commons or anybody else, must be looked upon as a speciality that we do not desire, that we cannot admire, and that we want to annihilate. That is my principle: 'annihilate' is the only word I can use. If the magistrates or anyone else ever attempt to do such things as these, we must shove them on one side as we should a viper, a reptile of the very highest order — what you might call a mammoth elephant — a lion, a tiger, a leopard, or anything of that kind. Shove them on one side. Don't pay any attention to them. They are attempters . . . The old Act was enough for us. Town and Empire, and Empire more especially, is my object. We look upon the town and the country and all that sort of thing as a little piece of rubbish put in, but the Empire is our business — the Empire outside, inside, and so on — one homogeneous mass, and we mean to pound it until it is ripe."

Till his death during an air raid on Lynn in 1941, E. P. Brice was Diggle's righthand man on the commercial and management side, coming to Lynn in 1910 after youthful help to John Diggle in his land survey and smallholdings work. Deprived of the family business, Frank Thew's elder son, Dyker Frank, found a niche in the Winfrey papers: at Kettering in 1927 and later at Peterborough and Wellingborough, with a spell in between at Brighton on the *Sussex Daily News*. In 1941 Sir Richard invited him back to Lynn to edit the *Advertiser* on Diggle's retirement, Ray Parkin being in the chair of the *News* (since 1931). Meanwhile, in 1929, Pat Winfrey and Thew were together appointed to the board: "a good stroke of business" said Sir Richard. At that time *News* and *Advertiser* were selling 17,000 copies per week between them.

At Spalding, some of the fire and force which Sir Richard personally poured into the *Guardian* were lost when he moved to Peterborough. To avoid what he considered excessive charges made by Cooke at Boston, Spalding production was transferred first to King's Lynn and then to Peterborough. The Diggle touch was also missing, and in 1907 Arthur Hallas, who had come from Bury St Edmunds as editor a year before, was victim of a drowning tragedy. Not till 1910, when H. L. Gethin left Peterborough and *The Citizen* to mount a rescue operation, did the tide flow again. He went reluctantly at Sir Richard's request but his "Irrepressible Pen Pictures" made the *Guardian* boom, just as Diggle's earlier tilting as "Boy of Low Farm" had pushed *The Citizen*. With caricatures by Bailey, a local artist, Gethin skilfully dissected the characters of chief figures in the neighbourhood and in some quarters there was competition "to be done". Medically rejected as a Kitchener volunteer, he and his wife carried the paper alone through World War I, and his appointment in 1918 as the country's first full-time secretary of a county branch of the National Farmers' Union (Holland N.F.U.) was a loss to journalism. Did he regret earlier irrepressibility? Perhaps, for he bequeathed this wisdom to youngsters eager to tilt at windmills: "Don't be too dogmatic. Remember that other people, however senile or silly they may seem, hold views equally strongly but have not your opportunity to express them . . . Above all, be very gentle with defaulters."[1]

Among the last young editors Sir Richard sent to Spalding were W. L. Joy and H. R. Parkin, both trained by Loomes at Peterborough. Like many Winfrey choices, Parkin came from Liberal-Nonconformist stock, his grandfather being a politically-active Congregational minister at Rushden, Northamptonshire, and his father, George Parkin, a Liberal enthusiast and speaker whose bright prospects were ended by early death. He started the League of Young Liberals and became its national vice-chairman, and in the two general elections of 1910 stood for Parliament in the difficult Stamford division. Parkin got out the jubilee issue of the *Spalding*

[1] *Spalding Guardian* 26 September 1931

70

Guardian (26 September 1931) and computed that over 50 years it had taken 650 million letters to fill its columns. So it was forgiveable if a few were occasionally out of place. It explained why "Rock of Ages" was sung very feelingly at General Booth's funeral by a large crow, and why a motorist who lost control in the market place could smash a widow into a thousand pieces. Did it also excuse the report that a councillor's apology for absence was because of an engagement with the Countess of Ayr when, in fact, it was with the county surveyor?

Joy's flamboyance took him to Paris and the *Continental Daily Mail* before returning to the fold as editor-in-chief at Kettering in 1944. Among his East Anglian exploits was driving an early Austin Seven car as far as it would go round the composing room. This was in the late 1920's in the Boston works where the Spalding paper — for reasons which follow — was again being produced. The *Boston Guardian's* support of Pat Winfrey in the 1923 and 1924 elections was too lukewarm for Sir Richard's liking. Though his brothers and sisters all had positions in Doncaster and Boston Press Ltd, the company's newspapers missed Joseph Cooke's driving force and Radical faith when he died in 1912. His son, another Joseph Cooke, and his brother Gilbert were main figures in the company, and Jo Cooke II was also a director of the *Peterborough Advertiser*, Sir Richard having introduced him as manager in 1909. But politically and commercially the life of the *Boston Guardian* was ebbing away.

It was too much for the Winfrey stomach. He insisted that Young Jo and the rest of the Cooke family should sell out to a new company of local Liberal businessmen which in June 1925 was registered as the Lincolnshire Guardian Printing and Publishing Company, Jo Cooke and he being on the board. Sir Richard sold the *Spalding Guardian* to this company so that once more the Spalding paper was printed in West Street premises at Boston which Jo Cooke I had built. At the same time the family sold their *Doncaster Gazette* to the *Yorkshire Evening News*. As anger cooled, Sir Richard repented of this move and in 1936 sold the business to Westminster Press Ltd, then owners of the pre-eminent Lincolnshire newspaper, the *Stamford Mercury*. For a time he and three of the Boston directors sat on the *Mercury* board with J. B. Morrell, Arnold Rowntree, W. R. Derwent and other Westminster figures, and Sir Richard was involved in the ceremony in January 1938 when the Marquess of Exeter drove into town from Burghley House to open the *Mercury's* modernised premises and switch on its new rotary press. The two *Guardians* and the *Mercury* were then all produced at Stamford. It had been a sad little chapter. "I did a foolish thing" was how Sir Richard wrote it off.

Peterborough was far different. True, its two main pillars had gone when Sir Richard took control of the *Advertiser* in 1896 — Slatterie Clarke, 42 years after launching it, and Edward Newton, 37 years after coming from the *Birmingham Daily Press* to succeed Slatterie's son Conquest as editor. Newton and three senior men expected to be offered the business and were shattered when each man on the staff received a note in Clarke's own hand saying everyone was being discharged on sale of the paper and thanking them for their "irreproachable services". Humane but outspoken, Liberal yet never narrow, ever readable and never unclean, the *Advertiser* was the kind of paper Gladstone had in mind in campaigning for a cheap Press. It was the first penny paper in Peterborough and when Newton followed his chief into retirement, Sir Richard trusted their lieutenants to carry on. W. H. Bernard Saunders, sub-editor, had joined 23 years earlier. Frank Loomes, chief reporter and assistant sub, had been with the *Advertiser* for fifteen years; manager and cashier, Edward George, had had fourteen years; foreman and make-up man — John Lamb Blake and John Dyson respectively — each had more than 40 years service.

Saunders should have taken the editorship but instead joined Sidney Smith in ownership of the *Peterborough Express* and ambitiously started four associated titles for neighbouring centres: a *Gazette* for Crowland, a *News* for Market Deeping, a *Chronicle* for Whittlesey, an *Observer* for Ramsey. They also took over the *Peterborough Evening News* which was put out, like the *Kettering Evening News*, by the *Evening News* at Nottingham in the mid-1890's. Saunders soon realised the folly of this excursion into proprietorship and in a matter of months was confiding his troubles to Sir Richard, who "at once took infinite pains to put me again on a sound footing."[1]

While Saunders, back in the fold, was launching the mid-weekly *Advertiser*, Sidney Smith abandoned the four new weeklies and sold the *Express* and the *Evening News* to Henry Butterfield of the Tory *Peterborough Standard*. In 1911 the evening paper disappeared and the *Express* was incorporated in the *Standard* in 1917. Saunders hastened their end by his work with the mid-weekly, which was renamed *The Citizen* in 1903 and had a Saturday football edition from 1909 to 1914.[2] Though settled as general manager, filling the gap between Edward George's retirement in 1900 and the arrival of Jo Cooke II from Boston in 1909, Saunders was more literary than commercial and loved research and writing, becoming a Fellow of the Royal Historical Society. He produced three books on Huntingdonshire lore and in 1889 founded *Fenland Notes and Queries* which he edited for two years till Sweeting, for long editor of *Northamptonshire Notes and Queries*, took it over. But his first book, on bird nesting, was written and illustrated when he was fourteen.

Naked gas flames and open coal fires lit and warmed the office, and Saunders broke so many of the new-fangled gas mantles when they came into use that colleagues refused to let him fix electric light bulbs in their turn. It was good to be back in the chair of *The Citizen* in 1909 and to stay there for another 20 years before retiring at 75. Leo, eldest of his ten children, trained on the *Advertiser* and was producing the *Kettering Guardian* and allied newspapers when these were amalgamated with Sir Richard's Northamptonshire papers in 1923. Bernard was a devoted Catholic, daily attending Mass on the way to the office: an unforgettable sight with black skull cap, full white beard and flowing cloak — "a man without guile" according to Sir Richard. It was equally

[1] *Peterborough Citizen* 18 February 1914.

[2] To meet the daily clamour for war news, Sir Richard started the four-page tabloid *Peterborough Evening Citizen* in 1914, a month after the First War began. It ran for two years before succumbing to wartime restrictions and lack of staff.

unforgettable to see this gentle man in anger. He once handled the preview of a film which showed a young fellow
taking his girl friend home where she took off her dress and
stood in black frilly petticoat. For its day it was daring: for
Saunders it was impossible. Forthwith he closed his columns
to the cinema's paid announcement. "I am the editor. I will
not have adverts for immoral plays in my paper," he shouted
hotly, brooking no argument and caring nothing if the
cinema never advertised again.

His dallying with the *Express* had left Frank Loomes to
take the *Advertiser* chair and to develop the character and
gifts which for 54 years were dedicated to the city and its
premier newspaper. On Christmas Day 1935, home again
from hospital, Loomes reached his 74th birthday; and on
New Year's Eve Sir Richard told an *Advertiser* staff party
that the board had just accepted his resignation. But Loomes
was too ill to be there. While others paid after-dinner tributes, he struggled to dictate a simple paragraph to his
daughter Mary for the next issue about a Christmas favourite, the sprightly robin. But he had to give up. "It's no good
Mary. The yellow matter is all muddled up with the grey,"
and he bade her finish it herself. He wrote no more, and died
at the end of his first week of retirement.

Saunders had gone three years before. The opposition
Standard summed them up as "glory boys — men who would
go through fire and water metaphorically and brave all the
plagues of Egypt for their newspapers. They could give
nothing but their best."[1] Loomes would take an *Advertiser*
home fresh from the press, smooth his hands over the pages
as if in caress and say to his wife, "Isn't it lovely!" Its five
pages of village paragraphs carried the banner "News from
Five Counties". It regularly included a special page on some
natural or historical feature, or new development or concep-
tion. Some now seem prophetic: "Dam the Wash" among
them. Its picture displays were first-class and from his
Autolycus notes Loomes breathed extra life into the whole
issue. He coined the phrase "Go-Ahead Peterborough" and
ran one campaign after another to make it so. Diggle told

[1] *Peterborough Standard* 3 January 1936.

74

him he would never get fat "for you're such a worrit. According to you no street in Peterborough is properly lit, no balance sheet properly prepared, no ankle properly turned, no sewer properly flushed, no sermon properly delivered, and nobody properly buried."[1]

Dignified and leonine, he told each new reporter that his first duty was to be a Gentleman. He must turn up on time and he must turn in only the best reports. A "Please see me" note marked failure in one. Copy flung back through the editor's hatch was judgment on the other. Somewhere on the scattered folios would be scribbled "Who wrote this b——— muck?" As devoted a Catholic as Saunders, he not only served with acceptance under a Protestant management in an Anglican cathedral city but was for long one of the most remarkable personalities in provincial journalism. After marrying a widow at the age of 50 he was the backbone of her pioneer infant welfare efforts in the suburb of Fletton. Leg-pulled over it though he was, Fletton's first Baby Week in 1916, with its slogan "Baby Week makes Baby Strong", inspired National Baby Weeks held annually since 1917 and slashed infant mortality figures,[2] whilst infant welfare work initiated by Mrs Loomes became standard practice in the country. She was the first Catholic woman magistrate appointed in Huntingdonshire, sitting for 25 years and honoured with a civic farewell and presentation organised by Pat Winfrey when she left in 1950 to live with her daughter Mary Barnard, herself a Norwich J.P. She was 95 when she died there in February 1973.

Loomes knew that when Mary Queen of Scots descended to her execution at Fotheringhay Castle in 1587 she handed her watch and a portrait of her son, later King James I, to the constable of the castle, Sir William Fitzwilliam. Both these relics were treasured in the Fitzwilliam home at Milton Park, Peterborough, and George Fitzwilliam collaborated with Loomes to preserve a shapeless block of masonry at Fotheringhay — all that remained of the Royal castle apart from a mound where the keep had stood. If Loomes had not

[1] Lynn News 10 February 1912.
[2] National Health magazine July 1925.

acted, American and other souvenir hunters would have left little of this last solid reminder of the tragic Queen, and his patient negotiation led to protecting railings with plaque being fixed in 1913. Though a sick man he stayed to edit, as his last *Advertiser,* the October 1935 issue commemorating installation of a new Foster rotary press. Sir Richard took premises round the corner in Queen Street to house this press, which made 32-page papers possible. Previous limit was 24 — and this only by marrying-up the Hoe installed in 1928 with the 16-page Foster which in 1919 had replaced the original eight-page Annand. Experts said this coupling of two presses was bound to fail but Ollie Halcrow proved them wrong. The idea came from Jo Cooke II whose reign as general manager ended in 1930.[1]

Charles Hughes succeeded Jo Cooke and with the passing of the Loomes-Saunders-Cooke trio, formed a new team with J. T. S. Flynn, editor of *The Citizen* 1929-1942, and W. E. G. Rippon, editor of the *Advertiser* 1935-45. All three were products of the Loomes school. Rippon was son of a Congregational minister at Brigstock, Northamptonshire. Flynn's city experience went back to 1902 and because of his pungent treatment of Town Council business there was never room enough for the public at council meetings. His special articles in mock Biblical phrases by "The Scribbler on the Tablets", with mixed-up names which deceived nobody, had a great following, especially among the "carticled larks" of the Town Clerk's department. Flynn's wartime death in 1942 left Rippon as editor of both *Citizen* and *Advertiser,* an arrangement cut short when he was killed in a 1945 road accident in North West Europe when visiting the war front. He had chronicled the career and reported the death of Sir Richard the year before and was elected to the vacant seat on the *Advertiser* board. In 1945 also, Charles Hughes himself retired, to live for another nineteen years with memories of chapters now closed.

[1] Joseph Cooke bought the *Herts & Cambs Reporter & Royston Crow* in 1930, and was still active as chairman of the company up to his death in September 1972, aged 91. He was for long affectionately referred to in Royston as "Mr Joe Crow."

10. THE WINFREY PRESS II
Northamptonshire, Suffolk

IN 1901, as already recorded, Sir Richard was invited to manage the Kettering company in succession to Thomas Collings. T. H. Chance, proprietor of the *Gloucester Journal*, had bought the weekly *Wellingborough News* when on the market in 1877, re-named it the *Wellingborough & Kettering News* in 1878 and pushed its sales in both towns, moving Collings from Gloucester to Wellingborough as editor in 1881. Kettering then had a population of 11,000 compared with Wellingborough's 13,700 but was mushrooming at such a rate that ten years later the figure had swollen to 19,400 against Wellingborough's 15,000.[1] Yet it relied on newspapers from outside until September 1882 when J. W. Linnett, a Northampton journalist, tackled the market with his *Kettering Observer*, printed in the town. In October, local Conservatives replied with the *Kettering Guardian*, J. W. Steff coming from Preston to launch it. He followed this in 1885 with his *Oundle & Thrapston Guardian;* in 1886 at Wellingborough with his *Post* as alternative to the *News;* and in 1891 with the *Rushden Times* and the *Finedon Courier*.

Liberal businessmen in the area formed the Northamptonshire Printing and Publishing Company in December 1887 to acquire the *Wellingborough & Kettering News* from Mr Chance, and Collings joined them as managing director and editor. They aimed at launching Liberal newspapers in the county and started with the *Kettering Leader* in April 1888, buying out James Waddington the printer[2] and taking

[1] *1971 figures:* Kettering 42,600, Wellingborough 37,500.

[2] A relative, John Waddington, had founded the *Northamptonshire Free Press* in Kettering in 1855. Moving to Leicester, he attempted a wider circulation for the paper as the *Midland Free Press* and this survived until 1917.

over his new print shop in Workhouse Lane (now named Dryland Street and headquarters of the company till its 1976 move to new premises in Northfield Avenue). "Kettering" was dropped from the *Wellingborough News* title. In the same year Collings launched the *Oundle Journal* and the *Thrapston & Raunds Journal;* sent A. J. Tompkins from the *Wellingborough News* office to start the *Midland Mail* for Market Harborough in 1890; and began the *Rushden Argus* in 1891 with Fred Cunliffe as editor, formerly Baptist minister at Walgrave near Kettering before joining the *Leader* staff.

Collings enlarged the six newspapers; calmed shareholders at their 1892 meeting by promising racing results would not include betting figures; founded *The Citizen* as a mid-weekly for Kettering in 1894, turning it three years later into a weekend football paper; extended the premises and bought his first Linotype machines; increased the company's capital from £5,000 to £10,000; and paid five-per-cent tax free on its shares. To keep other evening papers out, the board authorised the founding of the *Evening Telegraph* in October 1897 and two years later, with people hungry for news of the Boer War, the first rotary press was installed and company capital was again doubled, to £20,000. Steff was not the only competitor forcing the pace. At Market Harborough, where the *Advertiser* held the field, the *Mail* — and Tompkins with it — was sold by agreement to its Member, J. W. Logan. In March 1923, Tompkins was able to buy it for himself and in November absorbed the *Advertiser* also and merged the titles. On retirement in 1944 he sold the *Market Harborough Advertiser & Midland Mail* to the Kettering company which had been printing it for him on contract.

At Rushden, Charles Cross was making a good job of his *Rushden Echo,* and with it ran the *Raunds Free Press* and two other *Echoes* for the small towns of Finedon and Wollaston. Any journalist could start a paper without much capital if he had a printer to produce it and was prepared to slog away. Cross was such a man. He learned his craft working for the *Stamford Guardian* and persuaded Arthur Scholes, a friend from the *Stamford Mercury*, to join him in his Rushden venture in 1897. Scholes made and repaired violins to add to his income (he kept this up after leaving Rushden and made 99 in all), whilst Cross would rather lose money than offend his scruples, being determined to make the *Echo* a "vehicle of righteousness". He burned himself out in youth activities, adult education, village preaching and council work, and within a month of his death in 1929 his widow sold to the Northamptonshire Printing and Publishing Company. The *Echo's* subsidiaries had by then disappeared and in October 1929 the rival papers merged to become the *Rushden Echo & Argus*.

Meanwhile Kettering had its own casualties. Eight years was all Linnett could manage before asking the company to buy him out, and the papers amalgamated in June 1890 as the *Kettering Leader & Observer*. Three months later James Steff died, a victim of typhoid at 34, leaving a widow and three young children. Gamely, Ellen Steff carried on. For another 37 years she ran the papers from Kettering headquarters, Leo Saunders from the *Peterborough Advertiser* being her right-hand man when, at 70, she sold out to the N.P.P. Company in 1923. Steff newspapers at that time were the *Northants & Hunts Gazette* (title altered in 1913 from *Oundle & Thrapston Guardian*), which merged with the company's *Thrapston Raunds & Oundle Journal*; the *Wellingborough Post* (already incorporating *Rushden Times* and *Finedon Courier*), which merged with the *News*; and the *Kettering Guardian*, which merged with the *Leader & Observer* to become the *Kettering Leader and Guardian*.

By the 1920's the Kettering directors had therefore not only firmly established their own newspapers but had virtually the whole area to themselves. Further afield, Bedford beckoned but it was an unfortunate extension of interest. Rowland Hill, noted Bedfordian, magistrate and Liberal, wanted to sell the *Mercury* on the death of Augustus, his brother and co-editor. First of the Bedford papers to be started (in 1837) it had long before lost its lead. In hope of reviving it, the company bought the paper in March 1911 and produced it at Kettering as one of their string of weeklies, but by the end of 1912 they were glad to re-sell to the *Bedfordshire Times* company, the title being merged with the *Bedford & County Record*. With the paper came a short-lived directorate at Kettering for Sir George Royle, representing the old *Mercury* company. When the *Mercury's* Mill Street office closed, contents sold included five carrier pigeons with trap, nesting boxes, perches and other cote accessories.

The man who, more than any other, held the fort at Kettering headquarters through all these changes was Frank Hutchen. Fascinated by print and producer of schoolboy magazines, he preferred an apprenticeship under Waddington to helping in his father's leather business, and was on the printing staff at the time the company bought Waddington's works and launched the *Leader*. When the Winfrey regime began in 1901 Sir Richard found F. E. Fry and Hutchen in control. He gave the former a good opening on his new *Lincoln Leader* and appointed the latter managing editor, a dual position he held till death at 71. It brought him back to his desk most evenings. It meant he knew the whole job right through. It meant he could show a comp short-cuts in page make-up as easily as putting an editorial man right over name, event or back ground to either and that, if presses stopped before time, he would be the first to rush from his room to ask why. Sir Richard had to weigh Hutchen's many schemes for technical improvement against other claims. An extended composing room could not be delayed once the Steff newspapers were absorbed, and a new Foster rotary was erected in 1935 at the same time as sister units were installed at Peterborough.

But the stringent earlier years had first to be lived through, with sales fought for against a background of tight economies and two-and-a-half per cent dividends. There was no typewriter in the office till a Yost was bought in 1912. In World War I the ha'penny *Telegraph* was at times down to a single sheet, Tom Sturman learning to saw double reels in half to run a single width through his machine. With the war over, the *Telegraph* went up to one penny, the weeklies to three ha'pence. Dividends rose to seven-and-a-half (in 1919) and stayed between twelve-and-a-half and fifteen from 1923 up to the Second War. So it became easier for Hutchen to open his own photographic and engraving department, pioneered in 1920 by George Cragg, who later advised Loomes on a similar set-up for Peterborough. The impact of his "Beautiful Northamptonshire" series of photographs was achieved by curving fine-screen blocks over a saddle and tacking them direct on to blanks left in the stereotyped rotary plates.

Big innovation in 1921 was to install the new high-speed electric telegraph system developed by Frederick Creed, replacing handwritten Post Office telegrams ("flimsies") which conveyed national news from the Press Association's London office. Now it came direct by private wire at the rate of 150 words a minute, Morse signals emerging from the receiver as punched tape. This operated a translator which converted tape into typewritten messages. The *Telegraph* was the first provincial paper to install the new gear, a distinction due to Hutchen's personal persistence. World War II had to pass before teleprinters replaced it. Within days of the British Broadcasting Company starting its 2LO radio service from London in 1922, he had an aerial slung between masts on the office roof and bought one of the first wireless receivers in the area. When the BBC adopted the Fultograph system of transmitting still pictures by wireless in 1928, Hutchen bought one of the receivers — Captain Fulton's neat and inexpensive version of the experimental machines of the day — but quality of photograph received was inferior and the BBC stopped picture transmissions in October 1929. Meanwhile, the company exploited their publicity value by operating the equipment in shop windows.[1]

Folk wondered how Hutchen, on a vegetarian diet, could send such waves of energy through office and works. After carrying the enterprise through World War I, however, he was so run down that he took three months off to travel through South Africa. One result of this was his book *Under the Southern Cross*. Another was the arrival in 1921 of Fred

[1] The Fultograph machine and some of the original Creed equipment are preserved in the Kettering office.

Skinner to edit the major part of the weekly papers — pages which were common to all. His articles in the opposition *Free Press* at Spalding, based on war experiences in Belgium, had caught Sir Richard's eye and led to his appointment, and F. W. Skinner remained a pillar of the company till retirement in 1959. A by-product of his work was a readership succession rooted in his popular Children's Corner.

The important Wellingborough area was looked after by Victor Valentine,[1] ex-Kettering chief reporter who edited the *News* 1903-1931; and at Rushden the leading figure for more than 40 years was L. V. Elliott, a musician in his own right (died 1959). W. (Billy) Martin — retired 1930 — who left the *Kettering Guardian* in 1905 to join Hutchen as chief reporter, often wrote shorthand on his detachable cuffs and had to make sure to transcribe it before Mrs Martin washed them. Chief figure on the business side was Charles Wilson, a servant since 1891, accountant for 30 years, appointed secretary in 1924 and still a director at his death in 1945. One by one, except for editorial, F. A. Cooper inherited the responsibilities of both Wilson and Hutchen and carried them into the years of post-war expansion. Another memorable character was bluff Fred Felce, whose 59 years service stretched from printer's devil in 1900 for Charles Cross on the Rushden Echo to manager of the company's jobbing department and on to past-war direction of all EMAP commercial printing. In the small borough of Higham Ferrers he was for seventeen years mace bearer to the Corporation and was himself Mayor in 1947. He never forgot an encounter at the time of the *Echo* takeover in 1929. Sir Richard buttonholed him in the works. "I understand you ran this place for Cross?" "Yes Sir." "Now I want you to run it for me". That was all the briefing he ever had.

Frank Hutchen's flair was for management but though he did not stride editorial peaks where Frank Loomes was so at home, his finger was always on the readers' pulse. In 1934 he

---

[1] In his *Memories of Midland Politics 1885-1910* Channing, Liberal Member, names Wellingborough journalists who often drove back with him through the wooded lanes of Northamptonshire after village meetings: Valentine of the *News;* Holton, *Northampton Mercury* representative; and (less often) Peeple of the Tory *Wellingborough Post.*

openly disagreed with the directors, led by their chairman J. A. Gotch, when they criticised photographs of "bathing belles" in swim suits in the early days of beauty queen contests. Sir Richard over-ruled him and told the editorial team to raise the moral tone of the newspapers even if circulation was lost. But Hutchen's touch was never more justified than in 1940 when Lord Beaverbrook, Minister of Aircraft Production in World War II, wanted more Spitfire fighters for the Royal Air Force after the Battle of Britain. Hutchen asked *Evening Telegraph* readers to raise £5,000 — cost of one fighter. In four days it was done. Six days later there was enough for a second, and in less than a month his fund reached £25,000 — enough for five. A sixth took a month longer. Employees of John White, the boot worker who built up his own great enterprise at Higham Ferrers, were so inspired that they added a seventh on their own. Newspaper staff spent hours coping with cash sent to the office, much of it in coppers from small weekly collections. Beaverbrook marked this phenomenal success by sending to Kettering his friend Richard Bennett — he served as Prime Minister of Canada from 1930 to 1935 — to accept the sums raised.

Two years earlier Hutchen's elder son Alan — Sir Richard offered him the vacancy on the board following his father's death — had become chief electrical engineer at *The Times* after service with the *News Chronicle* and *Star*, and Kettering was one of the offices earmarked by *The Times* as a war-time production centre should they be bombed out of Printing House Square. Sir Richard knew Colonel J. J. Astor, its chief proprietor — created Lord Astor of Hever in 1956 — as a young Member entering Parliament, and told him he liked agreements simple enough for a single sheet of paper. "It's just this", he told him. "From 6 p.m. to 9 a.m. the plant is yours, and from 9 a.m. to 6 p.m. it is ours. It will cost you £500 every day you use it, and £1,000 a year if you don't." Under a similar arrangement with H. H. Aldridge, its chairman, Sir Richard reserved the use of *Peterborough Advertiser* presses for the *News of the World* for £250 a year. But neither Kettering nor Peterborough were called upon to shelter their Fleet Street friends.

Soon after a three-month World Brotherhood mission in the United States in 1926, Sir Richard faced the General Strike. In appreciation of loyalty to himself and the newspapers in continuing production he introduced superannuation schemes drawn up for him by the Public Welfare Society of London. This was a pioneering effort eighteen months in advance of the pension scheme launched by the Newspaper Society. The strike call was obeyed at Kettering by Linotype operators but other employees tried their hands at keyboards, whilst Peterborough men worked late to set matter for the next issue before starting a token stay-out. So the papers still appeared.

When the Winfrey chapter at Bury St Edmunds started with the formation of the new company in 1903, Bankes Ashton was nominal editor of the *Free Press* with Alfred Hallam full-time editorial man in charge. In support were two reporters who also acted aś sub-editors and proofreaders. To strengthen the team Sir Richard moved in Charles E. Turner, ex-Stamford apprentice who found a niche in the Winfrey Press at King's Lynn. He served Sir Richard at Bury till 1906 and after spells at Peterborough and Kettering moved on to national journalism, the last 40 years in Manchester on the *Guardian* from which he retired as News Editor. His 48 years continuous service on the executive of the National Union of Journalists (1920-68) and as a trustee for nearly as long put him in a class of his own among British journalists. Bankes Ashton took Turner with him in his gig to report country courts he attended as solicitor. This, or going to village meetings with the Liberal candidate in a four-wheel cab, was luxury compared with miles covered by bicycle. He was nineteen, earned 27s 6d per week, paid £1 board and lodging, and was as well off as any other young reporter of his day. At that age he stood in for Hallam on his holidays and in May 1904 Sir Richard sent him congratulations on the way he produced the paper. It was the week when the town was agog over prominent Nonconformists who refused to pay their education rate. The Bench ordered goods to be distrained upon and sold, but rioting played havoc with the auction and both Turner and

84

auctioneer fled through a back exit before an item could be sold.

Arthur E. Hallas, who managed the Bury Theatre before coming to the *Free Press* on the business side and saw its first Linotype machine installed, was moved in 1905 to the *Peterborough Advertiser*, and then as editor-manager of the *Guardian* at Spalding, where he was drowned while swimming in 1907. Sir Richard called young Fred Patrick from Kettering office to fill the gap at Bury. Patrick's steadily successful service there as manager 1905 to 1945 assures him of a worthy place among Winfrey lieutenants. Often enough, after seeing the *Bury Free Press* to bed, he would walk round the town and return with a handful of advertisements for the next issue — despite lifelong lameness. The company was consistently prosperous and when Edward Smedley, office manager at Peterborough, succeeded him in 1945, Patrick could look back on a good run of 20-per-cent dividends. Pat Winfrey's first directorship was at Bury where he and Patrick joined the board together in August 1923. Pat had just celebrated his 21st birthday and was still at Cambridge but spent part of the vacations at Bury learning all branches of the business.

Following Alfred Hallam, Patrick's editorial colleague was W. T. Cox, a dandy nicknamed "Dilly", one of West Suffolk's characters with the stature of a jockey and, surprisingly, a reputation as amateur boxer. On a Saturday in 1918, Sir Richard summoned Tom Linford, chief reporter at Lynn, to lunch with him at Peterborough. Cox, it appeared, was becoming secretary of the West Suffolk War Agricultural Committee: would Linford go to Bury as editor? All other editorial staff had been called up and if Linford did not go there would be no-one to get the paper out. Linford's journalism had started in 1899 on the *Hunts County News* with Edgar Hall, its editor, and Charles Hughes, his apprentice, in the early days of Sir Richard's control at Huntingdon. He had proved himself at Lynn, going to the *News* when Diggle took it over in 1903. Five times in the First War he was rejected for military service because of heart trouble. At Bury, he and Patrick built up the circulation of the *Free*

Press from 9,000 in 1918 to 20,000 in 1945. Linford lost all his reporters to the Services in the Second War and added to his work the job of Local Officer for the Ministry of Information. Soon after the Bury service of Thanksgiving for Victory in Europe in 1945 he suffered a severe collapse and on medical advice gave up work at 60 and moved to Bedford, nearer his native Godmanchester. Patrick chose to retire to Kettering.

Sir Richard's policy of driving his men with what he called "a snaffle bit and a light hand" worked perfectly with these two reliable runners at Bury, and the position of strength they achieved together brought weaker newspapers into their grip. Seventeen miles away at Sudbury, birthplace of Gainsborough the portrait and landscape painter, Edward Lewis wanted to sell his Tory-tinged *Suffolk & Essex Free Press* with its Friday edition, the *Essex & Suffolk News*, and its associated *Stowmarket Courier*. In failing health at 73 but still known as "Young Bogey", he succeeded William Lambton Lewis — "Old Bogey", his father — in 1904, 42 years after Old Bogey acquired the *Free Press*. He had worked on it for some years under Robert Rudland, founder of it in 1855. The Station Road premises built by W. L. Lewis in 1867 were home to the *Free Press* for 100 years till an office was taken in the new Borehamgate Precinct in 1967, and Lewis had the arms of Suffolk and Essex carved in stone on the front of the building. His leading articles were anti-Gladstone and outspokenly Tory, hence the "Bogey" nickname coined by local Liberals.

Edward was as partisan as his father but his own son, E. L. (Ted) Lewis, had no wish to don the family mantle. After Sir Richard was invited to purchase the *Free Press* he stayed on as cashier for 28 years. The takeover was effective from January 1922 when editions were dropped and only the mid-week *Suffolk & Essex Free Press* was produced. A disastrous Sudbury fire more than doubled sales of the first Winfrey issue to nearly 6,000. It also destroyed the Rose and Crown Hotel, generally accepted as the original of "Ye Olde Town Arms" used by Mr Pickwick on his visits to Eatanswill. Charles Dickens almost certainly had Sudbury in mind when describing this little town where Pickwick stayed on his way to Bury St Edmunds, but though he had watched Suffolk elections in 1835 it is not so certain that local journalists inspired the characters of Mr Pott and Mr Slurk, vituperative editors of the *Eatanswill Gazette* and its rival *Independent*.[1]

Production of the Sudbury paper was moved to Bury where it was printed on a Cossar press erected in 1921. Its new editor, Frank Trinder, had earlier been with the Press Association. In 1910, just as he was leaving Scotland Yard after a call, the telephone rang with news that Dr Crippen had been arrested on an Atlantic liner after murdering his wife in London. It was the first time wireless telegraphy had helped in an arrest and Trinder was the first journalist to get the story. The ending of his eleven-year spell in 1933 brought to Sudbury George Hunt, chief reporter at Bury, where he had been given "£1 a week and a chance" in 1919 after learning shorthand in the Army of Occupation in Germany. As staunch a Baptist and as hard a worker as Linford, by 1949 he had taken the 1933 Sudbury sale of 3,000 to 7,500. Management positions at Peterborough and at Wisbech followed till, in 1959, retirement took him back to Bury and to part-time work for the *Free Press*. But it was at Sudbury, during sixteen years of sound editorship, that he made his mark.

Meanwhile Newmarket had created problems for Sir Richard. Its 5,000 inhabitants had no paper of their own till a local printer and stationer, George Simpson, diffidently launched his neutral *Newmarket Monthly Illustrated Journal* in 1872. Ten years later George Sharman, who was running Tory newspapers in the Isle of Ely, sent in a *Newmarket Advertiser* edition but this disappeared before World War I. By 1880 the *Newmarket Journal* was coming out as an eight-pager each Saturday for a penny, and in 1887 Simpson added a two-page evening called the *Newmarket Sporting News* to keep his extensive racing readership up-to-date

---

[1] John Greaves in *The Dickensian*, May 1962; also Edwin Pugh's *The Charles Dickens Originals*, chapter four. On the publication of letters including several sent to his wife by Dickens from a Kettering hotel, the *Kettering Leader* of 18 May 1934 suggested that Eatanswill was Kettering.

with course news, results and betting. Simpson's death in 1917 left his son Walter in charge of a promising business but an unhappy post-war rift between him and Newmarket businessmen led traders to plan their own advertisement sheet, to be called *News of the Market*. They asked Patrick to quote for printing it at Bury but the scheme fell through.

After Walter Simpson's death in 1926 Sir Richard could get no definite reply to offers to purchase, so he launched the *Newmarket Free Press* in March 1927 to give Newmarket people the alternative they wanted. Dilly Cox was back in journalism and became its editor. Walter Simpson's affairs were left in such a state that his son Frank had to act in the High Court to acquire the newspapers for himself, Sir Richard meanwhile bidding unsuccessfully for a second time. Frank Simpson improved the look of his *Journal* by arranging with the *Bury & Norwich Post* to print it on contract in their works at Bury St Edmunds. This Conservative weekly had Sudbury and Mildenhall editions and dated back to 1782, when it was founded by a young man from Norwich named Peter Gedge. His link with the beginnings of English provincial newspapering is worth noting for it was his grandfather, William Chase, who brought out the *Norwich Mercury* in 1713. Tourists make a point of looking for Gedge's epitaph on a tablet placed in St Mary's church at Bury in 1818: "Like a worn-out type, he is returned to the Founder, in hopes of being re-cast in a better and more perfect mould."

Local Tories were directors of the *Post* with the Hon Walter Guinness as chief financial supporter.[1] He was a son of the 1st Earl of Iveagh of Elveden Hall, close to Bury, a member of the famous Dublin brewing family and Tory M.P. for Bury 1907-1931, and was serving as Resident Minister in the Middle East when assassinated in Cairo in 1944. Several months before creation as 1st Baron Moyne of Bury St Edmunds in January 1932 — which meant the end of his electioneering days — Linford and Patrick received overtures from the *Post* (circulation 3,500). Its purchase was

[1] Colonel Guinness's divisional agent was Elton Halliley, father of film and television actor John le Mesurier.

soon negotiated and it appeared under the new ownership to the end of 1931, after which the title was amalgamated with the *Free Press*. The *Post* was then just short of its 150th anniversary. One result of this takeover was that Frank Simpson found production of his *Journal* had passed to his rivals. Bury directors contracted to print the *Newmarket Journal* for him for seven years at £20 per week and sold him the copyright of their unprofitable *Newmarket Free Press*, which ceased to appear from the end of 1931. Printing by contract continued until June 1955 when Frank Simpson and Reg Jeffery, who had joined him as partner after the war, sold the *Journal* to East Midland Allied Press, 30 years after takeover talk was first heard. In appearance more farmer than journalist, Frank Simpson died in January 1966. Biggest joke this Newmarket character told against himself was of the February day in 1941 when German bombs destroyed buildings in High Street. Chief of these was the Marlborough Club, where Simpson happened to be using the top-floor toilet. He came down amid the wreckage and was still enthroned in a sitting position — bruised and blaspheming — when they found him. He started the first of the *Journal's* many successful hospital appeals in gratitude for treatment after this raid.

Another result of the *Bury Post* merger was transfer of staff. Just before Christmas they had a farewell party (reported in their final issue) at which Walter C. Baxter, advertisement manager, "was the life of the evening." Ever since he touched off laugh explosions at school and innocently put classes out of control, Walter was one of Nature's purest wits. In India in World War I — he was the Army's smallest officer — Captain Baxter's concerts paved the way to nine years on the West End stage in such shows as "Hit the Deck" and "No, No, Nanette." Bury Tories asked his help at political meetings as an entertainer to ensure good attendances and retained it by offering him the *Bury Post* position in 1929. His newspaper career in EMAP came to fuller flower after the Second War as general manager at King's Lynn, where the Royal family at Sandringham were among thousands who came under his spell when on stage. Queen

Elizabeth the Queen Mother was at West Newton Women's Institute with Elizabeth and Margaret as young Princesses when Walter was there with his stories in Norfolk and Suffolk dialects. As they left to rejoin King George VI at Sandringham, Princess Margaret asked him to repeat one of them. "Why do you want to hear it again?" asked the Queen Mother. "So that I can tell Daddy at dinner tonight . . ." W. A. (Bill) Appel, who took Linford's chair in 1945 after work in the Cambridge Ministry of Information office under Pat Winfrey, had started reporting for the *Post* in 1923 but by 1929 had already joined the livelier *Free Press*. He went on to edit this, with oversight also of the Sudbury and Newmarket papers, for 25 years.

Some months after his 80th birthday, at what he called a belated party which he celebrated with the Bury staff in January 1939, Sir Richard and his colleagues looked back along the way they had come since 1903. After the 1914-18 war they had enlarged the premises four times and spent £15,000 on plant, whilst capital and labour had worked together to make progress smooth. Now the time was near when his son would take over the reins and he had a grandson coming on (Richard John was then seven). In April he passed on the managing directorship at King's Lynn to Pat while remaining chairman, and repeated this at Bury in September. Sir Richard remained managing director at Kettering and Peterborough until his death in 1944, when Pat succeeded him in both companies. At Kettering the chairmanship in 1944 remained with T. N. Bird but at Peterborough Lady Winfrey was temporarily voted to the chair until H. B. Hartley succeeded, Pat at the same time assuming the dual office of chairman and managing director at Lynn and Bury.

For 57 years Sir Richard skilfully managed his companies and his staffs. Everyone knew they could appeal direct to him and he knew each one of them. On office visits he took the little black book which recorded their wages. (Time was when he aimed at each centre to keep the total below £100 per week.) He took the latest company accounts. He took current letters and queries in a paper clip, extracted from the appropriate drawer in his room at home. He put them all in an old leather bag, its surface long since rubbed and poor but a bag his father gave him when first he went to London. In it, too, he put his lunch — a bottle of cider, glass, sandwiches, bread and cheese — to eat alone in the boardroom or to share with Pat. Before her marriage to Edmund Eades, an official at the Board of Education, Lucy Winfrey was Sir Richard's personal secretary, whilst for several years Ellen, the eldest daughter (later Mrs Geoffrey Willson) checked proofs in the *Peterborough Advertiser* readers' department.

Sir Richard appeared harder than he was for more than one of his lieutenants proved him well enough to say "He was like a father to me". Younger staffmen, taking a boardroom farewell as they left for the Forces, might feel he had neither sentiment nor sympathy, yet he was known to weep at his desk over these men of his called from home to fight. He paid allowances to add to Army pay and many sweating it out on skeleton staffs received war-time bonus payments. Top wages in all departments just before the Second World War were from £5 to £6. Apprentices started at 5s or 7s 6d. When Charles Turner entered the Winfrey empire in 1902 at 25s per week his old teacher at Pinchbeck thought this so remarkable that she called the whole school together to tell them about it. He did not look for star writers and hot reporters but shorthand was always a must. Tony Ireson, as a Kettering apprentice, muffed his note of lines from a poem Sir Richard once quoted. Its absence from the report being noticed, he was told to learn it by heart and recite it when they next met. Political understanding was also encouraged, editorial apprentices between the wars being asked to read recommended histories such as Sir Charles Oman's *England in the Nineteenth Century* and then submit essays to Sir Richard. Where he found a response he lent books on political and current affairs from his own collection.

To him the Hitler war was utterly ghastly. He was fearful about Europe, about England, about a world from which Liberal policies and Brotherhood ideals seemed to be vanishing. He was concerned about his newspapers, trying to curtail expenses and, at 80, obliged to face cuts in newsprint supplies and other serious restrictions affecting all the companies and to involve himself with staff shortages, fuel rationing, air raid precautions and the like. In 1941 the *Peterborough Advertiser* printed the *Spalding Free Press* when their premises were bombed — they had done the same in 1923 after the *Free Press* fire — and in 1942 the *Wellingborough News* office was badly damaged by blast. He became very deaf, was losing the sight of the left eye, was riding less and no longer dared go skating — a joy from childhood. So much had passed. Most of his political friends had gone, their causes seemingly eclipsed. Original directors of the companies he was called to manage had gone. Loomes, Diggle, Hutchen were among lieutenants who had gone. Patrick, Linford, Hughes were nearing the end of their careers. War swallowed up nearly all his bright young men and who could tell what the future held? But he had children and grandchildren. So long as war lasted he would gamely carry on while planning for them and enjoying such simple pleasures as he could.

11. SPRINGTIME FAREWELL

WAR clouds had not started to gather and his chief lieutenants were still about him when Sir Richard celebrated his 75th birthday in 1933. Earlier, to mark his silver wedding in 1922, the Peterborough staff presented him and his lady with a pair of ram's head pattern silver candlesticks. Sir Richard thanked everyone by private letter for this gesture — a reflection of the "family" relationship that existed between them all. But for the 75th birthday everyone in the five companies (Boston was then part of the Winfrey Press) signed an album handed to him with a 96-ounce inscribed silver salver. More than 200 — as many as could be spared from work — came to Castor House for a giant party which included inter-office sports in the grounds and lunch in the village hall. Pat Winfrey was M.C. for the programme and Bury won a bowls tournament which at Linford's suggestion became an annual competition for the R. P. Winfrey cup. Sir Richard came fourth in the 80-yard race for veterans. (The year before, on his 74th birthday, he enjoyed showing off form by letting Pat photograph him at diversions such as riding, cycling, playing tennis and chopping wood.)

As his oldest journalistic servant, Diggle toasted The Chief: one who knew his job whether dealing with accounts or contents of newspapers. "He knows when a report is well done and, alas, he knows when it isn't." In reply, Sir Richard catalogued the years since his first association with the papers: Boston 46, Lynn 43, Peterborough 36, Kettering 33 and Bury 30. Combined wages and salaries were running at £40,000 a year and how they could pay a dividend he really

93

didn't know! John Derry, Sir Richard's oldest friend and still writing at 79, was there to pass over the gift and to recall earlier ardours as political firebrands. He fell back on a phrase of John Morley to sum up Sir Richard's chief honour — that the larger part of his life's energies had been spent in trying to make more men happy, and happy in a better way. Lady Winfrey, then two years short of her 70th birthday, was more matter-of-fact. The salver was a gift, she said, which came from the real people who helped to make them happy in their home.

Castor House became the Winfrey home in 1919 when Ellen's 21st birthday party served as house-warming. The family moved in during August after 22 years in Peterborough at Sutton House and Sir Richard never imagined he would have another 25 years to enjoy the change. Castor, important as a Roman colony and of great archaeological significance today, was granted to the Abbot of Peterborough by King Edgar, and confirmed to the Dean and Chapter by Henry VIII when the bishopric was founded after the Dissolution. The Castor living was rich and as Rectors of Castor, represented by a local curate, the Bishops of Peterborough were able to enjoy it from 1613 to 1857. In 1685 they built Castor House as a summer residence and began to lay out its grounds and plant its cedars. In its eight acres of hillside woodland to the East stand both medlar and Judas trees and in the kitchen garden is a prolific cordon apple tree fifteen yards long. Coming into a fortune, Stephen White, Rector of nearby Conington and son of Judge Taylor White of Chester, bought the estate in 1796, the White family retaining it until 1910 when Colonel Frank White retired to Henley. Descriptions of nineteenth-century life at Castor House are only thinly disguised in *Love's Illusion*[1] , one of the novels by J. D. Beresford, whose father was Rector of Castor 1864-1897. Two brief ownerships intervened between the Whites and the Winfreys, those of Hinchcliffe, a businessman retiring from South America, and of G. F. Bonner, who changed his name from Bunheimer at the beginning of the First World War.

[1] Collins, 1930.

Back in the countryside, Castor House fulfilled something for Sir Richard. Its trees spoke to him. Coming back from abroad, he never missed a diary note on the appeal of its flowers. In long tramps, alone but for his dogs, he traced the twists and turns of every local footpath. In the kitchen garden or buried in the top wood he could be lost to the world. Across the road from the house stood the thatched George and Dragon inn which, as the Dragon House, became home for some years for George Newton, Sir Richard's groom-turned-chauffeur whose wife had been nurse to the young Winfreys. George took Sir Richard everywhere, including the newspaper offices, where his acid humour made him something of a favourite. There were times when, to make sure Sir Richard had his hair cut, Lady Winfrey told him to let George Newton trim it at home. The scene was unforgettable: The Chief sitting on a kitchen chair in the harness room reading *The Times* and wearing an old trilby hat — a simple device to prevent Newton taking too much off. A little to the West, on a corner plot where Stocks Hill meets the main street, Sir Richard built and endowed four Homes of Rest for retired employees. This was at the time of his 75th birthday when a minor operation reminded him again of his remarkable health. Pattinson homes at Windermere inspired the design whilst a small tablet on each pair of bungalows bears the words "In Gratitude."

When the family moved in, Ruth was still at Polam Hall, the unsectarian school with Quaker background which Sir Richard chose for the girls at Darlington, but Ellen and Lucy had left. In due course Sir Richard drew on the good offices of Sir John Simon, leader of the Liberal National Party, in paving the way for Pat, having passed the Bar Final, to enter Walter (later Viscount) Monckton's chambers on call to the Bar of the Middle Temple in 1925. The arrival of two grandsons, Richard John in 1931 and Francis Charles in 1934, brought a new dimension to life following Pat's marriage in 1929 to an Irish Protestant bride, Nora Margretta Russell. Mrs Gretta Winfrey was the younger daughter of Mr and Mrs John Joseph Russell of Ballygasson House, Dunleer, County Louth. From their home the Russells could look northwards across Dundalk Bay to where the Mountains of Mourne come mistily down to the sea. Here ponies and horses, with freedom to ride and a magical gift for handling, made Mrs Winfrey's girlhood glorious but, alas, the family were victims of the I.R.A. on a tragic night in 1923 when all were forced at gun-point to leave bed and home while house and buildings were fired. Helping to save the terrified animals is but one of her memories of that dreadful night.

Her father held office as Sheriff of the county for 30 years and included poetry-writing among his relaxations. Mr Russell's special knowledge of agriculture in Eire took him often to Dublin or Whitehall to help represent its needs, and through the breed societies he campaigned for improved livestock to replace scrub cattle common on Irish pastures. The Russell and Winfrey families had become acquainted in 1925 at the wedding of Mrs Winfrey's eldest brother Gerald to Mary Pattinson, only daughter of Sir Robert Pattinson, Lady Winfrey's brother. Gerald had met her in her home county during his time at Cranwell as a regular officer in the Royal Air Force. He took part in the early air pageants at Henlow and carried his enthusiasm for flying into civilian life, but his career was cut short by death in 1936 when he was only 32. A sequel in turn to Pat's wedding followed in 1930 with the marriage of Mrs Winfrey's sister Daphne, who had been bridesmaid with Ruth Winfrey, to the best man, Donald (later Sir Donald) Scott. The two men had been contemporaries at Mill Hill and Cambridge, and Scott went on to prominence as an agriculturist in the North of England, where he owned and farmed land near Morpeth, and also in Parliament, sitting as a Conservative for ten years. Like Sir Richard, in 1945 he had a war-time spell as Parliamentary Secretary to the Minister of Agriculture, and was knighted in 1955.

For 60 years Sir Richard made brief diary notes. In 1940 on his 82nd birthday, confessing to living a good deal in the past, he started working through his annual diaries from 1885 to condense them into one volume. By drawing on these private records and on his memoranda, correspondence, scrapbooks and long memory, Sir Richard was able to compile more than one volume of reminiscences. His travel book *Days I Remember* came out in 1941 but a more important volume was *Leaves from my life*, produced for private circulation in 1936 and dedicated to the two grandsons. In this, extensive extracts from the diaries link chapters on specific activities and the lot of the farm labourer and his family is particularly well documented. Early days at Long Sutton and Spalding are not omitted but a fuller account was given in articles written for the Boston and Spalding *Guardians* during 1926. These were re-published in book form in 1929 under the title *Memories of forty years or more ago.*

Long interest in public affairs involved contact with a host of figures and in 1943 Sir Richard published his last book, *Great Men and others I have met*, a selection of personal sketches of significant men whose lives had touched his and whose portraits crowded the gallery of memory. The list starts with Gladstone; includes six Prime Ministers among men prominent in Government and Parliament; and recalls famous preachers, Brotherhood pioneers, travellers and journalists.

As petrol became scarcer during the war, Sir Richard and Lady Winfrey went into Peterborough by bus to church but this was later withdrawn on Sundays. A horse and four-wheel shay partly filled the breach and the grandsons knew it well as useful for picnics. Office visits became a tiresome mixture of bus and rail journeys with someone meeting him by car at various points. Even if Pat could drive him there and back, he occasionally felt unequal to attending board meetings. His last was at Cambridge on 3 April 1944, when it was convenient for Bury directors to meet in Pat's Ministry of Information office. He went by train from Peterborough and rain fell that day after the driest March for 27 years. The following Sunday was Easter Day and thereafter the diary is blank. From a slight discomfort on reaching home from Cambridge, Sir Richard became daily more unwell and as spring blossomed in the garden, life slipped gently away. The end came on Tuesday April 18th — the end for one who had loved the country and the countrymen, and left a mark on both.

Violets and primroses from the garden at Castor were the only flowers seen at the funeral. One of Sir Richard's Free Church friends, Dr Sidney Berry (secretary of the Congregational Union), joined in a service at the Peterborough Baptist church on Friday, April 21st, to picture his crowded life and independent character. He was nurtured among men whose political and social service sprang from deep religious conviction and that tradition, said Dr Berry, lived on in the record of his public work. Their own age, and even more the age that lay ahead, called urgently for men of that stamp to give real leadership rather than to echo little catchwords of the moment. After cremation at Kettering, where Dr Berry again officiated in the presence of Northamptonshire sympathisers and office staffs, Pat Winfrey brought away the ashes. On the Sunday they were scattered over the grave of Sir Richard's parents at Long Sutton, almost under the windows of the house where he was born.

During life he made substantial provision for his children and added to this from his £46,000 estate, leaving the residue to grandsons Richard and Charles. A trust in their favour had already been set up by their grandfather in 1936. Legacies again reflected his close relationship with the *Peterborough Advertiser;* shares to Hughes, Flynn and Rippon, and £1 for each year of service to all members of staff. Long Sutton was not forgotten, £100 being left to the parish council to help maintain ornamental gates erected at the entrance to the Winfrey recreation ground by Sir Richard in memory of his parents.

Lady Winfrey lived on for a further seven years, reaching Sir Richard's age of 85 before her death in 1951. By this time R. P. Winfrey was building with impressive energy and vision on the foundations of the past and outlining the bright new post-war chapters of the East Midland Allied Press story. Castor House remains the family centre of it, fulfilling Sir Richard's hope when taking possession in 1919 "that it may be the home of my family long after I have shuffled off this mortal coil."

PART II: EMAP COMES OF AGE —
ONWARD FROM WORLD WAR II

Introduction

FOR the creator of East Midland Allied Press, one looks no further than to Richard Pattinson Winfrey. The silver jubilee in 1972 of the formal inauguration of the Group showed how ripe were the fruits and how sound were the roots of this association of local newspapers with their sister publications in the national leisure field. At this anniversary and again in 1973 when Pat Winfrey stepped down from the Group chairmanship, memorials to him were found in simply looking round.

To build on the foundations laid by his father meant a new career for him. As described in Part I, Sir Richard Winfrey, aged 85 when he died in 1944, had for 57 years exercised personal control of the newspapers. Not till age and war brought their imperious demands did Sir Richard begin to devolve company work upon his son. Pat was 41 when the death of his father left him in full management command. He had practised at the Bar till appointed Chief Regional Officer of the Ministry of Information in the Eastern Region in 1939 and was still so serving. Victory in war was yet to come. Newspaper production and circulation were severely hampered by lack of skilled staff and by rationing of newsprint and fuel.

They were obstacles to struggle through, but ahead lay modernisation and re-structuring of the business, expansion into other fields of print, testing of new means of production, and at every turn the challenge of fresh fields and new opportunities. To this record, each one on the staff could add his or her own story. Each publication merits its own volume. It is R. P. Winfrey's overall stewardship which is outlined here. Its results far exceed Sir Richard's pre-war expectations. As one of the Winfrey daughters exclaimed at Mr Winfrey's retirement from the chair of EMAP: "His father would be proud of him."

R. P. WINFREY: CHRONOLOGY

1902 Born at Sutton House, Peterborough, June 24th.
1911 Attended George V Coronation naval review with Sir Richard Winfrey.
1920 With Sir Richard for four-month tour of Canada.
1921 To Christ's College, Cambridge, from Mill Hill School.
1923 First election to newspaper company board: Bury St Edmunds.
1924 Graduated B.A., LL.B.
     Contested Holland-with-Boston Division for Liberals in July by-election and October general election.
1925 Admitted Middle Temple: career as barrister begins.
1926 Elected to *Peterborough Advertiser* board.
1927 With Sir Richard for Canadian newspaper tour.
1928 Appointed secretary, Sir Halley Stewart Trust.
1929 Contested Wellingborough Division for Liberals in general election.
     Elected to King's Lynn newspaper board.
     Married in Ireland, April 2nd.
1938 Elected to Kettering newspaper board.
1939 Appointed Chief Regional Officer, Ministry of Information, Eastern Region.
     Ceased practising at the Bar.
     Appointed managing director, King's Lynn and Bury St Edmunds.
1942 Appointed assistant managing director, Kettering company, on death of Frank Hutchen.
1943 Appointed to control Civil Liaison Department, American Eighth Air Force.
1944 Death of Sir Richard Winfrey.
     Appointed to succeed as chairman of King's Lynn and Bury St Edmunds companies and as managing director of Kettering and Peterborough companies.
1945 Undertook United States tour at Government request.

1946 Appointed trustee, Sir Halley Stewart Trust.
Appointed Justice of the Peace, Soke of Peterborough.
Resigned appointment under Ministry of Information.
Isle of Ely & Wisbech Advertiser acquired.
First London office opened: Strand.

1947 East Midland Allied Press Ltd inaugurated.
Invested with American Medal of Freedom.

1949 Toured Europe and published *Fighting North Europe's Battle for Food*.
Lincolnshire Free Press acquired.

1951 Death of Lady Winfrey.
Stamford Mercury, Boston Guardian, Spalding Guardian acquired.

1953 *Angling Times* launched.
Contract printing began with *Varsity* (Cambridge University).

1955 Succeeded T. N. Bird as chairman, East Midland Allied Press.
Trout & Salmon launched.

1956 Elected director, Press Association.
Motor Cycle News acquired.

1958 *Garden News* launched.

1959 Anglia Press Group inaugurated.

1960 Elected chairman, Press Association.

1962 East Midland Litho Printers Ltd formed.

1963 First building erected, Woodston site: to house first web offset press.

1964 *Garden News* first title off new press.

1965 Divisional structure for EMAP inaugurated.

1967 Sixty-fifth birthday: Castor House staff parties.
First preprint run for *Daily Express*.

1968 Succeeds Sir Stanley Unwin as chairman, Sir Halley Stewart Trust.

1969 Double-width web offset press production starts, Woodston.
Garden News first EMAP computer-set title.

1971 Abbeygate Travel Ltd inaugurated.
Two-Wheeler Dealer acquired.
First EMAP Family Day.

1972 EMAP silver jubilee.
Sea Angler acquired.

1973 Relinquishes chair of EMAP: remains director.
Retires from Peterborough Bench.
First retail shops acquired.
Bike acquired.

1974 *Motor Cycle Mechanics, Popular Motoring* and *Practical Gardening* acquired.
1975 New offices and works open, King's Lynn.
1976 New offices and works open, Kettering.
Goss web offset press production starts, Kettering.

12. ANOTHER RICHARD

R. P. WINFREY was born on 24 June 1902, a date also marked by the sudden illness of King Edward VII two days before his planned coronation, which had to be postponed. Two small sisters, Ellen and Lucy, already awaited him and a third, Ruth, was to follow, completing the family at Sutton House, Peterborough. Richard was a family name repeated in each generation. Pattinson was Lady Winfrey's maiden name, passed on to all her children.

From King's School, Peterborough, Pat moved on to Mill Hill and thence to Christ's College, Cambridge, where he read History and Law, captained the college boat (the start of a lifelong rowing interest), ran in the athletics team, was secretary — with the later politically prominent Selwyn Lloyd as treasurer — of the University Liberal Club, and graduated in 1924. Because of his commitments, he would stay in Cambridge for part of the vacations to catch up on reading, only to be interrupted by the interest taken in him by Americans and others touring the colleges. As he had John Milton's old rooms over the college gateway he could not always persuade them to go away. While still at Cambridge, Pat coached a number of successful college crews and also the Cambridge college servants for their challenge row against their opposite numbers from Oxford. The race was at Bedford, Cambridge using the Bedford School boat, Pat's chief memory of the fixture being not only the win for Cambridge but also the beery proceedings enjoyed by both crews afterwards.

The family had moved out of Peterborough to Castor House in 1919 and Sir Richard was coming to the end of his long years of service on the City and County Councils and also in Parliament, where overwork and his special efforts for agriculture had left him weary. He intended that Pat should follow him as a Liberal Member of Parliament. From their earliest days the Winfrey children could not avoid familiarity with Liberal Party work through the activities of their parents and through meeting Government and Party leaders at functions or around their own or other people's tables. David Lloyd George was no stranger to Sutton House. Pat sometimes met them, too, at the House of Commons when calling for his father en route to Mill Hill School. During air raids in World War I, Stanley Baldwin, a coalition colleague, later Prime Minister and Earl Baldwin of Bewdley, would come into Sir Richard's room. To Pat, who once during a raid saw him take out his false teeth and put them on the mantelpiece, he explained: "They won't chatter so much on there." However, sore gums rather than bombs were Baldwin's fear.

Pat's stout fight for the Liberals in the Holland-with-Boston and the Wellingborough Divisions is described in Part I. Despite his energy, backed by Sir Richard's unequalled expertise, the ebbing Liberal tide could not be reversed enough to win a seat. Although Wellingborough's preferences in the 1929 General Election were in this order: Labour, Liberal, Conservative, they spelled the end of any further Winfrey Parliamentary ambitions. Moreover, the new Labour Government were soon deep in the economic troubles of the Great Depression, which led Ramsey MacDonald to form the first of the National Governments which led the country into and through World War II.

By his withdrawal from the political scene Pat was able to concentrate more fully on legal work, practising on the Midland Circuit. In addition he had begun to help Sir Halley Stewart, Sir Richard's closest political colleague and founder of the Sir Halley Stewart Trust, and learned many lessons from this great Christian gentleman, industrialist and benefactor. He was appointed secretary of the Trust in 1928.

After their marriage in 1929, Mr and Mrs Winfrey first lived in the Temple in Fleet Street and then in Hampstead —

where their two boys (Richard John 1931 and Francis Charles 1934) were born — moving later to the Hertfordshire countryside at Waterdale House near St Albans. Whenever possible both were out with hounds, Pat's passion for the chase being even stronger than Sir Richard's, and to be independent of the normal horse box he designed the first four-wheeled car trailer to take two mounts. With his deep sense of family, Sir Richard's affectionate but insistent determination to guide his children's lives sometimes proved too much for Pat. A point was reached where the son made a priority of freedom to take his own way in the field of politics despite knowing it would cost him the sizeable financial settlement the father had in train, and everything was, in fact, settled on Sir Richard's grandchildren. His good friend Sir Malcolm Stewart, Sir Halley's wealthy eldest son, could truly sympathise and on the flyleaf of his book on the life of Alexander Stewart which he sent to Pat at the time he penned a brief tribute "to your indomitable independence and courage." The ups-and-downs of family relationships never threatened family bonds, however, and weekend visits and holidays and Christmases together were a conspicuous feature up to Sir Richard's death in 1944. In 1940 bombs falling around the house at Waterdale had brought Pat's family to the Manor House farm in Ailsworth, the village adjoining Castor. Later in the war they moved to the thatched Dragon House which faces Castor House, and occupied Castor House two years later when Lady Winfrey, by then a paralysis sufferer, moved over into Dragon House.

Pat had been appointed Chief Regional Officer of the Ministry of Information by Walter (later Viscount) Monckton, in whose chambers he had worked at the Bar and with whom he had a close friendship. Because he insisted on retaining his personal independence, however, he declined to accept a salary and his total war service was unpaid. Pat escaped from the MoI office at Cambridge each week to spend time at Ailsworth, to keep in touch with his father, to manage the newspapers, and when possible to hunt on his wonder horse Bestman, which was fed on brewer's grain and worked on the farm. Firewatching and round-the-clock information and censorship duties meant many nights for all the staff in the office, with secretaries turning their hands to cooking at breakfast-time. Under Sir Will Spens, Regional Commissioner, shadow government departments operated to give a regional service which, if enemy action cut them off from the capital, could take absolute control of the territory. The Ministry of Information not only helped the newspapers but provided information for the public on a vast range of topics calculated to help morale and the war effort, using posters, leaflets, films, loudspeaker vans, exhibitions, and panels of speakers, as well as maintaining a link with 1,800 invasion committees in the region.

After the Pearl Harbour attack in 1941 brought America into the war, there were more United States Air Force bases in the Eastern Region than anywhere in the country, and Thames to Wash became a vast defence area. The number of U.S. airmen based there at one time or another during the four years from 1942 totalled more than 300,000. Because the British food ration made private entertaining impossible the MoI took the lead in establishing with the wealthy and powerful American Red Cross social clubs where both sides could meet on common ground. In addition, with about 25,000 U.S. troops on leave in East Anglia at any one time, facilities were over-stretched and adequate leave arrangements had to be specially organised. Pat Winfrey played a major part in forging the excellent relations which marked the presence of the mighty American 8th Air Force throughout the region, and remained in charge of the civil liaison department until 1945. Apart from the added burden of desk work, this entailed constant trips with distinguished visitors to airfields and Town Halls, and to social and ceremonial events at both, including visits from King George VI, Mrs Roosevelt, wife of the United States President, and Mr Wynant, the U.S. Ambassador.

In 1945, with victory in Europe secure, the Foreign Secretary asked Pat on Lord Monckton's advice to accept temporary attachment to the staff of Lord Halifax, British Ambassador in Washington, for the special purpose of liaison with United States newspaper proprietors. A number of these — notably those of the *Chicago Tribune* — were either anti-British, or did not comprehend the colossal sacrifice of the British people both before and after America entered the war, and that under Lease-Lend her foreign investments had drained away from her into Yankee pockets. Unfavourable editorials and biased reporting sprang from this prejudice and ignorance and hampered negotiations conducted by Lord Keynes in Washington for a substantial dollar loan to prevent the collapse of the £.

Few people in England seemed to realise how small a proportion of the U.S. population was of Anglo-Saxon origin or what pressures there were against sympathy for Great Britain. Pat Winfrey's role was to help counter these pressures by meeting Press proprietors not as a British Government representative nor as an Embassy Press Officer but as an independent visiting newspaper publisher and personal acquaintance of Lord Halifax who, incidentally, had been friendly with Sir Richard when they had sat together in Parliament. Retaining his honorary status, Pat was personally briefed by Halifax, who was well-informed about the Press personalities he was to meet. Air services were still in the future and visiting these American publishers entailed thousands of miles of train travel, mostly at night to save time. The operation, however, gave RPW a valuable chance to see the organisation of, and technical processes used in, a large number of important publishing plants — including the earliest insight into photocomposing experiments at Cambridge, Boston, Mass. — from which he formulated ideas for the foundation and growth of EMAP. As for his work for Anglo-American relations, the United States Administration were sufficiently impressed for President Truman to award him the American Medal of Freedom with Bronze Clasp in 1947.

After Sir Richard Winfrey's death Pat continued on an honorary basis to serve the Ministry of Information until March 1946. His staff at Cambridge remembered him both as prodder and inspirer, as one whose irritation at red tape was usually to their advantage, whose acts of kindness and infectious humour were as memorable as his outbursts of temper under war-time strains, and whose informality and warmth eased relationships with other regional officers and staffs and with those outside.

Philip Schwabe and Bill Appel, journalists from Winfrey newspapers at Lynn and Bury who became MoI Press Officers, have already been mentioned. Among the panics they coped with was improvising alternative lines of communication for newspapers in the region when bombs on the London GPO suddenly cut off their usual London news channels. To Christine Marsh, daughter of William Marsh, Regional Officer of the Ministry of Fuel and Power and three times an Olympics fencer, fell the exacting task of being Mr Winfrey's personal secretary. Irregular hours were the order of the day. She could either drive him to his appointments or take dictation when he was at the wheel. If expected at the newspaper offices, managers knew they might have to spare a typewriter so that Christine could transcribe her notes. Back at Cambridge there would often be further dictation for Christine or the typist on evening duty. Her loyalty during those hectic days is still remembered.

Another senior staff member was Barbara Clapham, daughter of Sir John Clapham, Provost of King's College, whose sister Christina was on Sir Will Spens' staff. Sir John and Lady Clapham were generous in providing a home from home at their delightful house in Storeys Way, Cambridge, where there were opportunities of being present with many distinguished figures, of whom Lord Keynes was perhaps the most significant. Mr Winfrey was glad to retain Barbara's services at the end of the war by arranging her appointment in 1946 as executive secretary of the Sir Halley Stewart Trust. His flat in the Temple, now scarcely used, became her office, and from here she also started an accounting service for the newspapers in respect of business obtained from national advertisers by George Jackson from his agency in Cliffords Inn. From the Temple, Miss Clapham and her assistant moved in 1947 to 167 Strand, and in 1953 to 8 Breams Buildings off Chancery Lane where the East Midland Allied Press London Office was playing an increasingly important part in Group affairs. Miss Clapham continued this dual service to the Trust and to the Group until her retirement from both in 1974, her brother, Sir Michael Clapham, retiring at the same time from his position as Deputy Chairman of ICI Ltd and President of the Confederation of British Industry. Her elder sister, Margaret, was by then widowed. Her husband, the Rt Rev W. H. Stewart, had seen the birth of the State of Israel and shared the travail of the land as Bishop in Jerusalem from 1943 to 1957, when he returned to this country to assist in the Diocese of Peterborough.

The wartime friendship which Pat Winfrey enjoyed with Edwin J. Beinecke, Commissioner for the American Red Cross in Europe, ended only with the latter's death in 1970. Banker and industrialist, his office in Cambridge kept him in close touch with the new clubs for U.S. Service personnel manned jointly by the Women's Voluntary Service and his own Red Cross helpers. In 1943 Beinecke opened a Red Cross fete at Castor House under Sir Richard's chairmanship, when Castor and Ailsworth gave £600 towards the £750,000 the villages of England were asked to raise for the Red Cross. A quite different personality was R. H. Mottram, the Norwich-born novelist. Before moving to the wartime panel of official speakers he served for a time as Deputy Regional Officer and in his reminiscences[1] speaks of Mr Winfrey as a fox-hunting barrister whose pleasant breezy manner persuaded him in 1940 to throw in his lot with the M o I at Cambridge.

Rowing was one of the interests which kept Mr Winfrey in touch with Cambridge after the war. In 1951, when following the university boat race in a launch, he was the only person to snatch a photograph of the Oxford boat as it sank. A year later, with both Richard and Charles Winfrey rowing for Christ's, he coached the college eight. Moreover, as food rationing was still in force, he organised supplies of venison and game from Cambridge graduates and country fare from Castor as a gastronomical supplement for the university crew. Visits to Henley Regatta and the Leander Club

[1] *Another Window Seat*, Hutchinson 1957.

110

became part of the settled pattern of summer, and for convenience Mr and Mrs Winfrey took a trailer caravan with them as accommodation, just as they often did for other fixtures such as the Three-Day Event at Badminton. They were early caravan enthusiasts and the launching in 1963 of the Caravan Club members' magazine *En Route* owed much to Mr Winfrey's interest and to EMAP printing facilities.

Old links with the Temple were revived when Pat Winfrey was the moving spirit behind the production of *Twelfth Night* in the hall of the Middle Temple on Candlemas Day, February 1951. This was exactly 350 years after Shakespeare's own Globe Theatre company, by command of Queen Elizabeth I, had first performed the play in the same Hall. Queen Elizabeth the Queen Mother and Princess Margaret were there to see Donald Wolfit play Malvolio. He kept in touch with a number of pre-war friends at the Bar whose later careers made them household names, among them Lord Birkett, Lord Salmon and Lord Morris of Borth-Y-Gest. Another legal figure was Sir Stafford Cripps, who became a minister in Churchill's war-time government and whose subsequent austere reign as Labour Chancellor of the Exchequer lasted from 1947 until retirement in 1950. Because of his knowledge of racing, he invited Pat to be a member of the Royal Commission on Betting, Lotteries and Gambling which he set up and which reported in 1951, but business commitments precluded acceptance of this invitation.

In 1946 Pat, like his father before him, became a Justice of the Peace for the old Liberty of Peterborough and was elected chairman of the magistrates a year later. Because of an obligation to go abroad as a director of Reuters Ltd, he left the chair in 1949 but remained a deputy chairman and regularly presided at magistrates' courts. He was recognised as a strong chairman, justly but sternly dealing with burglary, hooliganism, obscenity, sex offences and the like, and having little sympathy for the soft view that crime should be excused rather than punished. It was his practice to invite newly-appointed magistrates to sit next to him on the Bench so that he could comment on the proceedings where necessary, and this leadership made many of them feel more secure. Pat's term was extended beyond his seventieth birthday so that he could once more become chairman of the magistrates, bridging the 1972/73 gap between the resignation of the Hon Peter Brassey and the appointment of Sir Ivor Baker.

Hunting was ever his great escape from the pressures of business and duty. Mostly it was with the Cottesmore, in the Rutland and Leicestershire country which yielded its every secret to him over the years. There were days out also with the Fitzwilliam, the Woodland Pytchley, the Quorn, and the Burghley during its revival by his friend the 6th Marquess of Exeter. Newspaper colleagues knew there would be complaints if they fixed business meetings for a fox-hunting day. If robbed of an outing, Pat would often get his pleasure secondhand by phoning the Cottesmore kennels for news of the day's sport, and burning midnight oil over business was often part of the price paid for this daytime pursuit. When fuel was rationed during the 1956 war between Egypt and Israel he travelled to the office by motor-cycle to save petrol for trailing a horse to meets, but changed to a light three-wheeled car for the bleaker days of winter.

Pat continued hunting long after Mrs Winfrey had to give up. He chose some splendid mounts, most outstanding being Atlas, the big grey which figures in the painting of Mr Winfrey in hunting pose which was one of his retirement gifts in 1973. By then leg trouble was bringing Atlas to the end of his usefulness. Out on another horse with the Quorn in 1965, Pat had a serious fall at a fence which led to treatment for the back and made some inroads into his amazing vitality. But neither this nor any minor mishap subsequently kept him from hounds. In the late 1940's and early 1950's Mr and Mrs Winfrey took pleasure in racing Barber's Moon, Lovat, and Natty Bell, trained and often ridden for them by Mike Vergette of Market Deeping. Barber's Moon had to be destroyed after a fall at Market Rasen but not before winning three races in succession in 1947, and Natty Bell achieved a similar hurdling hat-trick in 1951. The latter won a number of important chases and was qualified for the Grand National

28. When Methusaleh II was driven into Bury St Edmunds to publicise Pratt's High Test petrol in March 1933, Mr ''High Test'' was greeted by Walter Baxter as *Bury Free Press* advertisement manager. Walter booked a room with a double bed for the seven-and-a-half foot visitor to stretch in it from corner to corner.

29. Election campaigning in the Wellingborough division in 1929. Mr and Mrs Pat Winfrey stand second and third from right outside the Liberal Party committee room at Bozeat.

30. Right: Frank Loomes, Editor, *Peterborough Advertiser,* 1897-1935.

31. Above: Loomes seen in 1913 with Mr George Fitzwilliam of Milton Hall (on chair) at formal presentation of railings round the last relics of masonry from Fotheringhay Castle. This preservation scheme was pressed by Loomes, a Catholic, in tribute to Mary Queen of Scots, beheaded there in 1587.

32. General Smuts with Sir Richard at the General's farmhouse at Irene, Pretoria. This snapshot was taken in 1929 by Lucy Winfrey (Mrs Eades), using a Brownie box camera.

33. Sir Richard in the garden at Castor House. Fergus looks on as Venus is patted, tail wagging too furiously for camera to catch it. Venus died in 1932.

34. Guests at the *Peterborough Advertiser* centenary celebrations in 1954 included these two stalwarts: Charles Hughes, retired as general manager 1945, and Mrs Agnes Loomes, widow of his colleague Frank Loomes, died 1936.

Combined Certified Net Sales 96,000 Weekly.

East Midlands Allied Press

Managing Director :
Sir RICHARD WINFREY, J.P.

Advertisement Manager:
GEORGE JACKSON,
Tel.: HOLBORN 3611/2.

CLIFFORD'S INN,
FLEET STREET,
LONDON, E.C.4.

Castor Nov 20. 1939

Dear Atton. It was very nice of you to
write me. It is some years since I last
met Wilkinson - I always liked him.
I see by your paper he retired from business in
1920 - that even I did not know.
I left J. Bell & Co in 1885 - Wilkinson was
then a Turner - So I suppose he was
about 75 - Your paper does not give his
age.

Well - you are getting an old Retfordian!
I cannot remember - but were you there
when we had that bye-election. One
Liberal Candidate was J. W. Mellor?
I remember staying at the Stag - or was
it the Stag & Pheasant?

GROUP

MEMBERS.

Peterborough Advertiser.

Peterborough Citizen.

Northants Evening
Telegraph.

Kettering Leader.

Wellingborough News.

Rushden Argus & Echo.

Thrapston, Raunds &
Oundle Journal.

Market Harborough
& Midland Mail.

Lynn Advertiser.

Lynn News & County
Press.

Bury Free Press.

Newmarket Journal.

Suffolk & Essex Free
Press.

ONE
RATE
ORDER
BLOCK
ACCOUNT

35 and 36. The Atton to whom Sir Richard addressed this reminiscent letter in 1939, soon after the outbreak of World War II, was Frederic C. Atton, member of a Spalding family who joined the *Free Press* there as a trainee in 1887 and became editor and director of the *Retford Times*. Note letter heading reflecting national advertising activity in advance of post-war formation of EMAP, and combined newspaper sales quoted as 96,000 copies per week.

And how old are you? Where do
you come in the allten family?
I know it is yr eldest brother at
Spalding — & I am glad to see he
has done such good public work
as his father did before him.
I passed over the Boston & Spalding papers
8 years ago to the Stanimer group —
They had th Stamford Mercury. So
they now run the 3 together.
Just fancy I bought th Sp. G. of Joe little
5½ years ago. It makes me an
old man — as indeed I am — & to
think I shd. have lived to see there
another ghastly war! How hateful
it all is to me.
I write on this paper for you to see
what we are up to. We are in for
a very thin time in th newspaper world.

With warmest regards
yrs v. [?]
R Donaldson.

[Letter 151 addressed by [?]: I
recollect you had 4 Chancery Lane!]

37. When the *Isle of Ely & Wisbech Advertiser* (now *Fenland Advertiser*) was acquired in 1946, the composing room was little changed from this 1915 view. On left, compositor sets type by hand from the case.

38. Part of page one of the first issue of the *Wisbech Advertiser* issued on 2 August 1845 as an eight-page monthly. It became a weekly on 22 June 1855, selling 700 copies; and touched 7,500 as its peak sale of the century at Queen Victoria's diamond jubilee in June 1897.

And Local Chronicle,
PUBLISHED ON THE FIRST SATURDAY OF EVERY MONTH,
AND CIRCULATED ON THAT DAY THROUGH THE ISLE OF ELY, IN THE COUNTIES OF CAMBRIDGE, HUNTINGDON, LINCOLN, NORFOLK, SUFFOLK, AND NORTHAMPTON, AND IN MANY OTHER PLACES.

| No. 1.] | SATURDAY, AUGUST 2, 1845. | [PRICE THREE HALFPENCE. |

WISBECH AND ISLE OF ELY

TEA and GROCERY
ESTABLISHMENT,
MARKET PLACE, WISBECH,
NEAR THE CHURCH.

LOUTH AND MEDWORTH

HAVE received a choice assortment of RAW, CHRYSTALLIZED, and LUMP SUGAR, suitable for Preserving, and making Wine, which they are selling very cheap.

Heads of Families, Proprietors of Hotels, &c., will find by purchasing at the above Establishment, that the necessity of sending to London to procure Good Tea and Coffee at a moderate price, is entirely superseded, their ability, experience, and Cash, enabling them to offer their Goods on equal Terms with the best London Houses.

Burgess's Essence of Anchovies, One Shilling per Bottle.

N.B. The Business in High Street carried on as usual.

BRIDGE FOOT, WISBECH.

C. M. PLACE,
LINEN DRAPER AND SILK MERCER,

TAKES this opportunity to thank his Friends for all favors, and to remind them that he has a choice assortment of SUMMER DRESSES and SHAWLS, at very reduced prices. His Stock of CARPETS, DRUGGETS, COUNTERPANES, and the Furnishing Department generally, will be found worthy the attention of Purchasers.

The Summer Stock of BONNETS, SHAPES and PARASOLS, will be cleared off very Cheap.

All goods marked in plain figures and no deviation made.

FANCY
DYEING AND SCOURING
ESTABLISHMENT,
NORTH BRINK, WISBECH.

JUST PUBLISHED,
PRICE SIXPENCE,
THE PLEASURES OF TEMPERANCE,
WITH
OTHER SONGS AND OCCASIONAL POEMS.

UPWELL, NORFOLK.

Pleasant & Convenient Residence.

To be Sold by Auction,

BY MR. C. CHAPMAN,

AT THE FIVE BELLS INN, UPWELL,
On WEDNESDAY, the 6th of AUGUST, 1845,
Between the hours of SIX & EIGHT o'Clock in the EVENING,
Subject to such Conditions of Sale as will then be produced;

All that Substantial and Commodious

DWELLING HOUSE,

Well adapted for a Family Residence,

TOGETHER with a spacious BARN, STABLE WASH-HOUSE, and other requisite Outbuildings and a piece of highly cultivated and productive LAND lying contiguous thereto (part whereof is surrounded by a Quickset Hedge, interspersed with ornamental Shrubs, and Evergreens, and planted with a tasteful variety of rare and valuable FRUIT TREES, now advancing to a most vigorous state of bearing), containing in the whole FOUR ACRES and ONE ROOD (more or less), and commanding an almost UNRIVALLED ADVANTAGE of a Frontage next the HIGH STREET and on the bank of the navigable River tion, of TWO HUNDRED and SEVENTY EIGH FEET, situate within ten minutes' walk of the Chur at UPWELL, in the County of Norfolk, and now r occupation of Mr. EDWARD HARWIN, wh a ancy will expire at Michaelmas next.

¦¦ Further particulars may be known on application to the AUCTIONEER, Upwell.*

DEACON & CO.,

39. Henry Watkinson (died 1895) founded his *Free Press* in Spalding in 1847. Here he stands on the pavement outside his office and shop in Hall Place to bid a personal farewell to customers in their carriage.

40. Hoe two-reel rotary press installed at Spalding by the *Free Press* in 1903 and used for weekly production until 1950.

THE
Stamford Mercury:
BEING
HISTORICAL and POLITICAL
OBSERVATIONS
ON THE
Tranfactions of Europe
TOGETHER WITH
Remarks on TRADE.

The Whole being a Mifcellanny of Various
Subjects, Profe and Verfe.

Thurfday, May 13. 1714.

To be continu'd Weekly.

VOL. III.   No. 43.

Printed by *Tho. Baily* and *Will. Thompfon* at
Stamford in *Lincelnfhire*, 1714.

Price Three Half-pence.

41. Britain's oldest surviving newspaper title is the *Stamford Mercury*, founded c. 1712 and acquired by EMAP in 1951. This 1714 title page is of the oldest issue extant. The British Library's vast collection has a *Stamford Mercury* of 22 May 1718 as its earliest example of a still-published newspaper.

42. Below, left: In 1716 the Stamford printers launched a second title, the *Suffolk Mercury* at Bury St Edmunds, where it ran for about 30 years.

Suffolk Mercury
OR
St. *Edmund's-Bury* POST.
BEING
An Impartial Collection of the moft
Material Occurrences,
Foreign and Domeftick.
Together with
An Account of Trade.

MONDAY, February 3. 1717.
To be continued Weekly.   No. 43.

St. EDMUND'S-BURY.
Printed by *T. Baly* and *W. Thompfon*, in the *Great Market-Place*.
Price Three Half-Pence.

43. The Stamford-Bury link survives today through EMAP ownership of both *Mercury* and *Free Press*, part of whose first issue of 14 July 1855 is seen here.

44. Ceremony in Stamford Town Hall in June 1966 when the Mayor welcomed 61 United States newspapermen from Missouri, whose university had presented a journalism Honour Award to the *Stamford Mercury* a year before. After a tour of the works they saw a *Mercury* historical exhibition before lunching at Burghley House with the Marquess of Exeter (seen right). With Mr Winfrey (left) is Dean Earl English of the School of Journalism, University of Missouri.

45. Headlines are a 20th century phenomenon but one of the earliest examples in journalism is this treatment (reproduced same size) of news in the *Stamford Mercury* of 8 November 1805, inspired by the tragedy and glory of Trafalgar.

Friday's Express.

The Most Glorious and the Most Decisive
VICTORY
Ever obtained by the Navy of Great Britain:
Purchased; however, at the dearest rate.

Death of Lord Nelson.

London Gazette Extraordinary:

Admiralty-office, November 6, 1805.

Dispatches, of which the following are copies, were received at the Admiralty this day, at one o'clock, *a. m.* from Vice-Admiral Collingwood, Commander in Chief of his Majesty's ships and vessels off Cadiz:—

SIR, Euryalus, off Cape Trafalgar, Oct 22.

The ever-to-be-lamented death of Vice-Admiral Lord Viscount Nelson, who, in the late conflict with the enemy, fell in the hour of victory, leaves to me the duty of informing my Lords Commissioners of the Admiralty that, on the 19th instant, it was communicated to the Commander in Chief, from the ships watching the motions of the enemy in Cadiz, that the Combined Fleet had put to sea:

46. A 1952 look at the seventeen provincial newspapers produced by EMAP. The Group's first national publication, *Angling Times*, was still twelve months away.

47. Opposite: Photographed at Castor House the same year – executives, managers, editors and senior staff responsible for these newspapers. Together near the main door are Mr and Mrs Winfrey, who regularly planned staff parties in the grounds.

48. Howard Marshall, who urged the launching of *Angling Times*, sits (left) with Pat Winfrey in this group at a Castor House cocktail party in November 1955. With them to celebrate sales topping 100,000 for the first time are (L to R): Jack Thorndike, Brian McLoughlin, Graham Overland, Tom Stewart, Bernard Venables, Peter Tombleson and Sonny Cragg (photographer).

49. EMAP's first four national publications as they looked in 1961 before brilliant offset colour transformed their front pages.

50. Readers of *Trout & Salmon* include the Prince of Wales, here discussing trout fishing flies with Jack Thorndike, editor, at the *Trout & Salmon* stand at the Glanusk Park Game Fair in 1976. Fred Jarvis, advertisement manager, shares the conversation.

51. Ron Beacham, circulation manager, at Earls Court in the early days of *Motor Cycle News*. The *MCN* stand was a big centre of attraction and thousands of copies were sold.

52. Another milestone for EMAP national publications – the first issue of *Garden News* comes off the press on 4 July 1958. First to read it (L to R): John Bloom and Sandy Erskine, editorial; Peter Dann, London office; and R. P. Winfrey.

53. Civil Defence and pre-Service units claimed juniors and staff exempt from call-up in World War II. This 1944 group is of Kettering colleagues who served at home after working hours.
Front (L to R): F. A. Cooper, Deputy Fire Guard officer; F. W. Skinner, Special Police; Miss P. Curtis, G.T.C.; Major H. R. New-bould, Home Guard; Miss W. H. Chapman, S.J.A.B.; G. W. Cragg, Special Police; R. W. Bushnell, N.F.S.
Centre: D. C. Waring, Sea Cadets; H. B. Linnett, S.B.S.; S. Thompson, Army Cadet Force; Q.M.S. Bellamy, Pte Capell, Pte Ovenden, Pte Patrick, Home Guard; P. Dawes, A.C.F.; J. B. Beeby, Sea Cadets; G. W. Mobbs, Trailer Pump team.
Back: F. I. Phillips, A.T.C.; D. Clarke, Trailer Pumps; J. R. Williams, Rescue Service; R. J. Pankhurst, Royal Observer Corps; W. E. Neale, F. C. Burdett, Rescue Service; W. P. Hipwell, S.B.S.; R. J. Ayres, H. B. Furniss, Trailer Pumps. Only absentee, junior reporter D. H. Neal, A.T.C., was out on a story.

54. All smiles after the 1959 annual company meeting in London. Helped by P. T. M. Wilson, Fred Felce (fourth from left) displays the inscribed silver tray presented to him on retirement after 59 years in general printing. Fred Cooper's silver teaset marked 41 years service from office boy to executive director, with retirement still ten years away. Mrs Cooper is with him and other main board directors are (L to R): R. P. Winfrey, C. W. H. Aldridge, T. M. Ashton, S. Bayliss Smith and E. Smedley.

55. In an office ceremony typical of Group long-service presentations, Paul Weston, Kettering compositor, receives a cheque from Charles Winfrey to mark 25 years with the *Evening Telegraph*. Ollie Bennett, overseer, is on the left of this 1974 group and Paul's colleagues are Neville Eastland, Roger Bosence, Clive Harvey and Trevor Patrick.

Joseph Slatture Clarke
Printer & Publisher
Market Place
Peterborough

R. Sorwen, Esq
Stamp Office
Northampton

THE
Peterborough Advertiser,

MONTHLY   MISCELLANY,

AND LOCAL RAILWAY TIME TABLE.

No. 5.]   JUNE, 1854.   [Price 1d., or Stamped [post free], 2d.

THE
Peterborough Weekly News and Advertiser,   [SPECIMEN No.]

No. 1.   SATURDAY, MAY 26TH, 1855.   Price 1d., or Stamped 2d.

WOOLLEN DRAPERY,

The Peterborough Advertiser,

AND SOUTH MIDLAND TIMES.

No. 463.   SATURDAY, APRIL 2, 1864.

ERIC'S
SILK & WOOLLEN SPECIALISTS
SPECIAL OFFER of
FURNISHING
FABRICS
8, The Arcade, Peterborough

Peterborough Citizen & Advertiser

Incorporating PETERBOROUGH ADVERTISER (Est. 1854), PETERBOROUGH CITIZEN (Est. 1894), HUNTS. COUNTY NEWS (Est. 1896).

No. 7998   Telephone 3232   FRIDAY, NOVEMBER 21, 1917   Postage 1½d.   *   TWOPENCE

Currys
Cycles, Prams, Toys,
Radio, Electrical
and
Household Goods
Municipal Buildings, Bridge St.,
Peterborough.   'Phone 3998

BRIDE ARRIVES AT ABBEY   The Great   HAPPY COUPLE WAVE FROM THE BALCONY   Gas Stove

---

Peterborough CITIZEN AND Advertiser

The complete local newspaper for over 120 years   FRIDAY, JUNE 18, 1976   6p

---

PETERBOROUGH
ADVERTISER
THURSDAY, JULY 21, 1977

56. Fashions in mastheads.
Top: Monthly in 1854. Tax stamp and stamp officer's name on right and J. S. Clarke's address as printer on left.
Second: Weekly from May 1855.
Third: Title shortened.
Fourth: Titles merged in 1946.
Fifth: Masthead in modern type face.
Left: 1977 corner title piece to suit tabloid make-up.

but suddenly became blind and unhappily had to be put down. Lovat won three good races before receiving an accidental injury which resulted in his demise. Though Mr and Mrs Winfrey did not bet, Natty Bell was a great favourite with EMAP printers who did, and was known to them as The Bread Winner.

In settling down at Castor after Sir Richard's death, Mr and Mrs Winfrey had to discriminate between many opportunities to share in social and public life. As well as charity work, Mrs Winfrey served for a time on the old Soke of Peterborough County Council. Mr Winfrey became a member of the Council of the Peterborough Agricultural Society and in active ways helped to foster what became the highly successful East of England Show. He was pressed into service by the BBC in the Midlands as chairman of their Advisory Council and Appeals Advisory Committee, and during the 1950's was questionmaster or member of discussion panels broadcasting from towns up and down the country. Twice, in 1960 and 1969, he refused to pay rates demanded on the Castor property in protest against local authority neglect of Castor village where storm water flooded roads and invaded cottages. In taking this lead, the misgivings of the Lord Lieutenant and his fellow magistrates meant less than the spirited example set by his father and grandfather in their stands against the Education rate and the earlier Church rate.

Even before his appointment as secretary, Pat had given some help to Sir Halley Stewart in the affairs of his Trust. Secretary in 1928, hon secretary 1946, hon treasurer 1951, chairman 1968 — the dates mark chapters in a story of unwavering service to Stewart ideals extending over half a century. He was one of the few who attended each of the three receptions at which Trust fellows and grantees were guests, the first being in 1935 when Sir Halley himself was host at The Red House, his Harpenden home. The others were in 1968, marking the publication of Sir Halley's biography, and in 1976, celebrating the first fifty years of Trust activity. Both receptions were held in London at Apothecaries' Hall, and grantees and friends were welcomed to each by Mr Winfrey as chairman.

Over the years he became familiar with a remarkable range of pioneering activity, mostly medical and social, which the Trust aided, and made many friends among men and women leaders in these fields. Sir Halley's grip of finance and business, allied to his Christian idealism and social sensitivity, illuminated Pat's own grasp of affairs learned from Sir Richard and extended by legal experience. All helped to mould the Winfrey whose name is inseparable from the story of East Midland Allied Press — caution mixed with courage, impatience with informality, contempt for pretence with respect for Christian virtues; breezy, warm-hearted, fun-loving, compassionate in personal need, generous in friendship, masterful in pursuit of further goals, infusing confidence and will to match his demands. As someone said: "He brightens my grey days."

13. POST-WAR PROBLEMS

LIKE the rest of the British Press, the Winfrey newspapers could not even mark time during World War II. One third of the country's 9,000 journalists were absorbed into the Forces and a great many more were moved to different work. Newspaper printing departments were similarly drained of 14,000 men and women. The loss of Scandinavian newsprint, the need to conserve dollars spent across the Atlantic, and the drastic curtailment of Canadian supplies as Nazi U-boats decimated our shipping, led to a 75 per cent cut in paper supplies. The Newsprint Supply Company effectively controlled the provision and use of what paper was available by restrictions on the number and size of pages, on circulation, and on the ratio of news to advertisement space. Fuel, like food and clothing, was also rationed and the fuel crisis of 1947 — caused by prolonged snows and widespread floods — was a particular menace, with electric power liable to be reduced or cut off without warning, so that presses could not run and Linotype machines could not operate.

Newsprint control lasted for sixteen years and was not finally relaxed until the end of 1956, by which time cost replaced supply as the bugbear. Pat Winfrey's scheme to centralise printing of the newspapers in two main centres meant that in some cases page sizes had to alter both in width and depth to fit the cut-off of a different rotary press. In addition, column widths of up to fifteen ems were reduced to a common ten em measure in the interests of more flexible page layouts. All these developments had to be approved by a reluctant Newsprint Supply Company. One of its directors, Tom (later Sir Thomas) Blackburn, chairman of Beaverbrook Newspapers 1955-68, well remembered Pat's insistence on the reasonableness of these changes as they affected one newspaper after another. No-one in the Supply Company, he said, could possibly forget the *Lynn News & Advertiser* and other Winfrey titles as they repeatedly came up for discussion. They took it in good part, however. Blackburn even brought a party of Daily Express men to Peterborough in October 1950 to look round the *Advertiser* works, share lunch and dinner with staff from Group newspapers, and attend a show in a city theatre at night. A scratch team representing EMAP offices lost 1-8 in an afternoon football match in aid of the Printers Pension and Orphan Fund against an Express eleven which included international experience and the once-great Alex James of Arsenal ('Baggy' because of his long shorts), who was then writing for the paper. Prominent on the same page as the *Advertiser* report of this visit was a notice advising readers that fewer copies were to be printed because the newsprint ration had been reduced!

Before World War II ended with victory in Europe, Mr Winfrey paid a war correspondent's visit to the Western Front in 1945, cabling a news report to the *Evening Telegraph* at Kettering as Montgomery was preparing his epic crossing of the Rhine. This was the year of Britain's first general election since before the war and of the replacement of Churchill by Attlee. To illustrate British democracy at work the British Council made the film "General Election" with Kettering as location. It had a world-wide showing and prominently featured the *Evening Telegraph* office, printing staffs as well as reporters and sub-editors. Later that year Pat visited East and West Canada in search of contracts for future supplies of newsprint, and also studied latest developments in automated printing processes, both hot metal and photocomposing.

The initiative for a European tour in 1949 was taken by Mr Winfrey himself, leading to the publication of a series of seven articles in all his newspapers under the general title "Fighting North Europe's Battle for Food". The need was urgent, he felt, for post-war Europe to grow her own food rather than import it, thus saving invaluable Marshall Aid dollars for industrial recovery. Examples and warnings from the state of farming as he saw it in Belgium, Holland, Germany, Denmark and Sweden were explained for the benefit of agriculturists at home, and the articles were later republished as a booklet. It was a serious individual attempt to back the willing farmer against the bureaucrat and the politician, and led to many expressions of appreciation.

Production costs were below average because of the small papers of the war years and the loss of staff to the Forces. Coupled with unusual pressure on allowable advertising space, this meant that company finance was in reasonably good shape to meet the demands of post-war change. No serious problems arose in accommodating returning staff and wives, pensioners and other temporary helpers were glad to hand back jobs they had been brought in to hold for the duration. The Northamptonshire Printing and Publishing Company (as it was then known) had the largest payroll in the Group and from its offices and works at Kettering, Wellingborough, Rushden, Corby and Northampton sixty-six employees went into the Services, leaving little more than this number to produce commercial printing and the evening and weekly newspapers. Of these, at least fifty gave long hours after work to duties with the Home Guard or sections of Civil Defence. Besides those released from the Forces, the country everywhere welcomed home men liberated from prisoner-of-war camps: the Germans claimed to have taken at least two million prisoners in the West. Anxious to ensure that in the area of the Group newspapers these men were adequately honoured, Mr Winfrey arranged P.o.W. home-coming parties in the main towns. He appointed an organiser to compile lists of guests and issue invitations, and to plan evenings of entertainment.

Though continuing newsprint rationing seriously delayed post-war expansion of the separate newspaper businesses, Pat lost no time in bringing forward the idea that he and Sir Richard had often shared of formalising the control of the individual companies through a Group structure. Resources thus combined — whether of finance, plant or manpower —

117

could be more effectively deployed in the interest both of economy and growth. In the Spring of 1946, Joseph Stephenson of Peterborough, whose partnership had long been associated with the separate businesses as advisers and auditors, was asked to prepare the financial basis of a scheme of amalgamation of all these companies.

While Stephenson was working on this, the need for it was emphasised by an approach to Mr Winfrey by Grahame S. Gardiner of Wisbech with a view to the sale of his *Isle of Ely & Wisbech Advertiser*. This Wednesday publication, which issued a smaller supplement on Saturdays, had been founded by Gardiner's grandfather in 1845 and continued by his father, but Grahame had no son to become fourth-generation owner and editor. Family sympathy had been with the Liberals and thus favoured a Winfrey takeover. To achieve it, Pat arranged that the Peterborough, Bury and Lynn companies should each contribute a third towards the agreed purchase figure of £35,000, pending the formation of the Group which would include the Kettering company.

By the end of 1946 the directors of these four companies had accepted the Winfrey-Stephenson amalgamation proposals. These provided for the formation of a holding company, shares in which would be offered in exchange for shares in the separate businesses. On the basis of these holdings a share capital of £290,000 was fixed for the new company and no fresh capital was sought. There was hundred-per-cent support for the recommendations from the shareholders of each company — 180 in all — and the holding company was incorporated on 27 May 1947 under the name East Midland Allied Press Ltd., the new company being accepted for share quotation by the London Stock Exchange. The initials EMAP had already become familiar in the newspaper world. They represented a convenience title used since 1939 in negotiating national advertising, and also the East Midland Amalgamated Paper Company which had been started about the same time to handle business on behalf of all the newspapers.

The businesses thus brought together were as follows: The Northamptonshire Printing and Publishing Co Ltd (head office, Kettering) publishing daily, *Northamptonshire Evening Telegraph;* weekly, *Kettering Leader & Guardian, Wellingborough News, Rushden Echo & Argus, Thrapston Raunds & Oundle Journal, Market Harborough Advertiser & Midland Mail;* winter only, *Football Telegraph* — Pink 'Un to its enthusiastic readers.

The Peterborough Advertiser Co Ltd: twice weekly, *Peterborough Citizen & Advertiser,* with an edition replacing the former *Hunts County News.*

The West Norfolk and King's Lynn Newspaper Co Ltd (King's Lynn): twice weekly, *Lynn News & Advertiser.*

The Bury St Edmunds Printing and Publishing Co Ltd: weekly, *Bury Free Press, Suffolk & Essex Free Press* (Sudbury) and *Newmarket Journal* (on contract).

There were also commercial printing sections at Rushden (incorporating the department previously maintained at Kettering), King's Lynn and Bury St Edmunds.

The *Mail* and the *Advertiser,* merged at Market Harborough in 1923 and printed on contract at Kettering, had been taken over in 1944.

At King's Lynn the Tuesday *News* and the Friday *Advertiser* merged their titles in 1945 to become the twice weekly *Lynn News & Advertiser.*

At Peterborough a similar change was made in 1946 in favour of twice weekly editions of the *Peterborough Citizen & Advertiser.*

The old *Supplement* published by the newly-bought Wisbech company became the Saturday edition of the *Advertiser* in the same year.

Directors representing the individual companies formed the new EMAP board headed as chairman by T. N. Bird, who was also chairman at Kettering. R. P. Winfrey became managing director, keeping the same position in all the subsidiaries and also his chairmanship at King's Lynn, Bury St Edmunds and Wisbech. In addition to H. B. Hartley, who became chairman at Peterborough, other main board directors were T. M. Ashton, Bury; T. F. Chater, Kettering, and D. F. Thew, Lynn. Fred Cooper, successor on the management side at Kettering to Frank Hutchen, became secretary of

EMAP Ltd and of all the subsidiary companies.

Titles of the latter (apart from Peterborough) were streamlined to read: Northamptonshire Newspapers Ltd, West Norfolk Newspapers Ltd, West Suffolk Newspapers Ltd, and Fen District Newspapers Ltd instead of Gardiner and Co (Wisbech) Ltd.

East Midland Press Properties Ltd was formed to take over new business premises in Peterborough and all houses acquired for staff. Northamptonshire Printing and Publishing Co Ltd, the old Kettering title, was retained for the commercial printing operation as concentrated at Rushden.

The first EMAP annual shareholders' meeting, in London's Waldorf Hotel in October 1948, was held in the knowledge that the profit made by the new group exceeded the combined average profits of the previously independent companies, but there had been no relief from severe newsprint rationing to usher in the period of expansion for which EMAP was poised. A start had been made, however, by arranging to instal bigger Hoe rotary presses at Peterborough and Kettering, secondhand machines being bought because waiting for new presses to be made would entail a three-year delay. W. A. O'Brien joined EMAP from the Kemsley Group as mechanical superintendent to supervise these installations and to advise on improvements in the whole newspaper printing process.

East Midland Allied Press was formed in time to supply evidence as a Group to the Royal Commission on the Press set up in 1946 at the instigation of the National Union of Journalists who were concerned that monopolistic tendencies might inhibit free expression of opinion. In its first report to shareholders the company emphasised the complete political independence of EMAP newspapers — Sir Richard himself had come to this view — and the Royal Commission made the comment that though now under a common proprietorship, they clearly maintained an existence separate from one another.

The point was made even more strongly in the report of the 1962 Royal Commission on the Press. Though EMAP had by then considerably expanded and matured, the editorial freedom of each newspaper, backed by Group production resources, appealed to the Commission as a "notable example" of strength and economy. Appearing before the Commission, Pat Winfrey confessed to its chairman Lord Shawcross that he had sometimes been teased personally over differing points of view printed in Group newspapers [1]. His editors had a free hand in their respective areas and the only common policy was that they should avoid anything obscene or vulgar, and in politics and religion should give a fair show to everybody.

[1] A particular instance of this was the current recommendation by the Local Government Boundary Commission that the small county of Rutland should be abolished. The Group's Peterborough papers approved, but the more closely involved *Lincoln, Rutland & Stamford Mercury* strongly backed Rutland's fight for survival. The success of this secured the county's independence until the reorganisation of 1974.

14. BIGGER AND STRONGER

NEWSPRINT rationing ended in six months of voluntary control in 1957, during which the Board of Trade left it to the newspapers to make fair arrangements among themselves and their suppliers so long as small users of newsprint were not prejudiced. By then the equalised (i.e. averaged between home-produced and foreign) price of newsprint was almost six times the 1939 figure of £11 per ton, the increases being due in part to an unsatisfied world demand. In line with other publishers, EMAP newspapers began to announce increased selling prices and in due course, advertisement charges also. In 1951 the *Evening Telegraph* at Kettering, which was sold at 1d (decimal ½p) before the war, went up from 1½d to 2d, and the *Bury Free Press* led the rise of some of the weeklies from 3d to 4d (1½p). Its pre-war price of 2d persisted until 1948.

The newspapers themselves took on a brighter look. "Display" was the order of the day, and detailed editorial page layouts replaced the judgement of the make-up man on the stone who by tradition had assembled type into pages to simple designs evolved as he went along. Photographs — bigger, better and different — strengthened the appeal of these post-war papers. In 1952 it was reckoned that staff photographers serving the Group's sixteen titles had taken more than 47,000 pictures in the previous twelve months. The public were gratified to see so many of their own faces in print, apart from the pictorial presentation of news that had never before attracted a camera. Photographic exhibitions, staged in the Group's main towns (particularly in

1951, Festival of Britain Year) and opened by civic leaders or local personalities, emphasised the place of the papers in their own communities and also the emergence of a post-war breed of fulltime press photographers with a new contribution to make to newspapering. As Pat Winfrey would say at these opening ceremonies, "Photographic art in the Press has come to stay". The Group's bigger offices devoted window or reception area space to topical photographs, and orders for reprints revolutionised darkroom work.

Changes made to the sober *Isle of Ely & Wisbech Advertiser* — first addition to the Winfrey Press — typified the effects of the new approach. June 1946 saw the end of the old-style Gardiner publication, and the first July issue revealed an unusually thorough transformation. News replaced advertisements on the front page, column width was reduced from 15 ems to 11 ems (2½ inches to 1⅞ inches — all standing matter had to be reset to this measure during a hectic weekend in the works: Group standardisation on 10 ems came later), there were nine columns per page instead of six, news and advertisements were arranged in a fresh order throughout the edition, a centre social page incorporated a leading article, sport was given more prominence, more photographs were used, wider coverage of the area was undertaken, readers noticed a livelier treatment of news stories, and a start was made in applying editorial display techniques to each news page. Only four pages at a time could be run off on the old *Advertiser* re-wind flatbed press, necessitating a double run for its eight pages, and printing was therefore switched to the King's Lynn Cossar, completed formes being taken the fourteen miles in boxes to slide on to the machine. Fortunately this had the same cut-off, so that startled readers of the *Advertiser* who first saw the new-look paper on Wednesday July 3rd were at least spared handling pages of a different dimension.

The *Advertiser* relied for most of its news headlines on a 12-point bold Gothic letter (capitals only) produced by Linotype which — to put it kindly — was more useful than decorative. Display types, set by hand from the case, had been mainly reserved for advertisements. Raids on these for editorial purposes had to be restrained and news head-lines were soon being supplied from the Ludlow machine in the Lynn works, set from copy posted overnight and sent to Wisbech as a parcel on the bus. Later headlines were retained at Lynn and dropped into blanks left in the completed pages of type when they arrived for printing.

Although type might sometimes go inconveniently astray on the bus, this Lynn-Wisbech co-operation was an early though simple example of advantageous sharing of Group facilities. The Wisbech staff were never more glad of this than during the 1947 fuel crisis, when electric power was liable to be reduced or cut off locally without notice. If cuts lasted too long, metal in the Linotype pots solidified, and not a line of type could be set for at least an hour after current again reached the heating element. On the one or two occasions when this calamity fell on a press day the Wisbech paper was put to bed at King's Lynn. Galleys of type and advertisements, illustration blocks, and partly-completed formes, plus staff, were hastily packed into van and car and taken to the composing room at Lynn with copy still to be set. Because of this sisterly help there was no delay in publication, and a further lesson in Group cooperation was learned. That production of the *Wisbech Advertiser* and its moder-nised Saturday edition should be moved to the Peterborough works in 1949 and to the Lynn works in 1963 (though still run off on the Peterborough rotary press) was — again — symptomatic of Group development which left no staff or newspaper unaffected as EMAP came to grips with expansion.

Grahame Gardiner at Wisbech was not the only publisher to turn to Pat Winfrey when retirement beckoned. At Spald-ing, nineteen miles from Peterborough in the South Lincoln-shire fens, the elderly directors of the *Lincolnshire Free Press* found release in selling their newspaper and station-ery business to the Group in 1949. From the purchase price of £59,000 negotiated with Ernest A. Wilson, chairman of the Spalding Free Press Co Ltd, and his fellow director and company secretary W. Cecil White — they were editor and manager respectively — the shareholders received half the value of their holdings in cash and half in EMAP shares.

Wilson and White were to retain their seats on the Spalding board for five years at an annual salary of £500 each, but they died within a few weeks of one another in 1952. Their fathers had served the business from boyhood and with four other senior staff had bought it after the death in 1895 of its colourful proprietor Henry Watkinson. He was persuaded to launch the paper in 1847 by John Gardiner, who had founded his *Wisbech Advertiser* two years before and was a friend from Watkinson's days in Wisbech as a printer's apprentice.

The transformation of the *Free Press* was less immediate than at Wisbech. News did not replace advertisements on the front page until the first issue of 1950, when printing was transferred from the 1903 Hoe press at Spalding to the Foster at Peterborough. This, however, entailed a severe break with tradition, Tuesday morning replacing Monday afternoon as publication time. Monday evening was, in fact, so much devoted to reading the *Free Press* that it was avoided by organisers of local events. Fresh news types were taken from other offices to help dress the front page and column width was reduced to the Group measure of 10 ems. Solemn discussion on the changes followed at council meetings, sports clubs and women's societies, but where votes were taken they were fortunately all favourable to the new appearance of the old family friend.

In 1950 the Kettering company pushed an edition of the *Evening Telegraph* into Bedford, opening a small office there and challenging the London evenings on what was very much their own ground; and sent flongs of most of their pages to the Peterborough office where a local centre spread was produced to complete a Peterborough edition. But the big development of the year was the move of the Peterborough business from premises Slatterie Clarke (founder of the *Advertiser)* built for it in Cumbergate in 1874 to accommodation in Broadway, in the City's main thoroughfare. Careful development behind the main offices gave ample space on the ground floor for a double-width rotary press with stereotyping department, reel store and publishing area, and on an upper floor for Linotypes and composing. This Hoe press was four units of a machine kept in reserve store by Kemsley Newspapers. Its six other units were erected in an extension built at the Kettering premises and were brought into use in 1952. Office conditions at Kettering had already been eased by moving commercial printing to the Rushden works.

Pat Winfrey had clearly lost no time in establishing Peterborough and Kettering as the major rotary printing centres for the Group but further expansion was on the way even before the new Kettering press was operating. Sir Richard Winfrey's first experience as a newspaper proprietor had been as owner of the *Spalding Guardian* which he bought in 1887, and sentiment led Pat to seek to bring it once more into the Winfrey fold. As recorded in Part I, Sir Richard had sold the *Guardian* to the Boston company he initiated in 1925 after Pat's Parliamentary fights in the constituency, but in 1936 he let both the Boston and the Spalding *Guardians* go to Westminster Press, who thereafter published them in association with their other local title, the *Stamford Mercury*.

The Westminster directors sympathised with Pat's Spalding wishes but production and content of the three papers were integrated under the control of Stamford Mercury Ltd to an extent which made it preferable to sell the company rather than one of its newspapers. Westminster had a debenture of £30,000 invested in the Stamford company, and in 1951 EMAP purchased the ordinary shares for £27,500. This added three more titles to the Group, bringing not only Sir Richard's first newspaper but also the historic *Lincoln, Rutland & Stamford Mercury*, rival to *Berrow's Worcester Journal* for the honour of being Britain's oldest surviving newspaper and certainly carrying its oldest surviving title. Steadily developing from c.1712, the *Stamford Mercury* not only became supreme as the news and business medium of Eastern England but during the 1850's enjoyed the highest sale of any provincial paper in the kingdom. Richard Newcomb, father and son, were fifth and sixth in the line of owners, the latter's wealth, fearlessness and reforming ideals making him in particular a powerful champion of the under-privileged. For long after his death in 1851 — this was shortly before repeal of the stamp duty led the lower-circulation *Manchester Guardian* to change from weekly to daily publication and start on its road to power — the *Mercury* appeared impregnable. Newcomb's successors, however, had no such visionary as C. P. Scott among them to steer a fresh course and avoid erosion by new weeklies springing up in the region, and though today its grip on Stamford, Rutland and adjacent corners of Lincolnshire and Northamptonshire is close and increasing, return to that proud 19th century peak seems remote.

A jealously-guarded survival from those high-circulation days is the privilege — unique now to the *Stamford Mercury* and well-known to philatelists — of cancelling postage stamps on its newspaper wrappers with its private cancellation stamp incorporating the title of the paper. The privilege derives from Inland Revenue decisions of the 1850's when proprietors of the *Mercury, The Times* and *Illustrated London News* were the only three given permission to print the then newspaper tax stamp on their publications during normal printing, instead of taking blank paper to Somerset House for pre-stamping. For the *Mercury* this was relief indeed as the paper was made in its own mill at Wansford, near Stamford, and had to be carted to London and back at great expense. Newspapers bearing the revenue stamp were allowed through the post until the duty was repealed in 1870, when postal stamps requiring GPO cancellation had to be used. Post Office agreement to the *Mercury's* use of its own individually-designed canceller dates from this change.[1] Last private owner of the *Mercury* was Mrs Zita Florence Todd-Newcomb, who ended 130 years of Newcomb proprietorship by selling the paper in 1929 to Sir Arthur Wheeler, a Leicester financier. He bought for £16,000 and within twelve months re-sold for £21,000 in a deal with Westminster Press Provincial Newspapers. Bankruptcy closed Sir Arthur's career in March 1931 amid the general economic depression of the times.

In August, a few weeks after the acquisition of Stamford

[1] *The Story of the Stamford Mercury Postage and Revenue Stamps*, by J. H. Chandler, 1958.

Mercury Ltd, Lady Annie Lucy, widow of Sir Richard Winfrey, died at 85 after a two-year illness. A substantial shareholder, she had been unable for some time to take any part in the business or to share in Pat's plans for the Group, but there were men and women, particularly in the Peterborough office and works, who were truly saddened that her lively personal interest, thoughtfulness and friendliness were withdrawn for good.

15. GROWING PAINS

THE first three annual meetings of EMAP shareholders were held in London at the Waldorf Hotel, Aldwych, but in 1951 they met at the Angel Hotel, Peterborough (site since redeveloped) to facilitate a look round the new offices and works in Broadway. The 1952 venue was the board room of the Northamptonshire company in Dryland Street, Kettering, where alterations and extensions to the premises could be inspected and the new press and other equipment seen in operation. The company accounts for this fifth annual meeting included a pictorial review of the five busy years since the Group was formed. Besides Peterborough and Kettering improvements, a new look had been given to the offices at Boston, Bury St Edmunds, King's Lynn, Spalding, Stamford and Wisbech, and the commercial printing works at Rushden had been extended.

The eleven newspapers which Sir Richard Winfrey had published — twelve with the football *Pink 'Un* at Kettering — had increased to sixteen, including the *Newmarket Journal*, printed on contract until the copyright was bought by EMAP in 1955 for £5,500. Expenditure on plant and premises had been of the order of £55,000 over two years but the first year's net profit of £11,622 had grown to £17,747. Staff had increased from 400 or so to 525: 130 on the editorial side, 44 in photoengraving, 125 in commercial departments and 226 involved in printing. Combined circulation figures on the formation of EMAP approached 200,000 with up to 50,000 for the Saturday *Football Telegraph*. Removal of pegged circulation control in January 1949 and addition of further titles brought the certified combined sale in 1952 to around

241,800, and with a quarter-million sale and claim to a three-quarter million readership EMAP joined the Audit Bureau of Circulations.

To arm the Group's Fleet Street agents and to further the appeal to national advertisers, booklets issued in 1949 and 1951 were the first of a long line of promotional publications descriptive of the newspapers and of the population, industry and agriculture of eastern England. EMAP had good reason to call its rich territory "The Heart of England" for it led the country in production of footwear, bricks, grain, sugar and diesel engines — to say nothing of Newmarket's horses! Its soil put apples, peas and potatoes into England's pantries and flowers on to its tables, whilst dug from under it by the world's biggest excavators came mineral ores to feed its hungry iron and steel works at Corby and Wellingborough. Some Group newspapers traditionally took spaces at their annual trades fair or county agricultural show but from 1951 they had a physical presence at many more open-air events by using a portable darkroom with newspaper display trailer. This impressive juggernaut, an ex-German Army outfit introduced by Pat Winfrey, also carried a stop press machine. The years brought refinements of transport, equipment, organisation and technique, all listed in a company publicity manual and used until changes in circumstances closed down the Group Promotions Department in 1975.

With rotary printing concentrated on new presses at Peterborough and Kettering, farewells were paid to faithful but unwanted machines in other towns. Cossar flatbeds from Wisbech, King's Lynn and Bury St Edmunds were sold after going out of service in 1946, 1949 and 1951 respectively. The Hoe two-reel rotary bought in America for the *Lincolnshire Free Press* in 1903 for £2,250 — a figure which included all the stereotyping equipment — was dismantled in 1950 after printing was transferred to Peterborough. Editions of the *Free Press* had twice before been run off by the *Peterborough Advertiser*. Both occasions were over a period of weeks while the Spalding press was repaired following damage by fire: in December 1923; and again after German aircraft dropped fire bombs during a war-time raid in May 1941. Stamford's four-decker Hoe was taken to Ilford, Essex, for a further term of service.

Sir Richard had taken premises in Queen Street, Peterborough, round the corner from Cumbergate, to house the new £12,000 four-unit Foster brought into use for the *Peterborough Advertiser* in 1935 (three units went at the same time to add to capacity at Kettering). Superfluous after the Broadway development, the Foster found a new home in Bath. Kettering saw a still bigger operation in 1953 when two Hoes installed twenty or so years earlier were shipped to Bangalore and the three-unit 1935 Foster went to Scotland to print the *Falkirk Herald*. It is an ironical comment on the continued expansion of Group activities that not many years after Peterborough sold its Foster, more printing capacity became essential. In 1961 another Foster, purchased in Bristol and — like its predecessor in Peterborough — built new in 1935, was erected in premises taken in Princes Street, Peterborough, to ease the load on the Hoe at Broadway. The cut-off of 25⅛ inches determined the choice of these machines.

Smaller composing rooms in the Group were closed one by one, all but their best Linotype machines and founts of type disposed of, and page production concentrated in five centres: Peterborough, Kettering, Bury St Edmunds, King's Lynn and Stamford. Duplicate stereo plates for advertisements from the Group's London agents ordered for all EMAP papers were cast at Kettering and Peterborough and sent to the other centres. The two photoengraving departments performed a similar service for news pictures until Bury (1950), Stamford (1955) and Lynn (1956) opened their own block-making sections. The latter depended on one of the earlier Klischograph machines designed by Dr Rudolph Hell which had first been used at Kettering. By engraving into a plastic material its stylus could produce a small block very quickly but good quality was difficult to achieve.

Thus serviced, each centre, with its own moulding press, took pages to the matrix stage, leaving only the rotary printing plates to be cast at Peterborough or Kettering. Publishing staffs travelled with these, to see the issue off the press and bring the papers home, delivering agents' parcels on the way. New pressures were felt all along the line as one newspaper followed another on to the press. Printing schedules were tight, van journeys closely timed, editors' deadlines strict: everyone felt a new urgency — including advertisers slow with their copy. Within weeks of starting to run in 1952, the rotary at Kettering was printing not only several editions of the Evening Telegraph every afternoon, the five area weeklies on Thursdays and the *Pink 'Un* on winter Saturdays but also turning out editions of the *Stamford Mercury,* the *Spalding Guardian* and the *Bury Free Press* on Thursdays and the *Boston Guardian, Suffolk Free Press* and *Newmarket Journal* on Tuesdays. It was a new sight for visitors to see one paper billowing forth from one end of the press and, thirty yards away, another from the other end. Peterborough's four units rumbled away under a similar load: a daily edition of the *Evening Telegraph;* two issues weekly of the *Citizen & Advertiser,* of the *Lynn News & Advertiser* and of the *Wisbech Advertiser;* and the once-weekly *Lincolnshire Free Press.*

The comfortable days were slipping away when each local paper had its own works and everyone from editor and overseer to office boy shared a common interest and local knowledge. Now Linomen, readers and stonehands in the main centres had to adapt to the different demands and styles of the different newspapers they produced. There were more press days, more overtime, more argument. To encourage production the Group in 1953 started its incentive scheme for type-setting operators and stonehands. At the human level, Pat Winfrey's vision and personal qualities of leadership and persuasion, borne on irrepressible streams of energy, were never more valuable than at this convulsive stage of Group development, which would not have been possible at such a rate without the readiness of a loyal staff so often to go a second mile. Mostly, however, they felt that — under him — they were on the winning side and were all moving forward together. Advice to one new promotee was: "You do what Mr Winfrey wants . . . He's magnetic, that fellow."

Pat's paternal rule, like Sir Richard's, was based on knowing everyone who worked for him, from junior clerk to manager. Jokes, leg-pulls, interest and often aid in personal troubles, and a warm and sometimes disconcerting informality made him the idol of many even if insistence and directness made him on occasion the despair of others. Every Christmastime saw him touring offices in the half-dozen or so counties of the EMAP area to say "Happy Christmas" individually to each member of staff. Where offices had no staff social clubs he asked for these to be started, so that employees could together enjoy outings, parties and games. In winter he and Mrs Winfrey did their best to get to each annual staff party where they could thank everyone for a good year's work, lead the way on to the dance floor and set the pace in party games.

The cup he gave for inter-office bowls after the friendly match at Castor at Sir Richard's seventy-fifth birthday party in 1933 was played for annually till the war. Soon after the war this contest was revived and director colleagues added trophies for tennis, cricket and football, and for billiards, snooker and darts. The bowls and tennis tournament became the Group's main summer social event, directors, editors, managers, teams, sometimes wives and supporters, converging to prove that Mr Winfrey's ambition to see a genuine family spirit binding EMAP together was no idle dream.

Sometimes in the earlier years, as round after round was played off on the greens, he could not resist the chance to call office chiefs away from their spectating to share some current problem, either his or theirs. *Splash,* as the EMAP house journal was christened, was launched in 1950 following a suggestion at one of these impromptu meetings. Nine issues of the little war-time *Telewag* — the title was a play on Tallywag, which was how Northamptonshire people talked of the *Evening Telegraph* — had kept Kettering and branch office staff at home and overseas in touch from January 1944 to March 1946. *Splash* would fill a bigger role for the Group: ". . . a permanent record of our activities, both as newspaper publishers and printers and as a happy family indulging in sporting, recreational and social activities" as Mr Winfrey put it in the first issue. He felt that "one of the most admirable features of our Group is the happy association between the staffs of the different offices, and the growing interest and pride there is in the well-being of the Group as a whole."

The tournaments were also an opportunity for office chiefs to meet in relaxed surroundings, perhaps for the first time, for Group development opened the way to earlier promotion for a number of young men whose energy and freshness were essential to progress. Death or retirement had left few of Sir Richard's chief lieutenants to carry on into the RPW era and new appointments were urgent.

At Peterborough Alan Page, who had previously worked for a time at Kettering, briefly occupied the editorial chair in 1945 between the death of W. E. Rippon and the arrival of H. R. Parkin. In the same year J. R. Livingstone — he had come to this country with the Canadian Forces in the 1914-18 war, married and settled in England, and was appointed to Lynn in 1941 by Sir Richard — succeeded Charles Hughes as general manager, and Edward Smedley, office manager at Peterborough, became general manager at Bury, joining W. A. Appel at the start of his editorship with G. H. Hunt still in charge of the *Suffolk Free Press* at Sudbury.

At Kettering W. L. Joy had become editor-in-chief in 1944, renewing an association with the Winfrey papers broken when he went into daily journalism. He had been with the *Continental Daily Mail* in Paris until 1940, when the fall of France in World War II brought him back to the *Mail's* Manchester office. Joy became EMAP's first Group editorial adviser, and his adventurous journalism and flair for newspaper design, features and picture power made an impact on all his editorial colleagues. F. A. Cooper had inherited Hutchen's management work at Kettering in 1942.

Lynn management was entrusted to W. C. Baxter, promoted in 1945 from Bury. His editorial colleagues were D. F. Thew *(Lynn Advertiser)* and L. J. Bartley *(Lynn News)*, the latter a sub-editor promoted in the same year from Kettering soon after finishing his war service. Another ex-Serviceman who had scarcely settled down to sub-editing at Kettering was David Newton, who in 1946 moved to the chair of the *Wisbech Advertiser*, first post-war addition to the Winfrey press. The manager chosen, just out of the Royal Air Force, was A. A. Hughes, youngest of the four sons of Charles Hughes, retired general manager at Peterborough.

A further round of appointments marked 1949 when another ex-Army man, C. W. H. Aldridge, who had become Parkin's assistant at Peterborough where he had trained pre-war under Loomes and Flynn, combined the editorial and management roles at the newly-acquired *Lincolnshire Free Press*. Parkin himself succeeded as editor-in-chief at Kettering on the departure of Joy to Australia.

Bartley moved from Lynn to Peterborough, being followed at Lynn by J. R. Williams, his old subs table colleague at Kettering. Williams became sole editor of the twice-weekly *News & Advertiser* on Dyker Thew leaving the Group in the same year to become managing director of newspapers published at Colchester. A little later, Thew started a successful twenty-year career in insurance, from which he retired to Hunstanton, scene of his boyhood.

Edward Smedley was at Bury only three years before moving back to Peterborough as general manager when Livingstone's health led to early retirement in 1948. Tony Hughes moved from Wisbech to fill the gap at Bury, and R. D. Beacham, whose EMAP career had begun in the Wellingborough office of the *Northamptonshire Evening Telegraph* where David Newton also started, joined him as manager at Wisbech.

Fresh life was infused into the *Suffolk Free Press* by the in-office promotion of J. E. Bloom to succeed his chief George Hunt, who moved to Peterborough to strengthen the management team there. His function was to support Bartley in the new role of managing-editor which he assumed in this same year (1949) so that Smedley could be free to work full-time in harness with Pat Winfrey as personal assistant to the Group managing director.

Smedley had joined the *Peterborough Advertiser* company as a clerk in 1926, the year of the General Strike, and had the excitement of being handed a revolver and detailed by Joseph Cooke, general manager, to go with the van driver to ensure unmolested delivery of the *Advertiser*. Sir Richard's absences abroad were often chosen by Cooke to indulge in some extra expenditure. Smedley's appointment was at such a time, and he was searchingly cross-examined on Sir Richard's return as to who he was and what he was doing in the office. "I expect you are Jo Cook's extravagance for this trip," growled Sir Richard. "I hope I don't find any more."

Smedley's contribution to the war effort was in Civil Defence. His training distinction in achieving all three of the highest possible gradings was unique and led to a personal acquaintance with Herbert Morrison, war-time Home Secretary. As chief instructor for the Peterborough area in the later part of the war he lectured company directors and staffs on dealing with incendiary attacks, unexpectedly finding Sir Richard and his men from the *Advertiser* in the Town Hall audience one evening. "Hello Smedley," Sir Richard called. "What are you doing here?" Disgusted to hear that it was to lecture, Sir Richard barked: "I expected we should have a talk from an expert."

Pat Winfrey found that Smed's experience of business routine, his grasp and presentation of issues, his patient unravelling of problems, and his sympathetic approach to staff were qualities well suited to complement his own anxiety for progress, and relied on him to fill in detailed background essential to the broad strokes being added to the EMAP picture. They had worked closely together on purchase of the *Wisbech Advertiser* and the *Lincolnshire Free Press* and on formation of the EMAP parent company: similarly on purchase of the *Stamford Mercury* company with its three papers in 1951. Smedley joined the boards of these companies and was elected to the EMAP board in 1951, so becoming the Group's first executive director.

16. FRESH FIELDS

PEACEFULLY, unexpectedly, in his sleep, King George VI died on 6 February 1952 at Sandringham House after a day spent shooting on the royal estate. Princess Elizabeth was not crowned Queen until 2 June 1953, when the Group's special contribution to the occasion was a memorable pictorial souvenir. Its large illustrations of family and Abbey scenes, finely printed in blue, gleamed in regal contrast to the gold of the text. Its pages, tissue-interleaved, were held in the gold-printed cartridge cover by a tasselled silken cord. Though heavily pressed by their own coronation issues, the newspaper production staffs at Kettering took pride in the meticulous extra work involved. It was no surprise that the commercial printing company at Rushden, where the publication was run off, were quickly busy on a reprint. Only their "blue and gold" of the Elizabeth and Philip wedding in November 1947 could be compared to it.

Christmas 1952, first after the King's death, saw the Royal Family as usual at Sandringham. Before the new Queen could return to London she found herself on the doorstep of the catastrophic floods of early 1953 when high tides, lashed by gales, mocked East Coast sea defences from Wash to Thames and drowned thousands of England's best food-producing acres. Three hundred people died, hundreds more spent hours of terror in bedrooms and on rooftops as water surged through their buildings, many houses were destroyed and countless others damaged. EMAP staff were among the bereaved and despoiled at King's Lynn, where water swept streets and homeless survivors were fed and sheltered in schools. As inrushing tides bottled them up, fenland rivers and drains overflowed and in places broke their banks, to add to inundation inland. The flood disaster of 1947, when thawing snow and ice choked and broke the water courses, was comparable but missing from it had been the savagery of the sea.

The Queen was quick to tour the countryside with the Duke of Edinburgh and — via Sir Winston Churchill, then in his third premiership — to back the plea for Government aid. EMAP readers, as residents in or near the stricken areas or as halfday or weekend visitors, all felt the nearness of tragedy. The Group's support of the relief fund opened by the Lord Mayor of London took the form of a twelve-page pictorial record largely comprising illustrations in hand after use throughout the various newspapers. This souvenir, put together within a matter of hours, found an immediate sale at one shilling per copy, several reprints being needed and more than 80,000 being run off. As all costs were borne by EMAP, a little over £4,000 accrued to the fund, a result which — according to a personal message from Buckingham Palace — "amazed and gratified" the Queen. R. J. Winfrey had a special reason for remembering it all: he was among Cambridge undergrads who slogged away filling and positioning sandbags where breaches occurred or threatened along the banks of the Ouse.

As newsprint was still strictly rationed and could be used only for specified titles in prescribed quantities, RPW had explained to the Board of Trade that newsprint was to be used for a special publication to raise money for the Lord Mayor's Fund to help flood victims, many of whom were in the Group's circulation area, and had requested an immediate permit to acquire paper to replace the quantity used. When an official at the Board not only refused a permit but threatened legal proceedings for violation of the regulations, Pat telegraphed to the effect that unless the threat was immediately withdrawn and the permit issued at once he would go without delay to Sandringham — where the Royal Family were regular readers of the *Lynn News & Advertiser* — and acquaint Her Majesty with the facts of this "despicable conduct". As Pat contemporaneously recorded: "It appears that the stupid bureaucrat had enough sense to know that RPW meant what he said and saved his silly skin by climbing down."

But these were only incidents in a period when Pat Winfrey, after five years of forceful refashioning of the newspaper businesses into an efficient Group entity, and with his programme of rebuilding and re-equipment completed, felt that EMAP must push on without delay. As T. N. Bird, shoe trade chief and lay chairman of EMAP, would say of him, perhaps enviously: "It's remarkable what energy Mr Winfrey puts into his job — and what energy he puts into other people!" Spare flatbeds and rotaries had been sold to help finance the new Hoe units: now spare capacity on the Hoes would be sold to other publishers.

One of the earliest — and smallest — contracts, starting in the 1953 Easter term, was to print *Varsity*, 6,500-sale university newspaper produced 24 weeks of the year by students at Cambridge with a fresh editor chosen by themselves each term. Printing was at Peterborough after pages were composed in the Bury St Edmunds office. The *Bury Free Press* team found, however, that a friendly interest in the work of their eager guests was not enough to save them from pitfalls, and a stronger voice in the conduct of the paper was ensured when Mr Winfrey formed Varsity Publications Ltd to take it over, EMAP subscribing 51 per cent of the £100 capital. Dr Lauterpacht, Fellow of Trinity and lecturer in Law, agreed to be chairman of the company with D. R. Thompson, recently appointed general manager of the *Bury Free Press*, as secretary and students completing the board. *Varsity* quickly lost advertising and readership support in 1972 when the Cambridge Students' Union began free distribution of 10,000 copies of their new competing weekly, *Stop Press*. The two papers merged from Easter 1973, the independent *Varsity* and its link with EMAP having both ceased halfway through the Lent term.

At the Kettering office, production began in March of the weekly 60,000 *Catholic Times* with four editions. Pages were made up after the Wednesday *Evening Telegraph* was cleared from stone, and printing completed on Thursday mornings before EMAP weeklies crowded the Hoe. Page production was later switched to Stamford, the association being broken only because the proprietors set up their own printing works nearer London to start a daily Catholic paper. But they had to leave behind the smooth service EMAP had given them, and in 1962 the *Catholic Times* ended its 103-year run in a merger with *The Universe*.

Meanwhile R. P. Winfrey was being pressed by his friend Howard Marshall to take a publisher's interest in angling — something he had long been urging. Before he was thirty, Marshall had moved from Fleet Street journalism to radio, his pre-war Test match broadcasts setting an unequalled standard. On the outbreak of war, when Pat went to the Ministry of Information, Howard moved into somewhat related work by joining the Ministry of Food as director of public relations. In 1943 he returned to the BBC as director of war reporting, personally helping to cover the North Africa campaign and the invasion of Europe.

His most memorable broadcast was after crossing to Normandy on D-Day, when he brought the scene at once to life for a waiting nation, speaking in still drenched clothes from the beach to which he had returned. Howard Marshall concentrated on writing and public relations after the war but agreed to describe the funeral of Queen Mary and the Coronation — both 1953 events — in sound for the BBC. Just before the funeral broadcast, when moving to a position on the roof of St James's Palace, he suffered great discomfort after falling through a hole hidden by a tarpaulin, but his splendidly deep unruffled voice gave no hint of pain.

Though rugby and cricket commentating made him an institution, fishing was his most loved, most constant recreation and it grieved him that Britain's countless anglers had so poor a Press. It was a turning point for anglers and for the Group when Pat Winfrey, after long and searching inquiry and with newsprint becoming free from rationing, persuaded EMAP directors to launch *Angling Times* to fill the gap. Fifty thousand copies of the first weekly issue, dated 10 July 1953, were distributed to meet estimated sales, and readers bought 33,000. At Peterborough to watch that first paper off the press, Pat Winfrey and Edward Smedley became part of an unforgettable scene. Eager to help, they found themselves stooping together over the office counter, fulminating their feverish way through thousands of labelled wrappers to insert fresh ones or alter others as phone calls by a determined sales staff — persisted in to the last minute — persuaded newsagents to place or increase their orders. At the November annual meeting, shareholders learned that circulation had grown to more than 50,000. By the end of the year it was 60,000, and in November 1955, 27 months from launch, Mr Winfrey held an *Angling Times* party at Castor House to celebrate a sale of 100,000. He wanted another party as soon as possible to mark reaching 150,000 but Marshall was certain the figure would rise to 200,000.

Some have computed that angling, as the country's leading participant sport, has a three-million readership potential. By 1963, when *Angling Times* achieved a weekly sale of 171,567, awareness of this potential induced Echo Publications (London) Ltd to issue *Angler's Mail*, which exceeded 100,000 by 1971 but still left *Angling Times* with nearly 160,000. By then the *Mail* had been taken over by IPC Magazines but the intense competition which ensued could not topple *Angling Times* which continued with a sale about 50 per cent ahead of its rival and reaching 175,000 in 1976.

In 1953 EMAP extended its coverage by introducing *Trout & Salmon* as a monthly for the game fisherman, its sale exceeding 43,000 by 1976 and its readership later including the Prince of Wales. Another step in 1963 was to launch *Fishing* as a further title to explore aspects of the sport each month to a degree not possible with the busier weekly. In time the need lessened for this extra service and *Fishing* was not issued after 1969. But *Fishing Tackle Dealer*, a controlled-circulation magazine for the trade acquired from City Magazines Ltd in 1963 remains a valuable link with the commercial side of angling. Since 1970, when the title was changed to *Tackle & Guns*, the magazine has had blanket coverage of outlets for fishing tackle, guns, and other sports goods.

These enterprises, which led EMAP to the premier position in Europe as angling publishers, had brought new faces
into Group positions. Stanley Bayliss Smith, who agreed to
chair the Angling Times company and had become EMAP
financial director in 1951, was a partner in the London
accountancy firm of Cassleton Elliott & Co (now Josolyne
Layton-Bennett & Co), familiar to Pat through Cassleton
Elliott's association with Sir Halley Stewart and his Trust.
Admired both in the City and in West Africa for his unrivalled knowledge of taxation and financial matters, Bayliss
Smith had moved on from cricket and rugby football to
enjoy sea fishing from his Sussex retreat at Rustington, and
was soon at home with problems of the new publications. On
Howard Marshall's advice[1], editorial direction of *Angling
Times* was entrusted to Bernard Venables, angling writer
and illustrator, with Colin Willock, who soon moved on to
Lilliput, working with him as editor. Ken Sutton, another
ex-Fleet Street angling enthusiast whose initial circulation
and marketing operation was so successful, hints at the
excitement and pressure of the early days in his personal
reminiscences, *Angling in the News*, published in 1960.

Trout & Salmon called for special outside expertise, Pat
Winfrey sending his angler son Charles to Scotland on a
talent-spotting expedition which brought Ian Wood to the
chair. Bachelor, musician, painter, writer and record salmon fisher, by retirement in 1969 this sturdy character had
taken *Trout & Salmon* to a 30,000 sale in fourteen years. He
did it by trying always to merit the American Negley Far-
son's compliment when he offered to write for the magazine
without fee because of its "unpretentious rightness".

The back-up team for these publications, drawn from
existing EMAP staffs, proved worthy successors when the
newcomers moved on, achieving greater things in conditions not always so favourable. An honours board would
include such editorial men as Jack Thorndike, who held the
chair for fourteen years after Venables left in 1956; Peter
Tombleson, technical executive, who became full-time sec-

[1] Howard Marshall remained on the board of Angling Times Ltd until his death in 1973
but Parkinson's Disease had curtailed his activities for some time previously.

142

retary of the National Anglers' Council when formed in 1967 on the initiative of *Angling Times,* and Brian McLoughlin, who rose to manage all EMAP national publications before leaving the Group in 1972; with Ron Beacham, whose circulation wizardry lies behind the mounting sales figures for each title in the Group's lengthening national list.

A sixpenny booklet listing the 1954 open events for match fishermen was a tiny start to a long succession of *Angling Times* titles on where to fish, when to fish, how to fish and what to fish for, with the first *Angling Times Book* bringing peace to the bedside of thousands in 1955. Among best sellers have been Ken Sutton's *Fishing for Londoners* and the *Angling Times Holiday Guides.* The service given to the sport by *Angling Times* and its sister publications is beyond dispute. More anglers fish more securely and more professionally with more scope in better-managed waters than ever before. Youngsters are encouraged through the immensely successful Kingfishers' Guild; the solitary angler finds his contemplation mirrored in the printed page; the match angler has an up-to-date competition guide and all the opportunity offered by the nationwide Angling Times League; the manufacturer, trader, club official, fisheries officer and water administrator recognise the voice of authority and share a common source of reference; even the blind and the disabled find their interest in fishing catered for and fostered.

R. P. Winfrey had managed the Group almost single-handed until his helper Edward Smedley became an executive director in 1951, and expansion into the national field led to two more executives joining the parent board in 1953: F. A. Cooper, EMAP secretary and managing Kettering, and C. W. H. Aldridge, managing Spalding. With administration of the subsidiaries divided between them, they became a close-knit triumvirate under Pat as managing director, with informality paying off as they ran the Group together and developed the mutual understandings which make for quick pace and prompt decision.

Though united in those pioneering efforts which leave the Group ever in their debt, the trio differed markedly from each other: Smedley — serious in demeanour, portly in appearance, dedicated in service, ambitious for EMAP, leading Rotarian and active through life in the Scout movement; Cooper — immaculate, cautious, calm, fresh in complexion as in wit, an enthusiast for golf; Aldridge — slimness accentuating a taller than usual figure, technically gifted, coolly efficient and with coiled-spring energy: qualities befitting an ex-World War II Signals officer serving on Field Marshal Alexander's staff.

Impatient with isolationism lingering in some offices, Pat Winfrey called to everyone to "Think Group". Concentration of production wore down barriers. So did the new integration of management. Both were aided by a developing inter-office telecommunications system which became unique — essential in a Group with bases scattered over several counties. Because of the war, the Kettering evening paper had to rely on Creed punched tape — pioneered there in 1921 — for its Press Association news until teleprinters were installed in 1948. By the mid-1950's Kettering was linked by both teleprinter and internal telephone to its branch offices and also to Peterborough, where a local edition of the Northamptonshire Evening Telegraph had been started. Only Bury St Edmunds and its satellites were excluded from this system when completed in 1962.

Room-to-room conversation became possible for all staff throughout the Group as well as the transmission of copy and messages by teleprinter, equipment being owned rather than hired from the GPO. The Telex service, installed at Kettering in 1959 and at Peterborough ten years later, meant that material despatched to EMAP by Telex from distant parts of the country or overseas could be immediately repeated to any part of the Group. These facilities are monument in themselves to the then adventurous expertise of R. J. Pankhurst, who reigned over EMAP communications from 1924 and died a week after retirement in 1967. Much of the electrical equipment after the war was acquired inexpensively from ex-government sources, being Army and R.A.F. surplus stock, though the dealers and contractors proved tough guys for Pat Winfrey and Dick

Pankhurst to bargain with. At the latter's side for most of the time has been Wilfred Elmore, still at Kettering, whose bright assistant, Nigel Monk, was on hand to play a full part in the technical transformation at Peterborough when the age of photocomposing dawned there in the 1960's. Inter-office van runs and couriers using fast Kings Cross-Peterborough trains completed Group contact.

Telex was indispensable to the success of *Motor Cycle News*, the struggling weekly which fell into the lap of the Group in 1956 and whose sale of around 200,000 makes it today the world's top-selling motor-cycling newspaper. It was the brainchild of Cyril Quantrill, motor cyclist from schooldays, wartime signals despatch rider, sports editor of the Temple Press glossy weekly *Motor Cycling*, and of his friend Peter Baldwin, whose father was then running a family printing business in Tunbridge Wells. It was conceived while both were at the 1955 International Six Days Trial in Czechoslovakia, and the first weekly issue came out on Wednesday November 30th. The aim was a fourpenny newspaper-style publication dealing with the sporting side of motor cycling and out a day ahead of its two rivals. However, with inadequate printing facilities, possibly up to twenty inches of advertising per issue, a sale rarely above 9,000, and only one editorial man to help him, even Quantrill's devotion could not keep his profitless infant alive for more than nine months and he and Baldwin senior agreed that the forty-first issue on 5 September 1956 should be their last.

Meanwhile Quantrill's desperate search for someone to mount a rescue operation had ended with EMAP via Ken Sutton and Richard Arnold, motor-cycling friend of Quantrill and contributor to *Angling Times*. Motor cycles had never been part of Winfrey dreams but the paper's potential challenged Group management skills and on September 19th the forty-second issue — a week late — was composed in the Stamford works and run off on the Peterborough rotary, its eight pages enlarged to the Group's tabloid size as for *Angling Times*. Cyril Quantrill sold the title for £100 and joined R. P. Winfrey, Smedley and Cooper on the board of the EMAP subsidiary formed to take over the publication, Ken Sutton and Ron Beacham re-living their *Angling Times* baptism in boosting a countrywide sale almost from scratch. By Christmas the average weekly sale had almost reached 10,000; it leapt to 26,000 in 1957, to 46,000 in 1958, and exceeded 66,000 in 1959, by which time it was making a significant contribution to the profits of the Group. The 1,000th issue on 22 January 1975 reported an average sale of 156,000, and figures exceeding 200,000 were first reached early in 1976, with issues of 60 or 70 pages. Ron Beacham's big part in this success included hectic weekend trips with the family caravan to racing circuits up and down the country. At these he personally flaunted the paper and introduced the *Motor Cycle News* banners, now a permanent feature of the racing scene, sited so that television cameras could not avoid them as background.

To be on the bookstalls on Wednesday with results and reports of weekend events entailed slick reporting, fast communications, urgent editing and quick production and distribution. Until the Telex service offered automatic receipt of messages at any hour, copy-taking by telephone kept staff on the qui vive from Sunday tea-time and through much of the night and early Monday. But for his untimely death in 1961 Derek Denton, a young motor-cycling sub-editor drawn from the Kettering office, could have told a rare tale of those feverish days for he bore the brunt of shaping Quantrill's dreams into reality via the phone, the desk and the composing room.

Before long the success and growth of *Motor Cycle News* brought its own special problems, both to editor and management, and in July 1961, with sales at 76,800, came a mutual agreement to part. Quantrill ("I have always liked to do things my way") left EMAP and was soon editing *Motor Cycle Illustrated* for City Magazines Ltd, eventually joining the Duckham oil organisation. To succeed him as editor, Brian McLoughlin was moved from *Angling Times* where he had learned the national publication trade under Jack Thorndike. McLoughlin proved himself an enterprising organiser whose talent led in time to appointment to managing editor of *Angling Times* as well as *Motor Cycle News*, to general manager of all the Group's periodicals in 1969, and to a management post outside the Group in 1972.

An airlift of the paper to the Isle of Man with full T.T. racing coverage ahead of rivals had started in 1958; a stream of booklets and one-off publications on technical topics, on motor cycle history, on road racing, speedways and stars of the wheel, made their appearance; the Ministry of Transport, the trade, race organisers and competitors, found themselves the objects of bold new criticisms or advice; motor cycles were offered as prizes in reader competitions; *Motor Cycle News* figured at the Earls Court and Olympia trade shows from 1962 and in that year staged the first veteran and vintage rally at Stanford Hall, Rugby; the paper annually helped select the Machine of the Year and the Man of the Year; McLoughlin made the first furthest-ever trip for the Group in 1964 when he reported the Japanese Grand Prix and established a rewarding relationship with Japanese manufacturers. The date is interesting in view of the bike boom which hit Britain around 1970 and led to a 23 per cent rise in motor cycle registrations in that year alone. Biggest success of all was probably the Super Bike championship started by *Motor Cycle News* and by 1975, when televised live from Brands Hatch, the premier road race championship in Britain.

Competing giants whom Quantrill faced with his stripling paper in 1955 were *Motor Cycle* and *Motor Cycling*, then selling more than a quarter million copies weekly between them. By 1967 they joined forces as a weekly newspaper entitled *Motor Cycle* but could not prevent *Motor Cycle News* continuing to romp far ahead of their combined sale, which had dropped below 90,000 by 1972. Meanwhile it was a natural development in May 1971 for *Two-Wheeler Dealer* — produced by NJ Publishing Co Ltd since January 1970 as the official monthly publication of the National Association of Cycle and Motor Cycle Traders — to join EMAP under the wing of *Motor Cycle News*. A two-wheeler trio was completed in 1973 when the Group acquired the 50,000-sale bi-monthly magazine *Bike* from the Rev Marcus Morris's

National Magazine Co Ltd. This was founded as a quarterly in 1971 by Mark Williams for the lively lads and lasses falling increasingly under the motor-bike spell, to whom Ogri — *Bike's* irreverent and sometimes shocking cartoon strip character — was something of a ton-up hero. Through Mike Nicks, who moved to the chair from *Motor Cycle News*, EMAP have remained watchful that Ogri's conduct keeps within bounds. Williams stayed with *Bike* as contributing editor, monthly publication started in August 1974, and by the end of 1976 sales were more than 80,000.

The introduction of *Angling Times* and *Motor Cycle News* with their attendant titles firmly established EMAP in the leisure publication field. It justified Pat Winfrey's view that there was more for EMAP in the publishing world than merely good housekeeping for their existing provincial newspapers. The periodicals were Edward Smedley's particular responsibility. His avuncular behind-scenes carefulness was valued not only in the board room but also by staffmen needing sympathetic discussion of their troubles or enthusiasms. A succession of younger men drawn by him and Pat from the local newspapers to compete with Fleet Street editorial, advertising and circulation staff far beyond their own townships, soon discovered they lacked neither the grit nor the fire to beat them at their own game. But success is never automatic. *Auto News,* which in May 1966 endeavoured to serve the sporting motorist as *Motor Cycle News* was serving the two-wheel sportsman, was all too early overtaken by a new Government economic freeze. Results expected from *Boat News,* launched in March 1973 as a companion to *Angling Times,* did not mature. So the axe fell cleanly on them both, the first after seven months and the other after only five, despite all the energy and effort put into the respective editorial sides by Pat Beasley and Russell Hole.

17.   IN THE CHAIR

THE death of H. B. Hartley in 1955 severed a link with the earliest Winfrey days in Peterborough. Friend of Sir Richard, first secretary of the Peterborough Advertiser company and successor to Lady Winfrey as chairman, he was a founder director of East Midland Allied Press Ltd and was active in both to the end. Pat had organised a company dinner in honour of his 92nd birthday. Now at 94 came the end. He had been Peterborough's most brilliant after-dinner speaker, and had added the charm of polished wit and literary allusion to the lunches for directors, managers and editors at each EMAP annual shareholders' meeting. The vacancy on the parent board was filled by P. T. M. Wilson, a leading Kettering solicitor and nephew of T. N. Bird (EMAP chairman) and grandson of Thomas Bird (chairman of the Kettering company 1922/27). Peter Wilson had himself joined the Kettering board on the death in 1951 of his cousin Tom Chater, who was also one of the Kettering representatives on the Group directorate when EMAP was formed. The family link with newspapers went back to 1889: not long after the start of the Kettering company.

Until retiring in 1951 T. N. Bird had been a leading figure not only in the Northamptonshire boot and shoe trade but in wider fields and had amalgamated the Dolcis Shoes chain of retail outlets with his own manufacturing company. Now in 1955 he asked for release from chairmanship of the EMAP board though willing to remain a director, staying so until his death in 1958. R. P. Winfrey succeeded to the chair while continuing as managing director, the board appointing Tom

149

Ashton of Bury St Edmunds as deputy chairman and Edward Smedley as joint managing director to ease Pat's day-to-day burden. The Winfrey family reached another milestone with Richard John's call to the Bar at the Middle Temple, a year after graduating in History and Law from Christ's College, Cambridge.

To boost the flow of advertisement revenue into the Group provincials, Charles Aldridge led a small team in 1955 to Copenhagen — the first from Britain — to study success achieved by the *Berlingske Tidende,* one of Europe's leading dailies. On his return, the pages of each newspaper were re-arranged to focus more attention on classified advertisements (the word "smalls" was banned!) and departments set up to canvass for them by telephone. Tele-ad departments have since become a permanent feature of the British newspaper scene.

Another innovation was entrusted to R. S. Stephenson, journalist son of Joseph Stephenson, the Group's auditor. After five years in charge of the local pages in the Peterborough edition of the *Northamptonshire Evening Telegraph* he was installed at Kettering to supply editorial material to the Group's provincial offices as basis for advertisement features with attractive reader appeal. As his contacts developed, few publicity men remained ignorant of EMAP, and at one stage he was asked to address London members of the Institute of Public Relations on how to prepare more acceptable handouts. He and his successors in the Group, with the backing of advertisers, have kept readers well informed on a vast range of matters. Be it agricultural developments, new car models, radio and television sets, clothes for school children, presents for Christmas, where to go for holidays at home or abroad or for halfdays and evenings out; ways to tackle home decorating or gardening; advice on hair styles, cosmetics, spring-cleaning, car maintenance, insurance, caravans or house repairs; how to plan a wedding (they stopped short at advice on funerals) or a party or a camping tour; where to hire excavators, concrete mixers, taxicabs or evening dress — all was made available, with the story of Saint Valentine and the real meaning of Mothers' Day for good measure. The list may have been trimmed over the years but a number of substantial themes persist.

To encourage advertisers to use the fast-growing *Angling Times*, Bill Lumby was sent to open an advertisement department at 8 Breams Buildings, in offices taken for editorial purposes when the paper was started in 1953. Lumby also cooperated with George Jackson, the Group's Fleet Street agent, but in the New Year of 1956, against a background of higher production costs and the arrival of commercial television with its impact on national advertising, John Nuttall was appointed to the London office as Group Advertisement Controller to push EMAP claims more directly and determinedly. A Londoner with 25 years in advertising and an all-round practical experience — including work with Edward Hulton on *Picture Post* — he used his Fleet Street standing to good effect, thrusting the EMAP banner in the faces of the advertising world with every confidence. He contributed regularly to advertising conferences and also to the newspaper trade press, where the Group ran a sustained advertising campaign.

Measures to back Nuttall included a new EMAP brochure in 1956 statistically descriptive of the newspapers and economic life of the Group area, claiming solid coverage via a 258,000 sale reaching a million people; a readership survey published in 1957 (updated in 1961) proving that nine out of ten adults in the area read an EMAP newspaper; publication of Audit Bureau of Circulations figures for each newspaper instead of the single combined Group sale quoted since joining ABC in 1949; the appointment of Ken Sutton as EMAP's first Group Circulation Manager; and the advent of George Walker, who left a London advertising post to become the Group's first Provincial Advertisement Manager.

A retailer-cooperation service, believed to have no counterpart at that time, was inaugurated to try to ensure that products advertised in EMAP newspapers were, in fact, in the local shops. Experiments were also successfully made in the part of the Group covered by Midlands ITV to demonstrate the value of advertisers using television and the local

151

Press simultaneously. John Nuttall recalled[1] his dismay at finding, just before a 13-week run of Group insertions was due to start, that no retailers in the area had been approached by the manufacturer or knew of the product. The discovery led to cancellation of all the insertions! It also led to a comprehensive merchandising service being set up, with Peter Dann, Nuttall's colleague at the London office, cooperating in the advertising field with the new independent TV company, Anglia Television Ltd. EMAP made a modest investment in Anglia TV in 1958 (withdrew 1970), and a year later devised the Anglia Press Group to provide concerted advertising coverage within the new station's reception area. The proportion of EMAP circulation involved was 178,000 (augmented in 1961 by the *Bedfordshire Times* series at the request of Westminster Press Ltd, who later added part of their *North Herts Gazette* series, and in 1963 by the *Peterborough Evening Telegraph*[2]) and in 1976 the total stood at nearly 367,900.

Pat Winfrey had hoped for closer involvement with independent television and in 1958 had joined with newspaper groups based on Norwich and Ipswich in applying for the broadcasting licence for the region. It went instead to the Marquess Townshend, Norfolk landowner who chaired Anglia Television Ltd with the support (among others) of Laurence Scott of *The Guardian*. Pat's hopes for local commercial radio were similarly dashed. Ten broadcasting companies covering EMAP country were formed in 1961 in anticipation of the Pilkington Committee's findings but the issue of licences in the 1970's was much restricted, Leicester being the nearest, and the companies remained dormant.

The Winfrey urge for expansion led in 1956 to the Northamptonshire Printing & Publishing Company, which had been carrying on the Kettering company's general printing commitments under Fred G. Felce in premises at Rushden, being renamed East Midland Printing Company Ltd and given control of the general printing departments in the Bury St Edmunds, King's Lynn, Spalding and Stamford

[1] *WPN and Advertisers' Review* 20 July 1962.
[2] The *Peterborough Evening Telegraph* ceased to be an edition of the *Northamptonshire Evening Telegraph* and became an independent newspaper from 15 May 1961.

works. Fred G. Felce continued to make his headquarters at Rushden and was joined in management of the new company by Alan G. Butler, general manager of the Kettering newspaper, who moved to Bury to oversee the plant there. Under R. P. Winfrey's influence, the era of dance tickets, handbills, parish magazines and voters' lists — the latter a hallowed tradition at Rushden — was closing in favour of contracts from the Stationery Office, British Railways, banking and industrial concerns and London publishers, notably George Allen & Unwin Ltd and Butterworth & Co (Publishers) Ltd. At Bury, larger premises were taken and new equipment installed for letterpress colour work. A consortium of British printers paid the Printing Company a compliment in 1957 by asking it to produce *The Book World Today*, whilst its longest single job was the 1962 reprint of Bertrand Russell's ponderous *History of Western Philosophy*.

Pat and his colleagues toured other printing works and visited printing exhibitions at home and abroad as they felt their way forward. To travel with this larger-than-life person could never be dull and was likely to be hectic. He was too shrewd to deceive, too much a presence to ignore, too experienced in examination to side-track; blessed, too, with a marvellous memory for facts and faces. His cries for help, entertaining and exasperating in turn to others, were on more vital issues: spectacles missing, keys mislaid, papers out of order, tickets lost. When Charles Aldridge retired from EMAP in 1976 he spoke of R. P. Winfrey as the dynamo that drove the Group and produced all the sparks. "You may think that RPW stands for Richard Pattinson Winfrey, but for me RPW stands for Raincoats, Pullovers and Wallets. Those of you who have travelled the newspaper trail across Europe know of the debris that gets strewn along the way . . ."

To accommodate increasing business, the Printing company's Rushden operation transferred to larger premises in 1959. Fred Felce was by then 72, and with 59 years in print behind him — the last a period of unusual pressure — forsook management for retirement, remaining on the board and also on the Town Council at Higham Ferrers, his

153

pocket-size native borough. Fred's civic service to Higham as Mayor's Sergeant, councillor, mayor and alderman extended over 36 years and ended at his death in 1964. His experience, energy, commonsense, occasional irrascibility, good humour and integrity put him in a class on his own in EMAP. Felce had disbanded the general printing units at Spalding and Stamford but production and administration in three widely-separated centres (Bury, Lynn and Rushden) proved unwieldy and denied to the company the return deserved by a trebling of its business.

In 1963 Rushden was closed down and its order book taken to Bury, where a sheet-fed Solna 124 was now adding four-colour litho facilities. Its installation in 1962 was in line with a general movement in commercial printing, and also reflected R. P. Winfrey's early convictions about applying the offset principle in time to newspapers. Alan Butler continued oversight of the Printing company until moving out of the Group in 1964 first to Cheltenham and then to Bath to manage Pitman Press, reverting to newspapers in 1968 as general manager of the *Straits Times*. Increasing nationalist pressure in favour of Malaysians led to his return in 1972 and a welcome back to EMAP the same year. Meanwhile closure of the Bury general printing operation had been forced in 1966 when the GPO compulsorily acquired the premises for an extension of their sorting office next door. Luckily space was left for newspaper production but with no feasible alternative in Bury, the printing business had to be vastly scaled down to fit the constraints of the company's modest section at King's Lynn.

It was an untimely blow after the build-up of business and addition of plant, but employee interests were safeguarded and few redundancies followed. An incentive scheme introduced in 1955 had benefited staff and output following the work measurement bonus payments started for the newspaper production side a year or so earlier. Personnel Administration Ltd set up the system at Bury and then in the rest of the Group, their first expert on-the-spot being Ivor McKinnon. Ivor found his wife at Bury, and also a reciprocated regard for EMAP which led him into the Group when a

154

new management structure paved the way in 1965. The incentive scheme has been adapted and revised over the years in consultation with the craft unions and remains a valued feature of the EMAP production scene[1].

Two newspapering neighbours welcomed R. P. Winfrey to the board of the Press Association — the first Northamptonshire man to serve as a director — at his election in 1956. W. M. Young of Norwich, general manager of the *Eastern Daily Press* and sister titles, was struck most by the happiness of the EMAP set-up: proof, he felt, of Pat's mastery of the art of management. From Northampton, W. Cowper Barrons considered EMAP centres were models of mechanical efficiency. "They always were in the days of his father, the late Sir Richard Winfrey. Pat Winfrey is a chip off the old block," he said. Four years later Mr Winfrey was elected chairman by his Press Association colleagues and his one-year term of office was extended for a time after the annual meeting in 1961 because W. M. Young, chairman-elect, was ill.

Though his 12-year term of service as director, chairman and then member of the consultative committee covered the customary period, it was marked by some unusual features. Stories of this forceful newspaperman and hunting personality went the rounds in Fleet Street. Cromarty Bloom, the association's general manager, spent a time in the country air at Castor House during sick leave and saw something of EMAP. Pat broke fresh ground as chairman by visiting every Press Association centre in the land and insisting on improvements where necessary. His firm stand in dispute with the Exchange Telegraph over complete and equal sharing prefaced a new 40-year Joint Service agreement in 1962. The gusty preference he had for progress rather than protocol was an occasional embarrassment to Cromarty Bloom and his full-time colleagues but this could not long survive Winfrey warmth and friendliness.

Centenary celebrations in 1968 formed the climax of his link with the association. Mrs Winfrey was with Pat in June

[1] In 1951 the *Express & Star* at Wolverhampton was the first provincial newspaper office to introduce an incentive scheme based on time and motion study. EMAP drew on the Wolverhampton experience. By 1951 there were 30 schemes operating in general printing companies.

at a Guildhall reception after the hundredth annual meeting when both were presented to the Queen; and he was a guest at the Savoy banquet addressed by Harold Wilson as Prime Minister which closed the programme in November. Pat's friend and neighbour, the Marquess of Exeter, toasted The Next Hundred Years. Perhaps, however, the 1962 trip to Greece, Egypt and East Africa in September and October on behalf of Reuters Ltd, the associated agency, was the most rewarding opportunity. Reuters had men to meet and. agency centres and contracts to check. As well as these, Pat pursued two other interests — the antiquities in Egypt, and the then novel application of offset printing to newspapers in Nairobi. Sir Richard Winfrey had visited Egypt during tours in 1899 (four months after the Battle of Omdurman) and 1931, and had included East Africa in 1928 in one of his three trips to the continent. Pat felt he was following his trail as he saw the Sphinx and the Pyramids, Luxor and its temples and tombs, the Nile as far as the Aswan Dam then being built, the mountains and game parks of Kenya.

Management of EMAP affairs remained in the hands of the three executives, assisted from 1958 by Richard John Winfrey[1]. From Christ's College, where he was Captain of Boats 1952/53 — excursions included rowing in the 66th International Regatta at Hamburg in 1953 — he had spent a year in London studying for the Bar before starting National Service. Commissioned in the Royal Norfolk Regiment (he was leading cadet on passing out), Richard went to Cyprus in 1955 during the dangerous troubles preceding independence. On release from the Army he preferred printing to Law and within a year at the London College of Printing had completed with distinction studies normally taken over two years. Before joining the management team in 1958 he worked in some of the offices, tackling a range of routine newspaper jobs. The three executives also had the support of a board of management, set up in 1960 to facilitate regular consultation with Group specialists: Ray Parkin, editorial (he gave up active editing in 1960 to become Group Editor-

---

[1] R. J. Winfrey became a member of the Press Association board in 1976, just 20 years after his father's election as a director.

in-Chief); John Nuttall, advertising, and W. K. Sutton, circulations.

Richard Winfrey was married in September 1958 to Miss Jean Wild of Warmington, brought up in the countryside between Peterborough and Oundle. A year later his brother Francis Charles, younger by two-and-a-half years, was married to a Yorkshire bride, Miss Julia Jane Downs, met while both were in Cambridge. Charles went into the Army on leaving The Leys, being commissioned in the Carabiniers (3rd Dragoon Guards) and serving for a time in Germany. Returning to Cambridge, he graduated in Estate Management at Christ's — he rowed for the college at Henley — and then joined a leading firm of land agents as a chartered surveyor. In 1960, however, he was glad to follow Richard into EMAP, spending some time in production, editorial, advertisement and promotion departments before starting six months' experience in *The Guardian* office at Manchester. Sir Richard had sometimes taken both his small grandsons with him on office visits. "Would you like to work in the newspaper business?" he once asked young Charles. "Yes, grandfather, sometimes in the afternoons," was the reputed reply.

18. MORE TITLES

SINCE EMAP started a contract printing service for other publishers in 1953 with *Varsity*, the list of titles grew steadily. The goodwill generated at the top by R. P. Winfrey and his colleagues helped lessen friction over competing claims for service in composing and press rooms. At Kettering, stitching equipment developed by Timson Engineers Ltd, locally-based makers of printing gear, had made it possible in 1956 for the newspaper rotaries to produce stitched magazine-size publications. This mechanism was an adaptation of a stitcher-folder attachment which Pat had seen on the press in the Vatican which printed the daily, *L'Osservatore Romano*, and other Catholic publications. He was there to investigate a proposal that the *Catholic Times* should be a daily paper linked with *L'Osservatore Romano* facilities. The negotiations came to nothing but the Timson stitcher-folder produced a great deal of work until the contracts expired. *The Racehorse* changed stables to emerge from Kettering; *Trout & Salmon* came off in two colours; from 1957 *The Schoolmaster* (later known as *The Teacher*) was produced there for Sir Ronald Gould and the National Union of Teachers; Benn Brothers Ltd soon followed with their *Nursery World* (rudely named by some of the staff as The Bedwetters' Gazette); *Air Mail*, bi-monthly paper posted direct to members of the Royal Air Forces Association, was run off from 1960 after being taken to matrix stage at Stamford. In the spring of 1962 Kettering added two magazine presses from Speaight's closed-down works in London.

Peterborough started producing *The Methodist Recorder* for its quarter-million readers in October 1961, the paper's centenary year. It joined Group publications printed on a 1935 Foster rotary just acquired from Bristol and re-erected in a mere three weeks in premises taken in Princes Street. Without this press the Hoe at Broadway would have been grossly overloaded. Crowding of the offices at Broadway had already led to purchase of the Kit Kat Restaurant next door. Apart from regular publications such as *En Route* for the Caravan Club; staff magazines for the huge Corby steel works, Lyons the caterers and Midlands electricity generating workers, there were once-only productions of which an unusual example was *Midnight Express*, which described in prospect scenes at the end of the world. These all belong to the Group's letterpress era. An exciting new chapter was soon to open with EMAP's conversion to offset litho printing, but meanwhile a valuable reputation had been built up and valuable lessons learned.

Among these lessons had been the application of colour other than by manipulating the stop press mechanism. Experiments in running a second colour had started in 1950. With Charles Aldridge in charge and press foreman Sam Young backing him on the Peterborough rotary, the *Lincolnshire Free Press* had a blue-letter day, when its normal eight pages emerged with a four-page black and blue wrap-round on the bulb industry to mark Spalding's annual Tulip Time. The technique was familiar on the Continent but it was not common in local weeklies in Britain and in Spalding caused a sensation. Each forme for the wrap-round went through the moulding press three times: first, to produce a complete matrix as normal in case the experiment failed; second, without type to be printed blue; third, without type to be printed black.[1] A different experiment seen first in the Market Harborough weekly in May 1963 echoed successful attempts in the United States to print text matter on a yellow or other tint as background. Crude though these efforts may now seem, they reflect a growing awareness of the need for colour and the Group's determination to make it available despite the restrictions of the stereotyping process and the newspaper rotary press. Few arguments in

[1] *Splash* (EMAP House Journal) Summer issue 1950.

favour of offset printing were to carry greater weight. If reminders were needed, the emergence of Sunday newspaper colour magazines and of colour television in the late 1960's was adequate enough.

East Midland Engravers Ltd was formed in 1960 with R. J. Winfrey as managing director to administer block-making departments attached to each production centre. They extended their service to outside customers and for a time the company offered the Pleasing Colour facility, producing blocks for three-colour work which helped cut down the cost of suitable printing jobs. Specialisation in the Fluorograph colour process followed, only two other companies in Britain at that time using this American technique under licence. The process required art work to be produced with a Fluoro solvent as a set of paintings or drawings, each in one of the constituent colours on transparent film overlays. Starting with colours pre-separated in this way halved time spent on block-making. EMAP became leading practitioners of this system, which speeded up work on book jackets for the Printing company.[1] B. S. Biro was foremost among book illustrators enthusiastic in adapting to the new technique.

Pat Winfrey reserved some of his choicest phrases for checks of EMAP publications. Headings, text, layout, pictures, features, advertisements — all were liable to challenge. What ink-smearer had ruined *this* edition? In which coal mine with the lights out had *that* group of people been photographed? Engravers, photographers, editors — all had their heads knocked together in the interests of better illustrations and all of them were advised on re-touching methods by Hugh Ecob from the London College of Printing. In pursuit of excellence, EMAP started in 1961 the annual search for the Group's photographer of the year. On the mechanical side, Pat in 1960 appointed George Kingsman, also of the London College of Printing, to visit the Group and advise. With his easy manner, practical approach, wide knowledge, and capacity for hard work and exact study, Kingsman won the confidence of the Group and played a vital part in the conversion to litho.

[1] *British Printer* April 1963

160

Printing for the nation's bookstalls reinforced the urge for quality, emphasised again in 1958 by the launching of *Garden News*. Its first appearance on July 4th was a rewarding moment for John Bloom, its creator and editor. Starting with West Suffolk Newspapers and editor at Wisbech from 1954, Bloom's personal passion for gardening dated back to boyhood in Norfolk, and his conviction that ordinary gardeners like himself wanted to read news stories about other gardeners carried weight with the EMAP board. He left Wisbech for Stamford where *Garden News* was composed for printing at Peterborough. Pat spent the whole day at Stamford to help put the first issue of the paper to bed and took the last set of matrices to Peterborough where John Bloom pressed the button to speed the new publication on its way.

Both were cautious. A harvest seemed certain from their sowing but it might be slow to mature. The field was dominated by two giants, *Amateur Gardening* (Newnes) and *Popular Gardening* (Fleetway) with sales of 280,000 and 200,000 respectively. The colour magazine *Practical Gardening* (Mercury House Publications Ltd) was to add to competition in 1960[1]. By the end of 1958 *Garden News* claimed an ABC sale of 24,700. It touched 44,000 in 1961 and in 1966, with a figure of 60,700, was the only gardening weekly to show an increase. From the 140,000 guaranteed for 1975, the sale swept past the 200,000 mark for the first time in the spring of 1976. Another giant was on the scene.

The Giant Vegetable Competition had helped to put it there. Claims to have grown the biggest — be it marrow, parsnip, potato, radish or whatever — poured in to the office when the contest was launched in 1960. The appearance of Richard Winfrey and Ray Wells (advertisement manager) in the BBC TV Tonight programme, along with Cliff Michelmore and twelve outsize vegetables (including a pumpkin weighing 159 lbs), set the seal on a new and exciting championship, open to high and low alike. A variation later was the Giant Sunflower competition, the BBC Blue Peter team entering the 1972 contest for flowers reaching more than 21 feet skywards.

[1]*Practical Gardening* was taken over by EMAP in 1974.

Garden News worked well with horticultural societies up and down the country but broke fresh ground with its show guide, its Gardener of the Year contest (won in 1971 by a cripple), its champion show exhibitors, its Gardening round the World and allied series, its competitions and offers (in conjunction with leading seedsmen, tool-makers and horticultural firms), its first-class contributions on floral art and garden design, its bold support of the private gardener and allotmenteer under threat from town or road development — accompanied by a weekly range of more homely practical points. Newspaper format and colour added to its impact. Its leisure garden design at the 1972 Chelsea Flower Show won a silver Banksian award. Its garden viewing trips for readers took them into Europe and as far as Japan. And what of those in commercial horticulture? "There is a trade angle which makes *Garden News* compulsive reading. It lies in the independence of the editorial experts from the paper's highly competitive advertising columns."[1]

Since December 1973 Michael Barratt, BBC TV presenter of Nationwide and chairman of the radio Gardeners' Question Time, has had his own comment column. An earlier link with television showed Violet Carson — Ena Sharples of ITV's Coronation Street — on the dust jacket of John Bloom's *Gardening for Pleasure* month-by-month guide which in 1963 was the first book produced by *Garden News*. A *Garden News* rose grew in her Blackpool garden since its launch on the market in 1962 by Blaby Rose Gardens, Leicestershire. Mr and Mrs Winfrey were hosts at Castor House for the rose-naming ceremony performed there by the Marchioness of Exeter.

With yet another national weekly sponsoring related publications, the Group's specialist book titles numbered 44 by 1962, with an annual sale approaching 60,000 through the book trade in conjunction with Allen and Unwin Ltd. E.M. Art & Publishing Ltd was founded in 1962 to develop this business, bringing together the activities of six EMAP companies: three national periodicals providing text, Engraving making blocks, Printing producing the books for Publishing

[1] *UK Press Gazette*, June 1972.

162

to market. Only the more expensive bindings were done outside the Group. The number of titles rose to 75, all but ten on an angling theme. The publishing operation, however, though given a fair and thorough trial, could never be more than an experiment outside the main thrust of EMAP, and from January 1967 Ernest Benn Ltd took over the stock and responsibility for selling future books. At the same time, concentration on offset-printed newspapers and periodicals made rotary magazine-size treatment of one-off special subjects preferable, though the Printing company continued composing and machining for other book publishers.

About 400 people worked for EMAP newspapers when the Group was formed in 1947. The list was more than half as long again by the time *Garden News* joined the other national publications and management took a firmer line on enrolment in day-release technical college courses for new intakes of craft apprentices. For some it meant a weekly trip to the London College of Printing. Training for journalists was a problem pin-pointed by the 1949 Royal Commission on the Press and tackled by the National Council for the Training of Journalists set up in 1952. When the training scheme became compulsory for all apprenticed reporters in 1961, Dr H. C. Strick was succeeded as director by John Dodge[1], a former Kettering schoolboy who acquired a taste for newspapering in the *Evening Telegraph* office and joined Reuters after taking a Cambridge degree.

EMAP support for John was whole-hearted as he built up the training scheme, and EMAP editors regularly helped as organisers or examiners at the twice-yearly proficiency tests or at weekend courses. Ray Parkin served as chairman of the national Proficiency Test committee in 1964 and staged a succession of residential weekends for EMAP's own apprentices. Group editors helped tutor Dodge's first residential week's course deep in the Norfolk countryside at Wymondham in 1963 — historic as the initial move towards the much longer residential courses at selected colleges of further education which became the norm. Richard Parkes

[1] John Dodge left the N C T J in 1969 to set up training in advertising and public relations for CAM, the new Communications Advertising and Marketing Education Foundation under Lord Robens.

(1966) and John Blackwell (1968), successive personnel managers, and Ron Hunt (1969), Quentin Clarke (1971) and Philip Hoare (1975), who followed one another as editorial training officers, furthered the association and were active in promoting practicable innovations. These led in 1975 to the Group establishing an in-house training headquarters at Peterborough for its own intake of juniors, with the help of visiting lecturers and the blessing of the Training Council and the Printing and Publishing Industrial Training Board. Reporters and sub-editors annually compete for EMAP editorial awards first offered in 1967 following the success of the contest started in 1961 for Group photographers.

The newspapers themselves figured in the national honours for newspaper design first awarded by the newspaper industry in 1953, successes being scored over the years by *Bury Free Press,* the Kettering evening and weeklies, *Lincolnshire Free Press, Lynn News & Advertiser,* and *Wisbech Advertiser.* Star performer was the *Peterborough Evening Telegraph,* re-tailored on becoming independent of its Kettering counterpart in May 1961. Before the end of that year Award judges hailed it as "a newspaper of real typographical personality" and only two evenings — from Glasgow and Sheffield — were placed ahead of it. A year later it was short-listed, and in 1963 came second only to the *Belfast Evening Telegraph,* making it England's best-designed provincial evening. By then it had doubled its daily sale to 14,000 and, with the City chosen for 100 per cent expansion, went on to become the country's fastest-growing evening with a 30,000 sale by the mid 1970's.

Meanwhile courses, conferences and seminars, both inside and outside the Group, carried the training message into every department and to all levels of staff and management, the conversion to offset printing involving a particularly heavy programme for which £50,000 was allowed in 1968 alone. John Stockley joined in 1974 to give fresh impetus to sales training in the offices and in 1975 ran the first contest to find the EMAP Ad. Rep. of the Year, with awards for excellence in categories of advertising performance.

19.   MAKING THEIR MARK

EXPANSION accelerated promotion within the Group and a line of young men — some already mentioned in chapter fifteen — could thank R. P. Winfrey for his enterprise in creating fresh opportunities. After Messrs Aldridge, Cooper and Smedley became fulltime executives, management openings occurred at Peterborough for F. E. Turner, who had forsaken Law to learn newspapering at Bury; at Kettering for A. G. Butler, whose production experience had led him into management at Bury when Tony Hughes started a new career with the Halle Orchestra (later with Australian broadcasting); at Bury for D. R. (Tommy) Thompson, groomed at Kettering by Fred Cooper; and at Spalding for W. E. Cook, son and grandson of men who had worked for Sir Richard and a pillar of the production and sales scene at Peterborough. Spalding production moved to Stamford and Walter Cook ran the two businesses together from 1957 after S. H. G. Andrews, who was managing the *Stamford Mercury* when bought from Westminster Press, moved to Kettering. Alan Butler's move to the Printing company created this Kettering vacancy.

In 1962 W. C. Baxter's retirement ended a happy 17-year stint at King's Lynn where advertising men succeeded, Desmond Wilcox first and D. F. Roberts in 1968. Desmond Wilcox had a period of management with the periodicals before following Sydney Andrews at Kettering in 1970, where a 15-year incumbency led to a quieter period for Andrews at Stamford before retirement. To replace him at Stamford, F. B. Potter was moved from Kettering, where he was assistant manager after coming into the Group via *Motor Cycle News* advertising.

Walter Cook and Frank Turner had meanwhile in 1965 swopped their respective management roles at Stamford and Peterborough. Sadly, illness led to Turner's resignation from Stamford and to early retirement. The Cook family had another generation in the Group in Walter's son David, on the advertising side of the national periodicals, and Walter gave post-retirement service in other ways after being succeeded as manager at Peterborough by L. A. Coles in 1975. Douglas Roberts went outside to transport management in 1976, leaving an opening for John Robertson, Group Accountant since 1972 and EMAP company secretary a year later, to figure in line management at King's Lynn.

For many years production of the nationals was by arrangement with the provincial newspaper companies and the move of Desmond Wilcox from Lynn in 1967 was the first formal appointment of a general manager on the periodical side. Brian McLoughlin took responsibility from 1969 to 1972, when he moved out of the Group to be followed by Bryan Hope from IPC Business Press. In less than a year Hope was back with IPC and Robin Miller, who had worked his way up from reporter to editor and editorial manager with the periodicals, filled the gap with a success which led in 1976 to his election to the EMAP parent board.

Editors were equally mobile. Raymond Parkin's reign over the Kettering newspapers lasted from 1949 to his appointment as Group Editor-in-Chief in 1960, when R. G. Howe moved over from King's Lynn. Howe instituted Editorial Services for the Group from Peterborough in 1973, and R. J. Hunt took the Kettering chair in 1974 after a brief incumbency by Paul Bach from Thomson Newspapers in South Wales.

Ron Hunt had left Leamington to become the Group's first editorial training officer in 1969 and promotion to editor-in-chief of the West Suffolk papers followed in 1971. W. A. (Bill) Appel's long service there had ended in 1970 with Tonie Gibson succeeding from Spalding, but Gibson had only a year at Bury St Edmunds before an invitation came to Peterborough. Hunt was followed at Bury by Malcolm Scott of the *Newmarket Journal*. In retirement in 1972, Bill Appel helped produce the *Journal's* centenary supplement and could look back on supervising special centenary publications in 1955 for both the *Bury Free Press* and the *Suffolk Free Press* at Sudbury.

Most detailed of the Group's centenary productions was the 1954 *Peterborough Advertiser* supplement — the last editorial task undertaken by L. J. Bartley before moving out of the Group to old haunts at Bexhill as editor of the *Observer*. L. W. Wainwright severed a long connection with the *Lincoln, Rutland & Stamford Mercury* to succeed Bartley, but returned to Stamford in 1961. J. B. Cooper filled the gap at Peterborough, moving from Wisbech (1958-61) after three years at Sudbury (1954-57).

Peter Sutton (1961-65), A. C. (Sandy) Erskine (1965-70) and Anthony Crook (1970-71) had built up the *Peterborough Evening Telegraph* and John Cooper was editor-in-chief of both *Advertiser* and *Telegraph*, the appointment being continued by Tonie Gibson (1971-76, when he left to launch a park-farm project in Peterborough) and Alex Gordon (promoted 1976). Cooper's transfer to King's Lynn in 1972 followed the untimely death of Percy L. Greenfield, formerly a sub-editor at Kettering, who had succeeded Ron Howe there in 1960.

The *Suffolk Free Press* at Sudbury had seen the first editorships of both John Bloom (1949-54) and John Cooper (1954-57), and they had also followed each other to Wisbech, Bloom to start *Garden News* in 1958 and Cooper to move to Peterborough in 1961. Sudbury continued steadily from 1958 under Geoffrey Brown.

The Newmarket Journal, long produced under contract at Bury St Edmunds for the Simpson family, passed into Group ownership in June 1955, bringing W. A. (Jimmy) James with it as editor. When James transferred to Wisbech in 1961, J. H. Sindall was promoted from King's Lynn to Newmarket and stayed till 1969. Illness interrupted service in the *Journal* chair given by Roy Gillard (1969-71) from Kettering, and E. W. (Ted) Robinson (1971-72) from Bury, who had once been chief reporter of the *Newmarket Free Press* started in opposition by Sir Richard Winfrey in 1927. Their successors

167

were Malcolm Scott (1972-74) and Martin Price (appointed 1974). Jimmy James excelled as Group Agricultural Editor on giving up the Wisbech editorship in 1963. As chairman of the Guild of Agricultural Journalists of Great Britain, he presided in 1972 when the International Congress of Agricultural Journalists met in London and Oxford.

Those subsequently in charge at Wisbech were Sandy Erskine (1963-65), F. H. Ward (1965-74), Piers Carter (1974-76) and David Ayres (appointed 1976). The *Wisbech Advertiser's* Saturday *Supplement* had been transformed into the livelier *Saturday Pictorial* in 1953 (Coronation year) but in 1962 was merged with its Wednesday companion the *Isle of Ely & Wisbech Advertiser*, and the new *Advertiser & Pictorial* switched publishing day from Wednesday to Thursday. A return to Wednesday publication in 1972 was followed in 1975 by change of title to *Fenland Advertiser* and wider distribution as the Group's first free newspaper. The Cambs Times Group had already produced their free *Peterborough Standard* advertisement paper and extended this in 1976 to the Stamford area.

David Newton left Wisbech in 1954 for Stamford, his turn there ending in 1961 with the year-long quincentenary celebrations of the Borough and inclusion among those presented to the Queen as editor of one of the world's oldest surviving newspapers. His subsequent work as Group History Editor has contributed to this record. Leonard Wainwright then returned from Peterborough to Stamford to complete his service to the Group and in 1969 John Sindall, whose career had started in the *Mercury* office, followed his old editor into the chair.

Charles Aldridge had been editorially in charge at Spalding until his promotion in 1953 brought C. J. (Sidney) Franks into command of the *Lincolnshire Free Press*. Franks spent all his working life in the service of the *Free Press*, joining in 1927 and dying in harness in 1966. Soon after EMAP acquired the *Spalding Guardian* and the Stamford and Boston papers from the Westminster Press Group he became editor of both the Spalding papers. They have been run in tandem since that time under the editorships of Tonie Gibson (1966-70) and David Young, appointed from Peterborough in 1970.

Last editor of the *Spalding Guardian* in Westminster Press days was Peter H. Tombleson, whose knowledge of fishing gained in the Fens was so valuable when *Angling Times* was launched. On his initiative the *Guardian* began in 1951 to sponsor popular dance competitions for choosing a Tulip Time Queen each Spring. Her greatest moments are when reigning over the much-televised floral parades which annually attract thousands of tourists to Spalding.

Harry G. Skepper, to whom Jo Cooke I and II and their Boston newspaper careers were familiar, had edited the *Boston Guardian* during the ownerships of both Sir Richard Winfrey and Westminster Press and was believed to hold the record for a one-man newspaper report — nine-and-a-half broadsheet columns of Boston Borough Council! His retirement on transfer of the paper to EMAP brought Cyril T. Linford to Boston from Bedford, where he had pioneered an *Evening Telegraph* sale for the Kettering company[1]. Son of Tom Linford, former Bury editor, he saw the *Boston Guardian* through its centenary celebrations in 1954 and edited its final issue dated 26 March 1958, the title then merging with that of the *Lincolnshire Standard* at Boston and ownership of the *Guardian* passing to the Standard Group.

Pat Winfrey needed these men to help forward EMAP expansion, and the frequency of their moves reflects this convulsive growth. No-one was transferred without his approval or without his or executive consideration of the human issues involved — a holiday missed, a house with room for Granny, a wife's health, a child's schooling. Each move (national publication staffs are listed later) entailed a shift of supporting personnel. Times of change were not the only ones when private acts of kindness went beyond normal company limits. A Christmas Eve accident which robbed a Printing company man of his hand saw Pat at his side in hospital and reassuring his wife the same afternoon. Supervisory staff glad of an inexpensive extra break from work

[1] The Bedford office closed in 1956.

could use the holiday caravan set aside for them on the Norfolk coast. Some had beneficial trips abroad — more valued before packaged holidays brought travel within everybody's reach. Harold Blake, who led the Kettering news staff with great distinction, was flown to America for the latest treatment before Parkinson's Disease ended his life so tragically in 1952.

Help of this kind preceded the formal schemes of today. In addition, Dr (later Professor) Harold C. Stewart, long associated with R. P. Winfrey in the Sir Halley Stewart Trust, agreed in 1955 to act as medical adviser to the Group, putting staff with serious or stubborn illnesses in touch with best available opinion. In 1954 Dr Stewart had opened the Sir Halley Stewart Field for public use at Spalding, the Trust having bought this open space to preserve both it and the memory of Halley, who had fought his most famous campaigns as a Liberal in this division with Sir Richard Winfrey's help. Winfrey Avenue alongside recalls both Sir Richard's link with Spalding and Pat's part in the presentation to the town. Professor Stewart's work at St Mary's Hospital Medical School, London, as a pharmacologist was to distinguish him as a leading authority.

General managers of subsidiary companies and editors of their newspapers in many instances joined the respective boards and had opportunity to acquire shares when they became available, a practice encouraged earlier by Sir Richard. When further five-shilling shares were issued in 1960, 100,000 were reserved for employees other than directors, and 165 of the 509 staff to whom the offer was made took it up. Their wish to have a finger in the company pie gratified Pat, who made a point of it to the Royal Commission on the Press in 1961. There was, in fact, some embarrassment because over-demand for shares had entailed rationing of the allocations. When a further 25,000 shares were made available in 1976, the 174 members of staff who applied more than twice over-subscribed for them. Three hundred employees out of a total of 1,500 were by then EMAP shareholders. The scheme to reward staff for making valid suggestions to improve methods or develop business was launched in 1961 and given fresh impetus in 1975.

Long service from the staff has been characteristic of the Group and reflects the family spirit which continuing expansion and an evolving industrial scene have not yet extingushed. Inscribed gold watches to mark 40 years' service were presented from 1959, starting at Kettering where three of the five men concerned each had 47 years to their credit. From 1973 there have been two levels of award — to the value of £50 after 25 years and £100 after 40. In that year 26 staff were still working after 40 or more years with Group companies, and five more joined the "Forty Club" within twelve months.

Although demands on production became continually heavier, EMAP remained remarkably free from labour troubles and staff enjoyed benefits freely if not always immediately negotiated within a prospering business. Mutual confidence survived a severe test in 1959 when trouble over new national agreements with the print unions led in June to the industry's worst-ever stoppage. It took 17 days and all Lord Birkett's humour and practised persistence as independent chairman at meetings of Newspaper Society and union men to hack a way through the tangle. Meanwhile, with almost the entire printing industry brought to a halt, no local papers appeared for more than six weeks, though management and journalists in some parts of the country did their best with duplicated news sheets[1]. An outstanding exception was EMAP, where employees accepted an interim arrangement with union approval and worked normally.

Pat Winfrey always felt that the Newspaper Society should negotiate with the trade unions independently of the British Federation of Master Printers, whose members operate in quite different circumstances. It was the Newspaper Society's inability to concede this point on behalf of the provincial Press that persuaded Pat to withdraw the Group from membership and go it alone with his own staffs, despite recrimination from contemporaries. EMAP

[1] The refusal of some local authorities to acknowledge these sheets was among considerations which led to the passing of Mrs Margaret Thatcher's Public Bodies (Admission to Meetings) Act, 1960.

remained independent until journalists in the Kettering and branch offices withdrew labour for ten days in May 1974 over the dismissal of one of their number. However, sales of the *Northamptonshire Evening Telegraph* dropped by less than five per cent despite a truncated news service. The Group subsequently resumed membership of the Newspaper Society and had some help when Kettering threatened — but did not take — strike action in mid-August 1976 in pursuit of a closed-shop agreement in favour of the National Union of Journalists. It was the first such attempt in the industry since Michael Foot piloted the Trade Union Labour Relations (Amendment) Act on to the statute book. Newspapermen everywhere looked on with close interest and, as editor on the spot, Ron Hunt crossed swords with NUJ men on television as well as in the daily and trade Press. Backing him, the EMAP board remained adamant in the view that closed shops were a potential danger to Press freedom.

At the end of that August, members of the National Graphical Association working in the United Newspapers, St Regis Newspapers and EMAP Groups withdrew labour in support of a ban on (mostly) advertisement material not prepared for publication by members of their own union. An interim settlement between the Newspaper Society and the NGA brought them back after a week during which, for the first time ever, all publishing activity in EMAP was halted and a loss of £175,000 incurred. It was from the ranks of the NGA that the Group appointed its first Employee Relations Adviser in December 1974. Gordon Frost joined EMAP from school at King's Lynn and had become Production Training Officer at Kettering and prominent in NGA affairs in Northamptonshire. Now he helped EMAP to keep abreast of legislation affecting employees and to sustain the two-way management-staff understanding which has always been a marked feature of the business.

POSTSCRIPT. The 24-week-long strike by members of the National Union of Journalists employed by Northamptonshire Newspapers Ltd, the longest in NUJ history, ended on 23 May 1977, by which time the manuscript of this book had gone to the printers. It is not possible here to trace in detail the course of this dispute, which was more than once thoroughly aired in Parliament, the national Press and on television as well as at TUC headquarters. Without loss but with much credit to EMAP, it highlighted extremist trends in the NUJ for all to see; the revulsion felt by most other EMAP journalists against industrial action in "a happy firm"; and the sturdy insistence of R. J. Hunt as editor on bringing out his *Evening Telegraph* singlehanded throughout the 24 weeks. His editor colleagues in the Kettering company, Quentin Clarke and Brian Paine, likewise produced their *News-Echo* and *Harborough Mail* weeklies as solo efforts.

20.   OFFSET PIONEER

IN his report to the shareholders in 1961, R. P. Winfrey hinted at technical advances in printing that could prove as revolutionary as the invention of type 500 years earlier[1]. "We shall keep ourselves alert and well-informed about these new developments," he said. In fact, his alertness kept EMAP to the forefront in applying offset lithography to newspapers and achieved for the Group its biggest leap forward into eminence, for offset printing in England had till then been confined to transferring designs to tinplate and to sheet-fed printing of fine colour illustrations.

In 1959, however, Baker Perkins Ltd, Peterborough-based engineers, were asked by the late John Crabtree to build the Spearhead newspaper press for East African Newspapers, published in Nairobi by the wealthy Aga Khan for the Muslim population of Kenya and Tanzania. Son of Charles Crabtree, John had left his father's firm to design and produce web-offset presses[2], after consulting with the inventive Klaus Aller of the Aller organisation in Copenhagen, and its general manager Nils Norlin. Managing director in Nairobi was Michael Curtis, who had left the chair of the *News Chronicle* ahead of its closure in 1960 and had the help of George Kingsman of the London College of Printing as printing consultant in this country. With this press on his doorstep, Pat Winfrey took a close interest in its testing and

[1] William Caxton set up England's first printing press in 1476 after learning printing on the Continent, where movable metal type was first used by Johann Gutenberg of Mainz in 1450.

[2] Stereotyped plates carried on a rotary press cylinder print direct on to paper as it unreels and passes through the machine. Lithographed plates with their finer detail print on to blankets round an intermediary cylinder from which the printed image is immediately offset on to the web of paper running on its other side.

his encounters with George Kingsman in the Baker Perkins works led to the latter's association with EMAP a year later.

Crabtree's design was not without some faults, Kingsman being left to say when the press should be shipped, and Pat stayed late into the night to watch final tests at Peterborough before dismantling for transport. He heard in due course that the Spearhead was being operated in Nairobi by Swahilis who could not read the text they were printing, and that each page of every paper had to carry an illustration to ensure they positioned the plates correctly on the machine. During his visit to East Africa in 1962 on Reuter business Pat saw the press working and also early models of Photon photocomposing equipment, production from both owing much to the competence and genius of the manager on the spot.

Meanwhile RPW's Wolverhampton friend Malcolm Graham was planning to open a new plant at Ketley and to launch the *Shropshire Star*, and their mutual interest in web-offset led to a joint trip to Copenhagen followed by a visit by Nils Norlin with Pat to the Baker Perkins works. Orders for new presses — one each for Ketley and Peterborough — were placed by both men later in 1962. They were the first to take two broadsheet plates round the cylinder and comprised four units and the new-type four-colour satellite unit which was the master-stroke of the design. The Hoe company of New York had to be asked to produce the folder EMAP needed for delivering both magazine and news formats — hence the urgent cross-Atlantic dash by RPW, Richard Winfrey and George Kingsman — and while this was being constructed an American-made Ampress folder was a satisfactory substitute, its disadvantage being the magazines were delivered with a folded edge which needed trimming.

One unit of the Halley Aller Lithomaster Senior Web Offset press was on the Halley stand to run off the *Halley Herald* and EMAP's *Litho Leader* (both with spot colour and compiled to explain press and publishing potential) at IPEX, the International Printing Exhibition staged in London during July 1963. The contracts press, in which the Baker Perkins Halley subsidiary was closely involved, incorporated the first satellite colour unit to be made and used on production, and with it EMAP were pioneers of web offset four-colour on newsprint. The satellite comprised a large central drum with four separate sets of page plates and inking rollers spaced around its circumference, each set printing one of the four basic colours: yellow, magenta, blue and black. Each colour was printed in turn as the web of paper passed round the drum, their combination producing all the shades required.

Activity in the Group intensified while the press was being built. Winfrey intentions, apart from adding brilliance and colour to *Garden News* and other periodicals, was to develop a contract service for other publishers. Print quality carried EMAP beyond the point reached by experimenters such as Woodrow Wyatt at Banbury and Charles Dalton at Welwyn, whose papers had been printed offset with some colour from 1962. Staff fears were allayed as talks were given in each office and the meaning of this new chapter became clear. Normal Longfoot was the first drawn from EMAP rotary press staff to adapt to offset production, he and Peter Mancer, Bill Quill and other colleagues attending courses and training with the help of the Printing company's sheet-fed Solna press and of visits to the Aller works in Sweden and Denmark and offset plants in the States. With Derek Smith, staff engineer, they sacrificed hours of spare time to learn the anatomy of the contracts press as it was put together, while Michael Smedley, Engraving company man at Peterborough, mastered plate production methods. Son of Edward Smedley, he had worked through the Pleasing Colour and Fluorograph experiments and was chosen to head the new litho plate-making unit.

To take charge of the litho development, one of the dormant broadcasting companies was in 1962 re-named East Midland Litho Printers Ltd, R. P. Winfrey chairing a board comprising Messrs Aldridge, Cooper, Kingsman and Smedley with R. J. Winfrey as managing director. Richard had been elected to the EMAP parent board in 1961 along with Ray Parkin and John Nuttall, the latter having added control

57. Richard Pattinson Winfrey M.A., LL.B.

58. Tea-table group at a 1965 Castor House garden party to meet incoming Group personalities. L to R: Ivor McKinnon, to head the new Contracts division; George Russell, appointed Finance director; and Philip Coles, new EMAP lay director. Ladies: Mrs Russell, Mrs McKinnon and Mrs Coles.

59. Miss Barbara Clapham in her room in the EMAP London office, then in Breams Buildings, where she accounted for national advertising for the Group and served the Sir Halley Stewart Trust as secretary, holding the double appointment from 1946 to 1974.

60. Sir Halley Stewart, returned as M.P. for Spalding in the 1887 and 1892 elections with Sir Richard Winfrey as colleague and campaign organiser. He had founded the Liberal *Hastings Times* and in 1887 urged caution over the latter's purchase of his first newspaper, the *Spalding Guardian*.

61. Pause for pictures during the annual EMAP bowls tournament at King's Lynn in 1961, won by *Peterborough Advertiser* players. Inter-office bowls matches, quickly resumed after World War II, were forerunners of the current range of Group competitions.

62. Family Day fling! Committee and helpers set to enjoy themselves and please visitors to Woodston from Group offices. In this 1974 line-up, all based at Woodston, are (L to R): Tonie Gibson, editorial; Henry Hewitt, production control; Peter Yeomans, maintenance; Lionel Coles, advertising (chief organiser); Peter Glover, circulation; Ken Thomas, editorial; Walter Cook, general manager; and Alex Milne, composing.

63. Reeled-up and ready to run. An early picture of EMAP's first Halley-Aller web offset press soon after erection at Woodston in 1964. To the left, three printing units; foreground, Ampress folder and delivery unit as originally used; to the right, fourth printing unit, then still awaiting four-colour satellite to complete the line.

64. Web offset preprint colour units which made Woodston the largest preprint plant in Europe, printing colour pages on contract for national newspapers as well as supplying Group publications.

65. Reminder of the EMAP site at Woodston when buildings were first erected in 1963. Windows facing to the left are of process department and canteen with offices over, with press hall behind and bindery alongside. The wooden hut provided further offices. Hedge at top of picture marks limit of site.

66. By 1970 the original modest press building is dwarfed by the preprint section behind it and by the double-width press hall (dark roof) in centre of picture. To right of the latter, the Banbury building houses contracts composing and bigger canteen. Beyond, surrounded by grassed areas, the main office block accommodates executive suite, *Evening Telegraph* and *Advertiser* floor, and newspaper composing. Garages and vehicle and maintenance workshops complete the complex on right. Wooden huts at foot of picture have since made way for bindery extensions.

67. Staff garden party groups photographed at Castor House on Saturday 29 July 1933 to celebrate Sir Richard Winfrey's 75th birthday on August 5th; and on Saturday 22 July 1967 to mark R. P. Winfrey's 65th birthday on June 24th.

Sir Richard (wing collar and bow) is with Lady Winfrey in centre of row sitting. John Derry, oldest surviving political and journalist friend, is on his left, and Tom Diggle, King's Lynn newspaper veteran, sits on Lady Winfrey's right. Both men paid tribute to the Chief.

68. Sitting on either side of Mr and Mrs Winfrey, centre of lower group, are Mr Richard Winfrey, now deputy chairman and chief executive of EMAP, and Sydney Andrews, then managing Northamptonshire Newspapers, who made presentations on behalf of EMAP offices.

Long-serving staff figure in both photographs, one easily-distinguishable example being Tony Ireson. As junior reporter at Kettering he stands tallest on the left above, and as editor of *Garden News* sits below in light suit on the grass near R. J. Winfrey.

72. Presentation by EMAP directors of canteen of cutlery to Edward Smedley on retirement in 1966, his 40 years service taking him from *Peterborough Advertiser* book-keeper to Group managing director. Sitting with him are Richard Winfrey, R. P. Winfrey and T. M. Ashton, EMAP deputy chairman.

Standing (L to R): Brian McLoughlin, *Motor Cycle News;* Peter Tombleson, EM Art & Publishing; Philip Coles, EMAP board; Derek Case, national division admin; Peter Wilson, EMAP board; Fred Cooper, provincial division executive; Ray Wells, provincial advertisement manager; Charles Aldridge, provincial division executive; S. Bayliss Smith, *Angling Times* chairman; Howard Marshall, *AT* director; Ivor McKinnon, contracts division executive; J. W. E. Banks, *MCN* director; Ken Sutton, *AT* director; George Russell, EMAP finance director; Jack Thorndike, *AT* director; John Sibun, national division executive.

Opposite.
69. Type for newspapers was set by hand from the case (compare picture 37) until Linotype and Intertype machines casting type from hot metal were installed from the turn of the century. The machines seen (top) at Broadway, Peterborough, were used until 1971.

70 and 71. Linotypes were superseded by computerised photosetters with associated correction screens, as seen (lower pictures) at Kettering.

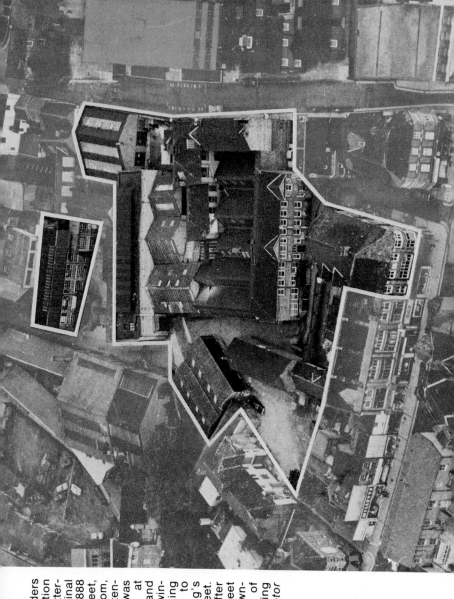

73. White line borders offices and production premises used at Kettering until 1976. Original main building of 1888 faces Dryland Street, which runs top to bottom, right. Subsequent extension and acquisition was piecemeal. Frontage at right angles to Dryland Street shows bay windows of offices looking down Huxloe Place to High Street, Kettering's main shopping street. Use was continued after 1976 of Dryland Street reception hall as town-centre office, and of upper floors fronting High Street for *Motor Cycle News.*

74. Kettering's new offices in Northfield Avenue are in three main sections, from left: reception, editorial and advertising; canteen, composing and accounts; press hall and process.

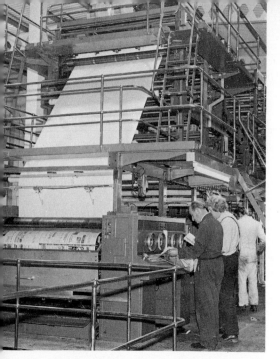

75. One end of the main (printing) deck of the Goss web offset newspaper press used at Kettering since January 1976.

76. Lower picture shows reel stands at floor level and two upper decks giving access for webbing up.

77. Happy choice in March 1973 as opener of the *Peterborough Advertiser* children's art exhibition – it represented the work of 1,000 local pupils – was the Duchess of Gloucester, who had married and settled at Barnwell Manor the previous summer. She was escorted by Richard Winfrey, EMAP managing director, seen with Ken Thomas, *Advertiser* editor.

78. This presentation to Richard Winfrey of an album of photographs showing stages in construction of the first Halley-Aller offset press, was made when trade Press journalists visited Woodston in April 1964. Sir Ivor Baker, then chairman of Baker Perkins Holdings Ltd, hands over the album watched (L to R) by J. F. M. Braithwaite, BP's managing director, and his colleague Angus Halley; with Nils Norlin, general manager of the Aller Organisation of Copenhagen.

79. A 1973 memory: Mr and Mrs Winfrey admire the presentation Waterford cut glass spirit decanter which was among surprise gifts on RPW's retirement from the EMAP chair. International Photon representatives arrived during a staff garden party at Castor House to honour a happy association with this gift and their presence.

80. Pleasant incident for Mr Frank Rogers during a tour of the Group in July 1973 was to congratulate Julie Fairhead on being top trainee journalist in the national proficiency test and first EMAP winner of the annual £250 Pfizer Award. Julie trained on the *Bury Free Press*, Mr Rogers meeting her during visits to offices after becoming Group chairman.

of the *Peterborough Advertiser* company to his duties in 1960. This gave Edward Smedley, from 1955 managing director of the *Advertiser* and a joint managing director of the Group with R. P. Winfrey, more time for EMAP affairs. Richard succeeded his father as joint managing director when Pat Winfrey shed some of his management functions in 1962 to give further freedom for the litho project with all its possibilities in colour printing and ultimately in re-winding pre-printed colour pages.

From his early thirties, therefore, R. J. Winfrey played a part in the project and helped from the start to evaluate and solve queries that endlessly cropped up. The Baker Perkins contracts press was the first of its particular kind, designed to do work not previously attempted. EMAP were on their own in that area of the litho field and the challenge of it, equipment tried, materials tested (ink, paper, metal plates, film, chemicals), methods checked, experiments made, failures examined, successes achieved, led to an unrivalled expertise shared from board room to shop floor. George Kingsman shone in these early trials but found EMAP men receptive and eager to the point of quickly becoming specialists in their own techniques.

No premises in the Group could absorb machinery needed for expansion and development and to accommodate it eleven acres were acquired on the outskirts of Peterborough, off the Oundle Road in Woodston. This site had the great advantage of being in the Fletton local authority area and therefore free from the jurisdiction — for planning and other requirements — of Peterborough City Council, whose political bosses were at loggerheads with the company's newspapers because of their stand for integrity in public persons and places. After years of bursting at the seams in crowded town centres round the Group it was a joy to have a purpose-built works with plenty of room for additions and extensions, where the lark sang and the air was fresh (when the seasonal sugar beet process ended across the road!).

Few opportunities were missed of checking web offset equipment in use or at exhibitions, and the trip to the United States in 1963 by Pat and Richard Winfrey with George

Kingsman was notable for ground covered. At Williamsport, Pennsylvania, the party saw America's most advanced off-set press, operated since 1962 by the Grit Publishing Company and built in technical partnership with Hoe of New York and Aller of Copenhagen. The trip included checks of setting matter by photographic means instead of by casting lines of metal type, and of progress with the Ampress folder being made to deliver printed matter in either broadsheet, tabloid or magazine size.

While the others flew over, Pat went by sea — he avoided long periods in aircraft because of a heart condition — but once there no time was lost. Pat ran the other two off their feet as the itinerary grew, and more than once the trio had to race across the tarmac from one plane to another for inter-state flights. Exhaustion, in fact, kept two of them from some engagements which the older man — then in his sixties — attended alone. From his American experience, R. P. Winfrey decided that the ideal photosetting system had yet to be developed and the relatively inexpensive A.T.F. keyboards made in the United States were adopted for the Litho company's original requirements. Punched tape from the keyboards produced text on photographic paper when fed into the A.T.F. photosetter. Headlines came from a Japanese Morisawa photocomposer which projected the image of a letter on to paper in contrast to the Ludlow which cast letters in hot metal.

While composing staff trained on this equipment, offset plates were made from proofs (repro pulls) of complete pages of text set traditionally in metal. By mid-February 1964 press erection was complete in the new Woodston building at Peterborough. It could produce magazines of up to 64 pages with spine glued on the machine as they came through. Publications with more than 64 pages, printed in sections, would be stitched on the Meuller gathering-stitcher in the new bindery. On February 28th *Garden News* became the Group's first litho-printed publication, an exciting trouble-free achievement only five weeks after press installation started. This printing record was celebrated three days later by a cocktail party at Castor House where

Pat Winfrey could congratulate executives and staff involved. Success spread a glow through the Group. With its first issue of the new press on March 19th, the *Wisbech Advertiser & Pictorial* won the Reed Paper Group award for its class in the 1964 web offset competition run by *Litho Printer* magazine.

From pioneering web offset for the Banbury newspapers, Peter Wildon came to Woodston in 1963 as works manager (until 1971), John Castle joining at the same time to attract contract work. City publishers found they could get to Peterborough with equal speed and less strain than to the outskirts of London. In due course house magazines, association journals, sporting and specialist publications streamed off the press, their superb illustrations from the satellite unit dried by naked flames flaring from gas jets as the webs raced through. These dryers, evolved by the joint expertise of Coates ink manufacturers and Timson of Kettering, went on to give admirable service. In 1965 a custom-built multi-purpose folder ordered from Timson supplemented the Ampress and added to versatility; paste-up of pages from photo-set text began in an additional building; double day-shift working started for both press and plate-making; and Richard Winfrey helped form the national Web Offset Newspaper Association and became its first vice-chairman (chairman in 1966).

While national Sunday papers planned colour magazines, the dailies preferred colour in their normal run of pages. Page advertisements in colour, gravure-printed elsewhere, were being run through many newspapers wallpaper fashion. Precise positioning on the sheet was not possible, so the design was continuously printed for cutting off at random. Offset colour from Woodston caught the eye of the Hon Gavin Astor of *The Times* (now Lord Astor of Hever), and Sir Max Aitken and Sir Thomas Blackburn of the *Daily Express* and in 1965, in association with them and EMAP, Baker Perkins started building a test plant in their Peterborough premises. Experiments followed in running and re-reeling colour for shipment to Fleet Street and inclusion in daily editions where the preprinted sections would fall into exact page position in each copy. Heatset inks needed to give top quality colour on newsprint running at a thousand feet per minute required hot air drying which, by taking too much moisture out of the paper, made it brittle and so reduced its suitability for re-running through Fleet Street presses in exact register. Development of re-damping units solved this difficulty.

The preprint project grew during 1966 into a partnership between Beaverbrook Newspapers, *The Times* and EMAP, the two dailies financing two presses and EMAP providing premises, staff and expertise. The first two Baker Perkins preprint satellites were erected in the new press hall built for them at Woodston (there was space for up to six: units three and four were added in 1969, unit five in 1971) and the first commercial run was for London sales of the *Daily Express* on Saturday May 20th, day of the 1967 Wembley Cup Final. On 15 July 1967 *The Times* first carried full colour preprinted at Woodston over two pages of a four-page supplement booked by British Overseas Airways Corporation. The *Financial Times* became a regular customer and in November 1968, for the first time, a complete edition carried a colour advertisement for Scotch whisky.

After Apollo 8, with Colonel Frank Borman in command, circled the moon for the first time in history during the Christmas period 1968, many newspapers printed space photographs taken by the crew, but *The Times* scored the greatest triumph. With day and night co-operation from the Litho company, the paper scooped the rest of the Press with its full-colour supplement preprinted at Woodston and incorporated in *The Times* of Monday 6 January 1969. Congratulations poured in from printers in Britain and on the Continent, and the full-page shot of a blue and white earth seen from low over the moon's grey-green surface became a collector's piece. Both *Times* and *Express* had colour coverage of the investiture of the Prince of Wales in the summer of 1969, this being the first time the *Express* carried preprinted colour on front and back pages for its whole circulation. By then colour coverage of Saturday football matches was being preprinted at Woodston on Sunday and appearing in selected *Express* circulation areas on Monday.

No wonder that as pioneer offset preprinters, EMAP more than repaid the initial interest taken by the *Daily Express*. As he neared the end of his chairmanship of Beaverbrook Newspapers in 1968, Tom Blackburn knew that the fantastic quality of EMAP colour removed for all time any question mark over national newspaper colour potential. Visitors from home and overseas trod a well-worn path to Woodston to watch the contracts press and preprint satellites with their sophisticated electronic controls, and to see the cameras, colour scanners and related equipment in the plate-making section. EMAP directors expounded technicalities to regular sessions held by INCA (International Newspaper and Colour Association, headquarters in Germany) and FIEJ (Federation Internationale des Editeurs de Journeaux et Publications, headquarters in Paris). R. J. Winfrey was asked to describe the colour potential facing newspapers of the 1970's and 1980's both in articles and at meetings. He told the Newspaper Society's 1968 technical conference that Britain was leading the world in full and spot colour, and in 1969 advised the Institute of Practitioners in Advertising that the Regional Newspaper Colour Marketing Association (he was its chairman) had just been formed to guide them in buying and using offset colour.

When the Newspaper Society Colour in Newspaper Awards were first offered in 1970 the *Daily Express* topped the class for web offset heatset colour advertising with a "rainbow" design for Formica preprinted at Woodston. Sir Max Aitken's jubilant claim that "We are producing the finest offset litho newspaper colour in the world" continued to be borne out by the 1971 and 1972 awards when preprinted pages for Benson & Hedges and the Ford Motor Company completed a colour hat-trick for the *Express*. The *Production Journal's* award for the best entry regardless of class added to the 1971 *Express* achievement and showed that offset colour quality had nothing to fear from any other printing process. *Express*/EMAP experiments in preprinting back-to-back colour (both sides of the same web) led to another colour "first" in 1971, starting with a northern edition wrap-round on Southport Flower Show.

With annual company reports sent to shareholders, Pat Winfrey included copies of glorious pages of colour printed for *The Times* to mark the opening in March 1972 of the Tutankhamun jubilee exhibition at the British Museum. The Litho company preprint men were now on three-shift working and re-reeling up to ten million impressions per seven-day week — dwarfed by presses which towered above them yet were tamed to hairbreadth sensitivity. They had appetites demanding 32,000 reels of paper and 200,000 kilos of ink a year and made Woodston the home of the biggest web offset preprint operation in the world.[1]

However, the picture is not without some greyer tones. Fleet Street dealings led to a scaling down in 1974 when Rupert Murdoch's sale of his 21-per-cent stake in Beaverbrook Newspapers was part of an arrangement by which *Daily Express* colour work would be carried out by Bemrose of Liverpool, colour-printing subsidiary of Murdoch's News International. Ample notice by Beaverbrook Newspapers of their intention to withdraw enabled EMAP to plan staff movement well ahead and to keep inevitable redundancies to a minimum. Two of the wholly-owned Beaverbrook units were sold and shipped to South Africa and the third, after purchase by EMAP, was dismantled and stored on site for future requirements. Beaverbrook's share in the two original jointly-owned units was acquired by the Group and the presses maintained a flow of preprint to *The Times, Financial Times,* EMAP publications and new customers. To R. P. Winfrey the Murdoch intervention was an undeserved, yet passing, blow. His first reaction to the initial message? — "No news is as bad or as good as when you first hear it . . ."

The *Express*/EMAP preprint project had scarcely passed the drawing board stage when plans for offset printing the Group's own publications began to crystallise. Whilst some preferred an adaptation of the successful contracts press, Pat Winfrey was attracted by another offset innovation, the double-width (four plate-wide) newspaper press. In 1966 the design was finalised and an order placed for a Halley-Aller

[1] *British Printer*, October 1970

five-unit press printing up to 80 tabloid pages with facilities for spot colour and for insetting full colour preprint. With a possible delivery of up to 45,000 copies per hour it would show letterpress Hoes a clean pair of heels. First newspaper to come off the press was the *Wisbech Advertiser* at the end of December 1969 but the milestone was nine months overdue and there was no cocktail party. Delivery of this newtype machine was delayed and this, with problems over performance which took time to solve, had serious financial consequences.

These troubles put back the switch from letterpress to offset and not only exasperated Pat Winfrey and his colleagues but played havoc with re-training programmes for most departments, prevented re-organisation of work on the ever-busy contracts press, and deepened cuts in profits made by increased costs and wages at a time of general trade adversity. Some financial recompense came from the suppliers but the pace of change was cautious as Stamford, Spalding, King's Lynn and Peterborough weeklies moved on to the double-width litho press during 1970 along with *Motor Cycle News*, followed by the Suffolk weeklies and the Peterborough evening in January 1971. From this early programme production grew steadily. Pausing for breath after a particular hustle on Tuesday 23 May 1972, the team figured they had achieved by far their biggest single day's work on this one machine: 398,915 good copies of five different titles in 15¼ production hours — a net average output of 26,158 copies per hour. These included 121,380 copies of *Garden News* incorporating a double colour preprint insertion.

To speed this ceaseless stream of print, advanced Ferag equipment from Switzerland made the despatch room the most mechanised in Europe, papers conveyed from the press to any of the room's delivery points being automatically counted and wrapped in bundles to conform to newsagents' orders. Canteen facilities on the Woodston site for men working all hours on the contracts and preprint presses occupied one end of a ground floor-only building put up in 1965. The rest housed office staff and a modest section where the A.T.F. and Morisawa equipment produced photoset text to be pasted-up into page form for some of the contract publications. Their output was supplemented by repro pulls of matter — mostly advertisements — set on hot metal Linotype machines.

Pat Winfrey wanted to match the double-width offset press with full-scale phototypesetting but needed reassuring where computers were concerned. Lord Thomson had launched the *Reading Evening Post* in 1965 as Britain's first computer-set newspaper but this installation dealt only with text matter. During 1966 Group executives made a special study of available hardware which could process accounts as well as text — researches supplemented by George Kingsman in 1968 when he took sabbatical leave from the London College of Printing for the purpose. A problem here was that computer manufacturers and newspaper publishers were virtual strangers to one another's techniques and requirements and Kingsman found himself equally obliged to brief as to be briefed. Here, as ever, he served as the technical ideas man, preparing as thoroughly as possible to meet challenges and cross-examinations by Pat and Richard Winfrey and their colleagues.

Meanwhile they were planning a new L-shaped building at Woodston to lead on from the new double-width press section, ground floor devoted to text and page composition, first floor to *Peterborough Advertiser* and *Evening Telegraph* editorial and advertising, and top floor to Group executives and telecommunications. The *Peterborough Advertiser* company's move from Broadway in January 1971 was the last into the new building. An ICL 1901 computer was installed for testing at Woodston in October 1968 to justify and hyphenate text as set on a tape-producing keyboard, Ray Dodkin (ex-RAF) having already joined as the Group's first systems analyst/programmer. His star pupil at Woodston, Bill Carter, ex-RAF communications technician and *Peterborough Advertiser* Linotype operator turned A.T.F. exponent, took over the computer room when Dodkin moved to Periodicals. Other roles for the ICL 1901 were to set, classify and up-date advertisements; to make out wages and salaries; and to carry out a variety of accounting functions, taking in decimalisation from February 1971. With it came two Photon 713 phototypesetting machines favourably reported on by Colin Budgen, then Litho company general manager, after checking working installations in the States. First Group publication to carry computer-set text was *Garden News* in its issue of 28 March 1969. Five months later the company ordered a second computer and a further Photon 713, the latter a model 100-8 capable of producing text at up to 100 lines a minute.

By the early 1970's the Woodston photocomposing room housed the largest Photon installation of its kind in Europe. The mutual understandings between Photon and EMAP dated back to that first Peterborough-built offset rotary which R. P. Winfrey had studied so closely along with George Kingsman. Other keen observers had included Harry Smith, also of the London College of Printing and an equal offset enthusiast. He joined Crosfield Electronics when they took over the agency for Photon equipment and as consultant to International Photon maintained a valued friendship with EMAP. Photons turned punched tape into photographic bromides of text ready for pasting-up, but first equipment to deal with original typewritten copy was the Datek keyboard. As this produced only unjustified tape, the operator could rattle through copy without pausing, as in Linotype days, to justify — space out words and letters — to a given column width. Computer function was to take Datek tape, with keyed-in instructions as to width, size and choice of type, and turn out a justified tape to run through the Photon.

Keyboarding and running off tapes for text corrections as marked by the reading staff, and pasting-up corrected lines over earlier bromides, were a laboured interruption until slickness was restored by the Hendrix visual display unit. When EMAP bought a Hendrix V.D.U. in 1972 it was not only the first to come to the Group but the first delivered to Europe, although more than 140 were by then being used in the United States. As it went through the unit, Datek tape rolled the text at reading pace on to a television-type display screen. From the Hendrix keyboard words could be corrected, sentences inserted, deleted or substituted and paragraphs re-set, leaving a clean tape to go through the computer. Nowhere was its benefit more heaven-sent than in up-dating classified advertisement columns. Apart from the Kettering series, the only EMAP provincials not photocomposed at Woodston were those produced at King's Lynn and Bury St Edmunds. At these two offices pages were taken to paste-up stage for plate-making and printing at Woodston, Singer Friden keyboards being used in conjunction with photocomposing units. Training for Lynn and Bury staffs included flights to the Singer Friden centre in Holland.

Keen operators and technicians found it good to belong to EMAP during the white heat of the Group's technological revolution. They mastered new techniques and helped train others. Young and old together adapted to different keyboard layouts, computer codes, lengths of tape and waxed bromides instead of galleys of metal type, and assembly of pages of text on a paste-up board with scalpel as tool. A new range of job opportunities opened at managerial and supervisory levels where potential was tested in developing situations. Colin Budgen, Merchant Navy master mariner turned printer, came in 1965 to manage the Litho company and Engravers, followed in 1970 by Graeme Pryor, Group work study manager and previously with the *Belfast Telegraph*, as general manager. He was succeeded in 1971 by local man Terry Boughton whose brother Derek was head of the composing room. Management assistant and earlier in Periodicals advertising, Terry was another example of EMAP boys making good. So was Ron Scotting, assistant general manager of the *Peterborough Advertiser,* who changed command in 1969 to take charge of double-width press production for the Litho company.

With two streams of work going through the Woodston composing room it became necessary in 1970 to separate contract from Group page production and to maintain a composing room for each. Work for outside publishers remained with Litho Printers but Woodston Newspaper Services Ltd was formed in October 1970 (financial half-year), with Ron Scotting as general manager, to handle

EMAP production and printing on the double-width press. Contract publications such as *Daltons Weekly,* for which double-width printing was more suitable, were run off by WNS Ltd as agents for Litho Printers Ltd.

In 1975 sophisticated Linotron 303 phototypesetters from Linotype-Paul began to replace the hard-worked Photons at Woodston and were part of new gear ordered for Kettering. Each of these sleek installations had its own inbuilt computer and printer, with links to one or more Linoscreen visual display units. The Linotron keyboard was designed not to produce tape but to transmit text direct to magnetic memory discs within the machine. Corrections thrown up via the display screens were keyboarded on the Linotron back to the disc, which then activated a clean bromide print for paste-up. However, serious teething troubles meant that this equipment did not begin to function as expected and there were immediate problems both at Peterborough and Kettering. If the old Photons had not been kept in commission at Peterborough — this was itself a problem as their manufacture had ceased — Woodston Newspaper Services production would have collapsed, and thousands of pounds were lost through delays and breakdowns.

Measures had to be taken to avoid production chaos over keyboarded material "lost" beyond recall in the machines, and keyboards were adapted to produce tapes to be run through whenever needed for the production of photographic text. The Linotron offered four times the capacity and 22 type choices compared with the Photon's eight, and claimed that these were not only available in more sizes but if a sub-editor's headline was too loose or too tight in the type size chosen, the machine could enlarge or reduce it to fit. It was the spring of 1977 before the Photons ceased to contribute to production in the Woodston composing room.

Behind other doors in the original contracts press building progress of a different kind was taking place among the plate-makers. Here Michael Smedley and his team from the Engraving company had their baptism during the first off-set press runs in 1964, searching determinedly through methods and materials for printing plates most acceptable to Halley-Aller sensitivity. As the Woodston complex grew, so did the range and weight of their workload. Process cameras, scanners for colour separation, automatic platemaking equipment — these were but some of the areas where technical appraisal never ceased. In October 1974, ten years on and with no further space for overflow, Smedley and staff met their most welcome visitor so far — Mr Peter Gibbings, chairman of Guardian Newspapers Ltd. He was there at the invitation of EMAP to open big extensions to the department and to congratulate the Group on catering for better conditions, bigger output, improved workflow and future expansion. His optimism over national recovery returned, he said, on finding firms like EMAP with courage and foresight to invest in new plant and processes despite the gloom and the doom. To supply plates for all the Woodston presses, the technical staff, who all had a say in the reorganisation, had cameras with computerised controls, machine processing of film, and bi-metal plate-processing equipment which was the first of its kind in the country when introduced. They were even more proud of the finely-disciplined and detailed system they evolved within the department to ensure print deadlines were met for any title on any press at any time.

R. P. Winfrey retired from the chair (but not from the board) of the EMAP parent company in 1973 not long after initiating redevelopment at Kettering to replace the Group's last letterpress plant in Dryland Street in the town centre. Northfield Avenue, main route through an open area not many minutes from the middle of town, fortunately had a good site where works and offices — mostly ground-floor, open-plan and through-carpeted — could be built with ample space around. For the evening and weekly newspapers, *Motor Cycle News* (whose editorial offices remained at Kettering throughout), and contract publications, EMAP planned a plant which would be one of the most technically advanced in the country, with a press which could print run-of-press colour or inset preprint from Woodston. Nothing less could be expected of a Group known in Europe as a leader in the web offset newspaper field.

188

After enquiries to Baker Perkins, Crabtree and Goss, the contract for a balcony-type, five-unit double-width press was signed with the latter's English subsidiary at Preston, Lancs, where Goss of America had bought up the highly reputable Foster press manufacturing firm. Pat Winfrey had seen Goss-made litho units from Chicago operating in Bologna, Italy, and the United States, and believed the American product was better engineered, utilised good class steel and offered a delivery date which could be relied on. The consequence of yielding to standard persuasions to "Buy British", "Back the Union Jack" and "Help full employment" by placing the order with Goss at Preston was sad though all too familiar. Because of such problems as the three-day week, strikes at Preston and strikes which held up steel supplies, the printing units had eventually to be made in Chicago and shipped to England. So in a roundabout way which reflects no credit at all on British industrial behaviour and added nearly £1 million to the country's adverse trade balance, RPW obtained the American-made machinery he preferred.

First production was the *Harborough Mail* of 22 January 1976, its 9,000 copies occupying only a few minutes of a press which could run up to 60,000 copies per hour. With automatic flying splice reel stands beneath its units, the Goss was 40 feet high, each unit weighing 22 tons and standing on concrete piles 40 feet deep. It added a new dimension to EMAP contract facilities and more sales power to Graham Daniels, ex-IPC successor to John Castle and director of contracts for the Group[1]. Among the early new titles attracted to Kettering was IPC's *New Musical Express* with a weekly run of about 200,000.

Innovation may have a less happy side and at Kettering, equipment problems took time to solve and photosetting output took time to build up. Staff did not leave Dryland Street — town-centre home of the company since 1888 — and farewells to letterpress were not said until the end of May

[1] E. P. (Ted) Cutting joined EMAP as litho marketing director early in 1977 from Mohn-Gordon Ltd, part of the big West German Mohn-Bertelsmann Group. He had previously worked in Chicago and seen the American web offset development at first hand.

1976, the first offset *Evening Telegraph* coming out on June 1st with full colour front and back. The move should have been ten weeks earlier but by then the National Graphical Association had only just lifted their countrywide ban on new photosetting installations. Months passed before equipment-performance approximated to promise and gloom lifted over late editions, reduced paging, abandoned advertising and lost revenue. But these were incidents in the march forward. Another was postponement of the official opening of the new plant by Lord Goodman. Arranged for 7 September 1976, this would have brought together publishers and trade union leaders, county figures and engineers, distributors and readers, and been one of the marks of his final year as chairman of the Newspaper Publishers' Association.

Eighteen years had passed since Pat Winfrey ran his rule over the Baker Perkins Spearhead press at Peterborough and started practical planning for Group offset. The Spearhead went to East Africa. "If they can do it there, we can do it a jolly sight better in Peterborough," he had said. His vision and drive; his adventurous confidence; his intuitive grasp of detail, opportunity and weakness; had transformed the Group and carried it far beyond the reaches where his father left it. Others profited — not least Baker Perkins, whose Halley-Aller project made them by 1967 Europe's most important makers of rotary offset printing machinery[1]. Pat's colleagues belonged to a more cautious school and the ultimate offset decision was left very much to him alone. By so much more, therefore, do EMAP and industry remain in his personal debt.

[1] *The History of Baker Perkins*, Augustus Muir (Heffer, Cambridge, 1968), pages 191, 194.

21. COPING WITH CHANGE

NOT all paths are smooth for pioneers and grind as well as glory marked the offset achievement. Top management felt the strain of pacing change without relaxing normal business pressures and this persuaded the board that company reorganisation was overdue. A cool look from top to bottom of the Group by P.A. Management Consultants Ltd — the probe, unhappily, was taken by some as a licence for complaint — led to their main proposals becoming effective during 1965, implemented in six months instead of the two or three years expected.

During this time illness and accident added to R. P. Winfrey's personal cares. In March 1965 he survived a serious fall at a fence when hunting with the Quorn and in May had to ask Charles Aldridge to deputise for him at the University of Missouri when the School of Journalism presented one of their Honour Award medals to the *Stamford Mercury*. It was the first weekly newspaper outside America to be so honoured. Awards had gone earlier to five other British papers — *Daily Telegraph* 1930, *Guardian* 1931, *The Times* 1933, *Daily Express* 1945, and the *Scotsman* 1963 — and though the 1965 honour emphasised the unique survival of a newspaper title it was also a tribute to modest local weeklies which are the mainstay of local life everywhere. Charles Aldridge presented to the university a 1717 issue of the *Mercury*, framed page by page to hang in the library, and in the summer of 1966 was able to introduce Dean Earl English and Missouri newspaper publishers to his EMAP colleagues when Stamford was visited during their European tour. Pat's 1965 programme also included a prostate operation in

London in August, dated to be over in time for the November conference of the Commonwealth Press Union in the Caribbean. He and Mrs Winfrey made business calls in the States before joining United Kingdom delegates in Bermuda led by Gavin Astor (Lord Astor of Hever), and the trip was a tonic. He enjoyed telling the Group's offset story. Hearing it, said Gavin Astor, made him feel like a Flat Earth Society member listening to an astronaut!

As advised by Personnel Administration and under R. P. Winfrey's continued chairmanship, a divisional structure was introduced to cover provincial newspapers, periodicals, and contract printing. Executive directors involved were Fred Cooper and Charles Aldridge, who continued oversight of the provincials; Edward Smedley, who remained in charge of periodicals; John Nuttall, who passed his *Peterborough Advertiser* company work to Charles Aldridge and concentrated on Group advertising; and Ray Parkin, who left the board on appointment as Group editorial consultant. A single Group managing director was favoured and Edward Smedley facilitated this ahead of programme by leaving the field clear for Richard Winfrey. Ivor McKinnon joined the Group to head the contracts division and George Russell, a chartered accountant with George Outram and company *(Glasgow Herald)*, brought a new look to EMAP business affairs as Group accountant and company secretary. Firm, wideawake and a glutton for work, he greatly strengthened the team. Philip Coles, a new lay member but an old friend of EMAP, added strength to the board as a respected Peterborough figure, director of local companies, and a former senior bank manager. Last post to be filled, early in 1966, brought Richard Parkes from the Army — he was latterly in the Ministry of Defence personnel and training advisory team — as the Group's first personnel adviser.

Edward Smedley remained a consultant to the board for a period after retiring from the national publications division in June 1966. Speeches, presentations and some emotion marked the annual company luncheon at Peterborough that month as Smed looked back over 40 crowded years — a long story of changes of premises, plant and places. But it was the people, he said, who had brought warmth and light and colour to them all. Successors to him in the periodicals division were John Sibun from Country Life Ltd, 1966 to 1967; Charles Aldridge 1967 to 1970 — additional to his provincials responsibility; and Ivor McKinnon, 1970 to 1973 when he became Group development director (left EMAP 1974). When with EMAP for part of 1973, Bryan Hope (ex-IPC) managed the periodicals under the ad hoc board (representing companies in the division), of which he was a member and Richard Winfrey chairman. Next in line as general manager was Robin Miller, elevated to the parent board as executive director in 1976.

Ivor McKinnon's mantle as managing director in charge of contracts was assumed in 1970 by Montague Josephs, who did not have a seat on the parent board but controlled both Litho Printers Ltd and its sister company Woodston Newspaper Services Ltd. When he left the Group in 1972 the gap was filled by Alan Butler on his return from Malaysia. His election to the EMAP board later that year was another happy example of a rise from the ranks. Printing managers ensuring that presses ran sweetly and output flowed smoothly for him were Alan Thorpe, who added preprint to contracts in 1974, and David Bray, successor in the double-width section to Roy Thomas when the latter moved to Kettering in 1976 to help tame the new Goss.

After completing the curriculum of the Manchester Business School, Charles Winfrey became a Group director in 1967 and spent the summer with the management team of Pennsylvania's leading newspaper, the *Allentown Chronicle*. On return he took charge of the Lincolnshire and Norfolk newspapers, adding the Suffolk titles on Fred Cooper's retirement in 1969 and Northamptonshire in 1974. Here he relieved Charles Aldridge, who had been carrying the evenings and weeklies at both Peterborough and Kettering and could now scale down his effort before retirement in 1976. F. C. Winfrey had something of Pat's cheerful informality and directness and the severe and unusual heart condition which interrupted his work in 1975 was a sadness to all. During 1976 he resumed oversight of the weeklies stage by stage and John Ryan, executive editor of *The Guardian*, joined the Group as managing director of the Peterborough and Kettering newspapers. A journalist with national and local weekly, daily and public relations experience, he had been in *The Guardian* London office since 1963 and was 1976 vice-chairman of the National Council for the Training of Journalists.

Three further non-executive directors were by now serving on the EMAP board. As a partner in the London stockbroking firm of John Prust & Co (later Laurence Prust & Co), Graham Ross Russell had handled Group affairs in the capital market for some years before election in 1970. A scholar of Trinity Hall, he had played rugby for the LX Club while at Cambridge University and later took the full curriculum at Harvard University Business School to gain the Harvard M.B.A. degree. John Prust's senior partner was H. R. Bourne, whose services to the Group started at its inauguration in 1947. His brief expressions of thanks to chairman and directors were a delightful tailpiece to many EMAP shareholders' meetings, often dignified by Shakespearean quotations. None was more apposite, perhaps, than these lines from *Measure for Measure*, heard in 1969 when the offset breakthrough had falsified all fears:

> Our doubts are traitors
> And make us lose the good we oft might win,
> By fearing to attempt.

Warm welcomes awaited Frank Rogers when he accepted a seat in 1971. A newspaperman to his fingertips, rising from reporting to work in harness with Cecil King and Hugh (later Lord) Cudlipp as managing director at 45 of the International Publishing Corporation Ltd, he had left IPC in 1970 on its merger with Reed International. The National Newspaper Steering Group, set up jointly by managements and unions to try to rationalise labour relations, were glad to have this distinguished Fleet Street figure as chairman, and in 1971 the Newspaper Publishers' Association, headed by Lord Goodman, chose him as their Director. This appointment ended at the end of 1973 after EMAP directors had asked Mr Rogers to succeed R. P. Winfrey as Group chairman. It was a non-executive position with Richard Winfrey as deputy chairman and chief executive, so that Frank Rogers was able to combine the office with service to the great Plessey Company Ltd as adviser on corporate affairs, including the entire range of external relations. He was keen to develop communications within the Group also, and to *Splash* supplements on the state of the business Richard Winfrey and executives added staff briefings round the offices. In 1974, *Emap News* replaced a weekly bulletin to take care each month of routine internal news items.

A friend of the Group who joined lay members on the board in 1976 was O. D. G. (David) Barr, senior in a legal practice in the Wisbech-King's Lynn area. He was already a West Norfolk Newspapers director and drew on a lifetime's enjoyment of angling for contributions to *Trout & Salmon* and similar journals. David Barr's arrival brought the strength of the EMAP board to twelve for the first time. Senior lay member was P. T. M. (Peter) Wilson, elected 1955, who had served on the Northamptonshire Newspapers board at Kettering since 1951 and been its chairman 1957 to 1972, when both he and R. P. Winfrey resigned. This opened the way for Richard Winfrey to become chairman at Kettering and for Charles Winfrey and Peter Wilson junior to take the vacant seats. P. T. M. Wilson had greatly extended the legal practice started by his father and stood high in the profession. Conspicuous among extra interests were the iron ore quarries which marked Midland landscapes. He served iron ore producers as secretary at area and national level and was among those consulted on legislation to restore worked land to farming. Corby had already mushroomed from a Northamptonshire village to a steel town of 10,000 before being granted urban powers in 1939 (designated a New Town in 1950), and as part-time clerk till then of the parish council he had a spread of new steel works and a flood of population — mostly from Scotland — among his problems. Pat Winfrey was the only survivor of the original 1947 parent board.

In 1966 F. E. T. (Peter) Dann, London office manager, assumed responsibility for all national advertising and Ray

Wells moved from managing *Garden News* to the new position of provincial division advertisement manager with George Walker as deputy. A shrewd businessman in his own right who steered his family into interests in retailing and plastics, Wells had arranged a string of offers for *Garden News* readers and then turned his fertile mind to reader competitions for the whole Group. From August 1964 EMAP provincial readers in swelling numbers entered a Mark-the-Ball contest based on football pitch scenes with the ball blanked out. Top award of £250 rose by degrees to £4,000 in cash or equivalent with a range of consolation prizes, and the Post Office, struggling with up to 50,000 letters per day for the competitions department opened in Stamford, had hopes of better wages from being upgraded! Following suit, *Angling Times* invited readers to Find the Float; *Motor Cycle News* to Find the Rider; *Garden News* to Find the Ball. Group newspapers benefited from the large paid-for notices introducing these innocuous weekly contests and giving winners' names.

The picture greatly changed in 1970, however, when proceedings under the Betting, Gaming and Lotteries Act 1963 against national newspapers running Spot-Ball contests led to a three-year wrangle without final resolution of the legal issues. Discretion meanwhile reduced the Group's interest to modified competitions each week in *Motor Cycle News* and *Garden News* and occasionally in *Angling Times*. In the provincial division awards were offered in an ingenious range of smaller-scale contests tailored to suit local offices and local circumstances. Ray Wells resigned from EMAP in 1971 to concentrate on his own affairs, leaving provincial advertising to the practised and good humoured George Walker. His retirement in 1975 brought promotion to Derek Abel of the Stamford-Spalding papers. He had served the Group well since starting at Bury St Edmunds — his father had been on the works staff there — and shared a happy nature through the charm and range of his water colour drawings.

Expansion more than doubled EMAP's list of periodicals between 1970 and 1974, starting with *Practical Photo-*

196

graphy, launched in 1954 and known till 1959 as *Popular Photography*. Pergamon Press sold to EMAP in 1970 soon after this monthly joined the procession coming off the contracts press at Woodston. Called from *Motor Cycle News* as editor, Martin Hodder took the sale of 41,000 past the 60,000 mark before going in 1976 to edit the IPC weekly *Amateur Photographer*, leaving PP's technical editor Robert Scott to take command.

Joining the Group in 1971, *Two-Wheeler Dealer* continued serving the trade as controlled-circulation magazine of the National Association of Cycle and Motor Cycle Traders. Colin Mayo, Association secretary, doubled as editor until replacing Charles Deane in the chair of *Motor Cycle Mechanics* in 1975, his *Two-Wheeler Dealer* successor being Alan Aspel.

Fastest-rising of the Group's periodicals was *Sea Angler* which A. E. Morgan Publications launched as a sportsman's magazine in February 1972 and sold to EMAP in October with a circulation around 12,000. Sales were doubled in little more than twelve months and trebled during 1976. Ted Lamb, a former *Angling Times* man who joined Morgans and was *Sea Angler's* editor, returned to London publishing in 1973, handing the magazine to Peter Collins. A fishing enthusiast almost from birth in Norfolk Broadland, Peter Collins was among the strong men of *Angling Times* as features and later assistant editor. For part of 1974 Ian Beacham, youngest of Ron Beacham's sons and Group-trained, edited *Sea Angler* and shared in its success story — a move which made him at 26 the Group's youngest editor — but handed over to Peter Collins again on being called to *Motor Cycle News* as assistant editor.

Before long the new motor cycle superstar Barry Sheene, whose family lived near Wisbech, was racing his way toward the 1976 world championship. Ian Beacham brought out a Super Sheene special in his honour and edited the champion's personal story published as a hardback at the end of the year. Four more one-off specials during 1976 led to *Motorcycle Racing* being established as a bi-monthly from 1977 — with Ian Beacham at the controls and a million motor cycle speed fans as target for its picture power and gleaming colour. After a 30,000 *Super Sheene* sell-out in a matter of weeks, a Paris publishing house bought the rights and produced a French edition.

EMAP acquired *Bike*, with its particular appeal to younger motor cycle owners, in 1973 and added *Motor Cycle Mechanics* in September 1974. Two other monthlies — *Popular Motoring* and *Practical Gardening* — were included in a £300,000 deal with Mercury House Publications which brought an extra combined sale of 275,000 to the Group. Staff of the three papers moved out of Mercury House into Fleet Street until editorial offices were found in Peterborough. Here in 1975 Colin Mayo succeeded to *Motor Cycle Mechanics*, and within two years promotion took sales from 95,000 to 112,000.

Stanley Russell, who had known EMAP as part-time editor of the Caravan Club's *En Route*, continued *Practical Gardening* and saw comparable growth, becoming editor-in-chief in 1976 on Geof Hamilton's arrival as editor from *Garden News*. Doug Mitchell stayed with *Popular Motoring* as London editor, Mike Twite moving to the chair in Peterborough after spells with magazines in the same field, including editorship of *Motoring News*. The magazine was re-designed, given an extended title: *Popular Motoring & Practical Car Maintenance*, and a brief to help the growing number of car owners — especially younger people — obliged to carry out their own servicing.

Management of all the periodicals via the *Angling Times*, *Motor Cycle News* and *Garden News* directorates was finally abandoned when Mercury House titles joined the division, EMAP National Publications Ltd being formed to supersede them. Robin Miller became managing director under Richard Winfrey and George Russell, chairman and vice-chairman, and others on the board were David Arculus, general manager (previously EMAP corporate planner), and Ron Beacham, chief circulation manager. Forty-four years had passed since Ron Beacham became the *Wellingborough News* office junior, and 22 since he started pushing *Angling Times* as the Group's first national publication.

They had never missed any issue, he said, and his eyes were on an aggregate divisional sale of one million. He saw this barrier broken in April 1976 when the seven monthlies and the three weeklies for April 10th (omitting the two trade journals) reached a total sale of 1,039,034, *Garden News* and *Motor Cycle News* at the same time becoming the first national weeklies to exceed 200,000. Frank Rogers could report to shareholders that *Garden News*, like *Angling Times* and *Motor Cycle News*, was now leader in its own field, and that the national publications were again contributing the major part of Group profits.

Switches of staff over the years between periodicals, and between provincials and periodicals, make a study in versatility and Group mobility. Some of those who found their feet under editors' desks have already been named. The three who followed Brian McLoughlin to *Angling Times* were Russell Hole 1969-72, Mike Hughes 1972-74, and Bob Feetham, who all came up through the ranks. From launch in 1963 till relieved by Roy Eaton in 1966, Jack Thorndike edited *Fishing* while running *Angling Times*. Ian Wood's retirement and the closure of *Fishing* in 1969 meant change for them both, Jack taking over *Trout & Salmon* with the support of Roy. In 1976 the two were appointed editor-in-chief and editor respectively.

McLoughlin had moved to *Angling Times* from *Motor Cycle News* in 1966, when MCN control was put into the hands of Peter Howdle. This stalwart had started helping Cyril Quantrill while still in the trade and in 1958 joined the *Motor Cycle News* team of pioneers. By mutual arrangement, he became associate editor in 1967 when Charles Rous took command. Typical of the breed drawn to work for the paper, Rous at that time held the world kilometre sprint record (750 cc class). His departure from the Group to *Motor Cycle* brought in Robin Miller in May 1970 just as the paper moved to offset production. The motor cycle boom was under way and by 1973, when Robin Miller became divisional editorial manager, he handed over to Peter Strong a sales figure which had risen from 98,000 to 136,000. Editorial succession since Pat Beasley took over *Fishing Tackle*

Dealer on purchase in 1963 (it became *Tackle and Guns* in 1970) was secured by Mike Hughes 1966-70, John Crossman 1970-76, and Cyril Holbrook — all four moving over in turn from *Angling Times*.

An invitation to John Bloom in 1966 to run *The Grower* from its London office was an opportunity for Tony Ireson to head the *Garden News* team. He had earlier brought his writing gifts to the paper after years with the Kettering company and was particularly respected in Northampton-shire for his descriptions of local life and history and for his 1954 volume on *Northamptonshire* in Robert Hale's county books series. John Parker 1970-71 — he left to edit the evening paper at Kettering — came between Tony Ireson and Frank Ward, the latter chosen from *Motor Cycle News* and followed in 1974 by his assistant Peter Peskett, an EMAP man from junior days. Frank Ward's appointment as editorial manager of the three Mercury House titles led to this change.

For most of the national publications the world became their parish and in early days editors personally booked tickets and hotels for themselves and their staffs. "It's like running a travel agency," grumbled McLoughlin. Campaign organisation, travel, accommodation, communication, promotion, and back-up facilities wherever needed in Britain or overseas, entailed a considerable on-going operation, with production disciplines always an added pressure. Restructuring of the national division under the new company and its general management eventually put the titles in three groups under Ray Dodkin, Russell Hole and Frank Ward as publications managers.

Phil Jenner, a Boston man who changed career a little late in life to help *Angling Times* sales, carved a special niche for himself as publicity manager and organiser of show stands and exhibitions. Olympia, Earl's Court, Isle of Man races, game fairs, fishing championships — all learned to admire the Jenner brand of efficiency and helpfulness which overflowed the bounds of duty. He retired in 1969 after ten happy years of making friends for EMAP publications but, with energy to match his love of the work, continued show attendance for another six years. He died in harness, in his London hotel room as he slept after the last day of the 1975 Boat Show at Earl's Court. "What is the secret of the success of your papers?" visitors would ask. "It's the team work and the good spirit I've always found in EMAP", Jenner would reply. "We're all good pals together." He was only partly right, for the secret lay deeper — in the stout heart and unslackening effort of men like himself . . .

22. STEPPING ASIDE

SCENES reminiscent of Sir Richard's 75th birthday garden party for his staffs in 1933 marked Castor House in 1967 for R. P. Winfrey's 65th. Guests — about a fifth of EMAP's strength of a thousand [1] — were drawn by lot from each department and saw Sydney Andrews, Kettering manager, hand Group gifts to the chairman — a silver cigarette box, a cheque to add to his collection of paintings, a book with subscribers' signatures, and a garden chair for Mrs Winfrey. Then the fun began: a pair of coloured braces (RPW never got on with trouser belts), a pair of "Castor House hunting socks" alleged to be specially designed by Mary Quant, and a shirt placarded "From German Trade Mission: all is forgiven. Europa Hotel."

Pat found the yellow webbing of the braces handy for autographs and addresses when making new friends on board ship and during trips. The shirt was reminder of a business visit with other EMAP men to West Germany. Flags of many nations fluttered along the facade of their hotel in Bonn and Pat's insistence that the duvet on his bed should be replaced by blankets was misinterpreted as an order to remove the German flag outside the window. Temperatures rose in the hotel but though it faced the Chancellery, stopped short of provoking an international incident. The two pastoral scenes bought with the cheque were reproduced in that year's Castor House Christmas card and so shared with the hundreds of Winfrey friends annually greeted at home and abroad. Gift from EMAP directors was a gold watch presented at the annual shareholders' meeting.

[1] Staff totalled 1,530 in 1976: 1,256 full-time and 274 part-time.

R. P. Winfrey remained in the chair for a further six years and was 71 when Frank Rogers succeeded him in 1973. The Group commissioned Luke Sykes, Huntingdonshire farmer, painter and amateur stage coach guard, to do a presentation portrait which showed Pat astride Atlas against a favoured Fitzwilliam hunting background at Tichmarsh, Northamptonshire. In August, as soon as possible after the annual meeting, Mr and Mrs Winfrey held garden parties at Castor House on two successive days for longer-serving staff and wives/husbands. Uninvited guests on the second day, smuggled into the grounds by Ron Scotting, were Harry Smith, Brian Mulholland and Frank Austin — three men from International Photon who plotted a presentation of their own in honour of a long pioneering association. They were grateful to Mr Winfrey, said Harry Smith, for all he had done not only for them but for the industry as a whole, and his own journey that day from Dorset and the gift of a choice cut glass spirit decanter bore out their appreciation.

Between these two personal milestones Pat Winfrey saw the Group's offset project completed at Woodston, and inaugurated at Kettering as far as purchase of site for new headquarters and placing of order with Goss for the new printing press, both in 1973. In 1971, with Woodston a settled centre of production and administration, EMAP affairs were orderly compared with turbulence in industry and country. Postal strike havoc, threats and big wage claims by the NGA, Natsopa, Sogat and NUJ, disappearance of the Daily Sketch, rebellion against Edward Heath's Industrial Relations Act, erosion of profit by gathering tides of inflation, an EMAP pre-tax profit down from £236,000 to £177,000 on a turnover which had increased from £3,437,000 to £3,998,000 — these were part of the background to Group thinking on further expansion.

Travel tours for readers were already being sponsored by some EMAP publications, and diversification into the travel trade started with purchasing agencies in Bury St Edmunds and Braintree and the arrival of the experienced John Dimmock as manager of a new Group company christened Abbeygate Travel Ltd. It needed no vast capital sums for machinery and production equipment, nor did extension into the book and newspaper sales trade in 1972, when Readwell Ltd was formed in conjunction with Messrs Mills and Whatmore to control and add to their Fairford Agency Ltd shops. R. P. Winfrey chaired Abbeygate Travel and R. J. Winfrey the Readwell company, George Russell being a key figure in developing the Group's new Retail Division. In his first statement as EMAP chairman in 1974, Frank Rogers reported that Abbeygate's growth to nine branches made it the largest travel company in East Anglia. Although one branch soon closed, the acquisition of Fourwinds Holidays was a significant development in 1976. The company operated tours for the middle and upper section of the market and had a good reputation for holidays tailored to suit the individual.

Fourwinds extended the range of these and at the same time strengthened the Group's position in the travel trade. For convenience and economy they moved from their Euston Road headquarters to Durrant House, Herbal Hill, Islington — former home of Durrant's Press Cuttings agency — the EMAP London office also transferring there after 23 years at Breams Buildings. Unexpected currency problems denied success to Eurotel, the agency started by the Group to sell villas along the Spanish Mediterranean coast, and this department was disbanded in 1974. Abbeygate expected financial gloom to affect holiday traffic also but found the reverse. EMAP readers not only responded to general travel announcements in Group publications but eagerly and often in groups supported holiday tours, cruises and winter weekends in the sunshine organised through their own local newspapers. The periodicals found the same success with specialist trips abroad — fishing holidays, garden explorations, motor cycle events, photographic forays and the like.

EMAP started in 1973 to take over selected smaller news-agency shops (with delivery service) as they came on the market in the area. Brian Reeve of the Martin group came to Woodston as general manager of these businesses which were all re-named Reids. When N. G. Mills and R. T. C.

Whatmore withdrew, Readwell Ltd became wholly-owned by EMAP and in December 1974, Reids newsagencies joined the bookshops under its wing, making ten in all. Apart from Cambridge, where the Group initiated and shared in a new shopping development, they were all within the provincial division's area, at Downham Market, Hunstanton, Kettering, King's Lynn (two), Peterborough, Stowmarket and Wisbech (two). Cliff Packwood succeeded Brian Reeve as general manager in 1976, bringing with him experience as regional manager for Dillons, the 200-odd shop chain operated by the *Birmingham Post and Mail*.

When the Group's freehold properties were revalued in 1974 the balance sheet figure for land and buildings rose from £872,259 to £2,421,294 — more than half the total capital employed. For the first time EMAP had their own professional to make the survey, Robert Balam being appointed managing director of the revived East Midland Press Properties company in October 1973. A chartered surveyor at home in both the construction industry and local government, he proved a shrewd ally at a time when the Group were more than usually occupied with building, buying, selling, leasing, extending and altering offices and retail premises. Woodston complex notwithstanding, Peterborough seemed never to stop outgrowing its clothes. Central Accounts settled in Broadway but the national division overflowed from Park House and its annexe into a further set of offices in Church Walk followed in 1975 by a suite in Aqua House by the main river bridge for staff from Mercury House. A year later, the whole ground floor of Woodston House — big office block between Aqua House and Group headquarters — was occupied by periodicals staff. Wooden huts they left behind on the Woodston site, first used by executives in the early days, were cleared in the path of extensions to the contracts division bindery.

For years the twice-weekly *Lynn News & Advertiser* and the Printing company had been bursting at the seams in Purfleet Street, King's Lynn, where no further extensions were possible around the property built for the *Lynn News* in 1893. After putting the Friday edition to bed on Thursday evening, 27 February 1975, Purfleet Street was smoothly and completely evacuated and on Monday morning, 3 March 1975, work began as usual on the Tuesday edition in new premises. For these a quiet tree-bordered corner was found on the Hardwick Industrial Estate, bounded on the outskirts of Lynn by a sweeping highway leading coastwards. Open-plan ground-floor layout saved steps and sped work flow. A milestone for the newspapers and printing companies, it was also symbolic of change and progress throughout much of East Anglia. King's Lynn itself had seen great industrial growth, whilst business and population spilling over from London continued to affect EMAP territory from North-amptonshire to the Norfolk coast. Lynn's Readwell store included an office for the newspaper so that a presence in town was more central than before.

Fred Haynes of Cranford, one of Northamptonshire's garden experts, bred a new rose for the *Evening Telegraph* in advance of 1976, Year of the Rose and of the Kettering newspaper company's move to purpose-built premises. Management presented a bed of new *Evening Telegraph* roses to each major town in the circulation area and clothed the bare borders of the new site with them. Moving day was not until the end of May 1976 when the Dryland Street premises, bought as a first-year move by the original North-amptonshire Printing & Publishing Company, were left behind by all but a small staff in the reception foyer. This was retained as a town office. Behind it, Ludlow and Linotype machines, composing stones, galleys and chases, foundry, rotary presses and despatch area stood eerily still. EMAP had ended letterpress printing exactly 500 years after Caxton had first set up his press in Westminster in 1476, and there was something dumbly reproachful in the sight of faithful and long-serving machinery awaiting clear-ance. Flongs of the last hot-metal *Evening Telegraph* pages and mallet and plane from the moulding press were among items grabbed as souvenirs. Extra rotary plates were cast. Fixed on a stand, two together made a substantial cylinder of metal as support for glass-topped foyer tables. Miniature replicas of the final letterpress front page, cast from identical metal, were framed for readers as collectors' pieces, available along with casts in the same metal of a typical street seller with bag and bill board. Authentic model for these three-inch figures was William George Dee, who first sold *Evening Telegraphs* in Rushden in 1943 and 34 years later, at 76, was still selling from his pitch in High Street.

As Dryland Street closed down that May and the Goss rotary was running itself in at Kettering, the Group ordered a new offset press for Woodston to share contract printing with the Halley-Aller. It had already done a noble job for twelve years, and over the last two Alan Butler and the Litho company had been ear to ground, assessing movement in the magazine field. Their research and their faith finally led them to West Germany, where Koenig and Bauer agreed to delivery by 1977 of a £1 million double-width heatset offset press. Plans for this custom-built Commander included full-colour satellite and additional spot colour facilities, with output up to 50,000 copies an hour. Frederick, the original Koenig, was engineer to *The Times* until returning to Germany in 1817 to manufacture printing presses at Wurzburg, and Andrew Bauer, a fellow Saxon, was mechanic in his Whitecross Street works, East London. Makers of the new EMAP machine take pride in looking back over 165 years of manufacturing history to Koenig's invention of the world's first cylinder press in 1811. With its sheet-feeding arrangement, automatic inking of type, and cylinder to obtain uniform impressions from it, Koenig's 1811 breakthrough heralded emancipation for a host of ink-smeared slaves toiling at traditional hand presses. Removal of the *Daily Express* satellites left room for the 105 feet of the Commander in the preprint hall.

A smaller-scale but much welcomed development at King's Lynn during 1976 was installation of a Japanese Komori Sprint four-colour offset press for the Printing company. This transformed production of magazine covers for the national publications and accelerated other work for the Group and outside customers, for most of which colour was being ordered. Bury St Edmunds, however, saw the reverse of the coin. Here a decline in orders for letterpress blocks led to closure of the Engraving company's operation.

In few senses could R. P. Winfrey be described as a retiring figure. He cared too much for the Group he had built up and too little for the leisured life he might have had to lose interest, conceal criticism or withhold advice. Though no longer EMAP chairman with the final word, he remained on the board, was the company's largest individual shareholder, chaired the Travel and Property companies, headed the Peterborough, West Norfolk and Lincolnshire newspapers, and was chairman of Woodston Newspaper Services which printed them. Liberal-Nonconformist watchwords about local newspapers acceptability in any home or circle always surfaced if he found the crude, the coarse or the bawdy in picture or report. National publications sometimes concerned him too, and protest against blatant explicitness in sex magazines handled by the Retail division led to a fresh management look at its list.

What are standards unless to mark where men stand firm? Without standards, how do men know where and when to stand? To Pat Winfrey, as to Sir Richard before him, there were things in business life other than profits. Conforming to a permissive society was not one of them. If convictions of this kind were not easily articulated, actions had made them clear years before. There was the case of the front page picture carried by *Garden News* in its early days. Coming across it in the composing room after the paper had gone to press, Pat Winfrey took exception to the bikini-clad glamour girl shown using a spade. He ordered a front-page re-make and instant recall of the whole issue, entailing interception of newsagents' parcels at as many delivery points as possible. John Castle figured in another incident in the early offset years. He had pulled off a valuable 600,000-run contract to print *Tit-Bits* but was told — and almost wept to hear — that its editorial standard and content made it unacceptable to EMAP as printers. The incidents passed into the lore of the Group: they illuminate part of Pat's character.

23. WHITHER EMAP?

CHANGE marked the provincial publications less than the nationals, the Northamptonshire weeklies being most affected because of natural erosion by the advancing evening. Between April 1973 and December 1974 the six titles were reduced to two, *Kettering Leader*, *Thrapston Journal* and *Corby Leader* being discontinued and *Rushden Echo* and *Wellingborough News* merged as *News-Echo* under one editor. An opposition *Corby News* survived only fifteen months before selling to EMAP and ceasing publication in December 1962. Market Harborough retained its *Mail* but the *News-Echo* future was less secure. Sadly, too, what had been Frank Hutchen's special pride, Kettering's Saturday sports paper the *Pink 'Un*, closed towards the end of the 1974 football season because of production problems. Sales rose to 50,000 soon after the war ended and football fans throughout the region waited for it in town and village centres every Saturday evening but demand had dropped to below 10,000 by closure.

Peterborough also showed signs of a swing to the evening and when union action affected production in 1975, Tuesday's edition of the *Advertiser* was dropped. In June 1976 Friday's edition was re-launched as a lively tabloid and from September switched to Thursday publication. Although the *Wisbech Advertiser* was the only Group paper converted to free circulation (as the *Fenland Advertiser*), West Suffolk Newspapers experimented with a new free paper for twelve months only in 1973/74, calling it *Bury Post*, the opposition title acquired on amalgamation in 1931.

Anglia Echo Newspapers at Haverhill, where the *Suffolk*

Free Press had put out a local edition since 1962, sold the *Haverhill Echo* to EMAP in 1976, thus rounding off the West Suffolk Newspapers operation and adding 8,000 to its total sales figure. Ownership of the paper, founded in 1888 as the *South West Suffolk Echo*, had passed to two men who were apprenticed to it before the turn of the century and it was Alan Claydon, descendant of one of them, who sold the paper in 1962. To acquire it, Anglia Echo Newspapers was formed by Douglas Brown, political editor, writer and broadcaster who left Fleet Street and went on to develop a contract printing and consultancy organisation with Halstead as an additional centre. His decision to forsake metal in 1971 and adopt computerised photocomposition and offset printing meant that the *Echo* staff came into EMAP well prepared for the Group's production methods. Announcement of the takeover was made in the presence of George Russell when the *Echo* staged an exhibition in Haverhill illustrating the paper's history.

A display on a bigger scale, repeated in several centres in Northamptonshire, marked the 75th anniversary of the *Evening Telegraph*. Prince William of Gloucester, living in neighbourly nearness at Barnwell Manor, agreed to open this at Kettering in October 1972 but his tragic death in an air race in August meant that the exhibition proceeded without the reception which would have brought him and many county and newspaper figures together. The fatality occurred less than two months after the marriage of his brother Prince Richard brought a new princess into the county[1]. In 1973 Princess Richard was a guest of the *Peterborough Advertiser* when she opened the exhibition of children's art sponsored by the newspaper. Since the *Lynn News & Advertiser* office was flooded with 2,156 entries from school children for the Group's first art show in 1963, these exhibitions were supported with enthusiasm wherever the Group staged them.

Involvement with readers took many forms, from investigating individual cases of hard luck to sponsoring appeals

[1] Prince Richard succeeded as the Duke of Gloucester on the death of his father in 1974.

and public entertainments in aid of charities. Largest-ever of these was Expo Steam, developed at Peterborough from a tattoo programme in 1972 to become the world's biggest rendezvous for steam traction engines. On one occasion, among first-class extra attractions making it an unbeatable holiday weekend event, a parade of vintage and veteran cars included the Rolls-Royce of the 1930's which R. P. Winfrey inherited from his father, recognised round the Group in earlier days by its wooden traveller-type body. Children had a chance "to see where Daddy works" among gleaming new gear in modern buildings when Woodston opened its doors to staff families on a June Sunday in 1971. Thereafter Family Day drew crowds of EMAP people to Woodston whenever it was organised.

Except for a dive in 1971 when provincial division costs outstripped increases in selling prices and advertising rates, the Group's annual pre-tax profit rose from £151,000 in 1967 to £1,067,000 in 1977. Turnover in the same decade rose from £2,394,000 to £14,800,000. Inflation distorts but cannot conceal the picture of growth projected by these figures:

	Turnover	Pre-tax Profit
1967	£2,394,000	£151,000
1968	£2,733,000	£228,000
1969	£3,082,000	£273,000
1970	£3,437,000	£236,000
1971	£3,998,000	£177,000
1972	£4,893,000	£380,000
1973	£6,769,000	£901,000
1974	£8,108,000	£935,000
1975	£9,741,000	£677,000
1976	£11,510,000	£724,000
1977	£14,800,000	£1,067,000

Loyalty and effort on the part of sales staff and teams and individuals in each office lie behind the statistics. Annual shareholders' meetings were held at the Waldorf, London, until 1965 when the Great Northern Hotel at Peterborough became the regular rendezvous, and at each one the customary vote of thanks to staff was more than a formality. EMAP outgrew dimensions which made personal acquaintance possible with everybody but Richard Winfrey was eager to get the message of appreciation over to the Group, using not only the annual meeting but *Splash, EMAP News* and office visits. As standards of living rose over the years, cash jingled in teenage pockets and marriages started earlier in life, so demand quickened for houses, furnishings, electrical goods, cars, holidays and entertainment. Telephone canvassing transformed the classified columns and provincial newspaper issues grew thicker and thicker as advertising spread over more and more pages — pages which became ever more expensive to produce and print. Advertisement managers in the Group were among first friends made by enterprising businessmen. As already noted, some moved on into general managership. Others stayed long at the wicket for consistently high-scoring innings — among them such Group figures as the genial Arthur Wood at Kettering and Keith McGee, national division advertisement manager at London office. When he joined the first Quantrill team as advertisement/circulation man, he push-biked round the City on a pocket money plus commission basis.

Banking and accountancy arrangements became a tangle as the EMAP tree put out branch after branch. After professional advice in 1959, calendar-month accounting was dropped in favour of four-weekly periods and budgetry control was introduced[1]. This gave readier checks of performance and regular statistics not before provided — a service which in due course computers made even speedier. No-one was more sensitive than R. P. Winfrey to business barometer changes and over the years sails were furled at his order ahead of squalls and storms which others might have risked. Donald Loakes took charge of the new accounting procedure after joining EMAP as its first Group accountant. He took book-keeping under his wing stage by stage, moving in 1960 from Kettering to the former Westgate Congregational manse in Peterborough, next to the church where Sir Richard had once worshipped, and in 1964 to Broadway.

[1] The company's financial year was changed in 1963 to end in March instead of June.

Here John Hope succeeded him in 1966, followed in 1972 by John Robertson until the latter's move to West Norfolk Newspapers in 1976 led to the promotion of his assistant Brian Allpress.

These three men also succeeded as EMAP company secretaries and backed George Russell — involved in top management all along as financial director and since 1967 as assistant managing director — in welding Group Central Accounts into a keen-edged management tool. Richard Winfrey shared the thirteen-week advanced management programme at the Harvard University Business School in 1972. George Russell followed him there in 1974, a fellow participant being Mike Collins, man in the command module when Neil Armstrong made the first moon walk in 1969 — hence the lively interest when G.R. produced moonshot pictures which were a preprint colour scoop for EMAP a year before. Joseph Stephenson's partnership audited Group accounts until his death in 1965 severed a personal link with Winfrey affairs going back to Sir Richard's *Peterborough Advertiser* takeover in 1897. Thereafter Stanley Bayliss Smith's firm, Cassleton Elliott & Co (later Josolyne Layton-Bennett & Co) conducted the professional audit.

At R. P. Winfrey's last shareholders' meeting as chairman he was able to point to a record pre-tax profit for 1973 of £901,000, nearly three times more than the highest previous figure. Frank Rogers a year later reported a rise to £935,000 but, though turnover had risen by 20 per cent — caused more by inflation, he said, than the addition of new business — the 1975 pre-tax profit dropped to £677,000. Industry was bedevilled by the economic problems which were to lead to the Labour Government's big international borrowings. Price Commission constraints on meeting swollen costs by advancing selling prices and advertisement rates were so crippling, however, that Frank Rogers felt driven to describe their damaging effects at a personal interview sought with the Minister of State[1]. However, results by other companies declined more than the 28 per cent shown

[1] Top selling prices reached in 1976 were: provincial — evenings 6p, weeklies 8p; national — weeklies 15p (nine times the pre-decimal fourpence of the 1950's), monthlies 40p, bi-monthly 50p.

by EMAP and Group policy was not diverted from investment in plant and buildings while giving readers better value in all the publications. Climb-back in 1976 justified this confidence and the periodicals, with their manly down-to-earth approach to leisure, continued to claim new records against national trends.

Bank borrowings which had helped buy machines and build premises were offset by an increase in issued capital, the City in February 1976 taking up one-and-a-half million 25p limited voting ordinary shares at 32p. It was the Group's first institutional placing, capital having always come previously from private sources or short-term bank borrowings — except for creation of £500,000 debenture stock in 1966 to replace 1956 and 1958 issues totalling £285,000. Many shareholders had family links with Sir Richard Winfrey's original newspaper associates, and in itself the Winfrey family holding was sufficient to foil any would-be slick and soulless predator. Two of Pat's three sisters, Mrs Ellen Willson and Mrs Lucy Eades, remained in active contact with the Group as directors of the newspapers at Peterborough and Bury St Edmunds respectively.

When surveying 1972 results R. P. Winfrey could look back on 25 years of Group history. There were glimpses of it in a small exhibition at the meeting. There were others in comparisons he quoted: net assets grown from £342,000 in 1947 to £1,760,000; 145,000 ordinary shares of £1 increased to 3,085,237 of 25p; staff of 400 with wages of £110,000 expanded to 1,350 drawing £2,100,000. Each original £1 ordinary share, worth £1.36 in 1948, was represented by thirteen shares of 25p — four ordinary and nine limited voting ordinary — and was worth £6.32. He reminded shareholders that the origins of the Group lay far back in Sir Richard Winfrey's acquisition of the *Spalding Guardian* in 1887 and its support of Gladstonian policies. His courage, enterprise and wisdom led less able owners to put their papers under his management. Despite the Hitler war, all were sound and ready for development after his death in 1944. All through and for more than 80 years, the Winfrey policy of ploughing back profits, of keeping in balance the

214

claims of capital and labour, of the business and its customers, had been a vital factor.

The year after, when Pat relinquished the chair in 1973, it was exactly 50 years since his first appointment as a director — of the *Bury Free Press*. He had a word of warning: the freedom of the Press was the right of everyone to hold conscientious beliefs and have them published. "When that right and that freedom are lost we are left with the Moscow and Mussolini way of life."

He had a word of exhortation: to keep faith with their forebears who founded newspapers not merely for commercial gain but to support ideals of character, personal conduct and public service.

He had a word of praise for all EMAP people: "We have an excellent team and an excellent business . . . My warm and affectionate and lasting thanks to my splendid band of colleagues."

He had a word for the future: "growth" would remain the keynote of EMAP. Fresh titles might be launched or acquired; other businesses might take them beyond East Anglia and the East Midlands. With their affairs in "applepie order" they might well be at the beginning of a new phase in Group evolution.

Headed by Frank Rogers and Richard Winfrey with their brilliance of gift, business ambition, proven experience and unquestioned standing, the Group's "new phase" is under way. Backed by every working colleague, their success is success for all in a third Winfrey-generation chapter yet to be written. It was Pat at the silver jubilee who looked ahead and said: "At its half-century, if courage, efficiency and vigilance persist, the Group can be one of the most formidable enterprises in the field of publishing and kindred activities."

PETERBOROUGH ADVERTISER : SOME MILESTONES

	Sale price	No of pages	Approx sales	PET sale	Notes
1854	1d	4	800		Launched May as monthly from Cathedral Square
1855	1d	4			Weekly from May 26.
1865			7,000		Pages 31" x 23" wide.
1874					Moved Cathedral Square to Cumbergate.
1875			12,000		
1883					Pages 30" x 24" wide.
1884		8			Pages 24" x 17" wide.
1896			15,000		Control passes to Sir Richard Winfrey.
1898					Peterborough Citizen launched (Tuesdays)
1915			18,000		Sale 25,000 with Citizen.
1918	2d	8			
1924			24,000		Combined sale with Citizen.
1930			30,000		do.
1939					War in Europe until 1945.
1945					Front page news from May 11.
1946					Titles merge as Tuesday and Friday editions of Peterborough Citizen & Advertiser.
1948	3d	8			Price rise July 20.
1950					Moved Cumbergate to Broadway, December.
1953					Newsprint control eased.
1957					Newsprint control ended.
1961		22*	39,000	7,000	Combined sale of two Advertiser editions. Peterborough Evening Telegraph launched May 15.

Year	Price	Pages			Notes
1963	4d		38,000	13,000	Price rise December.
1970	6d		33,000	21,000	Price rise September. Printed offset September.
1971	3p		31,000	22,000	Moved Broadway to Woodston, January. Price decimalised to 3p, February.
	4p				Price rise to 4p, November.
1974		28*	28,000	29,000	Evening paper overtakes Citizen & Advertiser sale.
1975	6p		16,000	28,000	Price rise July. Tuesday edition dropped July.
1976				29,000	Advertiser printed tabloid from June 25. Published Thursdays from September 16.
1977		40*			Combined evening and weekly sale: 44,000.

* Peterborough Advertiser average number of pages per issue.

PETERBOROUGH ADVERTISER :
FINANCIAL COMPARISONS
Covering all company titles

	1901 £	1938 £	1976/77 £
Newspaper sales	2,250	8,086	394,362
Advertisement sales	2,529	15,250	804,164
Wages and salaries	1,732	8,639+	331,800+
Newsprint purchases	1,032	3,797	219,810
Rates and Insurances	58	412	12,447

Last year before war slump.
+ Wages figures include National Insurance not payable in 1901.

EAST MIDLAND ALLIED PRESS LIMITED
Main board Directors from formation in 1947

T. N. Bird	1947-57	Chairman 1947-54
R. P. Winfrey	1947*	Managing Director 1947-62 Chairman 1955-73
T. M. Ashton	1947-70	Deputy Chairman 1955-69
T. F. Chater	1947-50	
H. B. Hartley	1947-54	
D. F. Thew	1947-48	
E. Smedley	1949-66	Managing Director 1955-64
S. Bayliss Smith	1951-70	
C. W. H. Aldridge	1953-76	
F. A. Cooper	1953-69	
P. T. M. Wilson	1955*	
J. Nuttall	1962-65	
H. R. Parkin	1962-64	
R. J. Winfrey	1962*	+Managing Director 1963 Deputy Chairman 1970
P. E. Coles	1965*	
I. C. McKinnon	1966-75	
G. Russell	1967*	+Assistant Managing Director 1967
F. C. Winfrey	1967*	+
G. Ross Russell	1970*	
F. Rogers	1971*	Chairman 1974

A. G. Butler   1973*   +
R. W. Miller   1976*   +
O. D. G. Barr   1976*
     * still serving December 1976
     + fulltime executives at December 1976

HONORARY PRESIDENT

By invitation of the board and in recognition of his long and distinguished contribution to the company, R. P. Winfrey has agreed to accept the title of Honorary President of East Midland Allied Press at the time of his intended relinquishment of all directorships in 1978. P. T. M. Wilson has announced his intention to retire from the board at the same time.

EMAP NATIONAL PUBLICATIONS

Title	Date founded if before EMAP control	Date founded or acquired by EMAP	
Angling Times		1953	
Auto News		1966	5.5.66 to 1.12.66
Bike	1971	1973	from National Magazine Co Ltd
Boat News		1973	7.3.73 to 11.7.73
Fishing		1963	last issue Dec. 1969
Fishing Tackle Dealer	1957	1963	from City Magazines Ltd; became Tackle & Guns 1970
Garden News		1958	
Motor Cycle Mechanics	1959	1974	from Mercury House Publications Ltd
Motor Cycle News	1955	1956	from Cyril Quantrill
Motorcycle Racing		1976	
Popular Motoring	1962	1974	from Mercury House
Practical Gardening	1960	1974	from Mercury House
Practical Photography —as Popular Photography 1954	1959	1970	from Pergamon Press
Sea Angler	1972 Feb.	1972 Oct.	from A. E. Morgan Publications Ltd
Tackle & Guns		1970	see Fishing Tackle Dealer
Trout & Salmon		1955	
Two Wheeler Dealer	1970	1971	from N. J. Publishing Co

EMAP PROVINCIAL PUBLICATIONS

Title	Date founded if before EMAP control	Date founded or acquired by EMAP	
Bedford Mercury	1837	1911	to Bedford Record 1912
Boston Guardian	1854	1925	to Westminster Press 1936, to EMAP 1951, to Lincs Standard 1958
Bury Free Press	1855	1903	
Bury Post	1782	1931	merged with Bury Free Press 1931
Corby Leader		1960	last issue 20.12.74
Fenland Advertiser		1975	see Wisbech Advertiser
Haverhill Echo	1888	1976	from Anglia Echo Newspapers
Haverhill Free Press		1962	discontinued 1976
Hunts County News	1886	1897	merged with Peterborough Advertiser 1926
Kettering Guardian	1882	1924	merged with Kettering Leader 1924
Kettering Observer	1882	1901	merged with Kettering Leader 1891
Kettering Leader	1888	1901	last issue 6.4.73
Lincolnshire Free Press	1847	1949	formerly known as Spalding Free Press
Lynn Advertiser	1841	1922	merged with Lynn News as twice-weekly 1945
Lynn News	1859	1893	
Market Harborough Advertiser	1854	1944	merged with Harborough Mail 1923

Continued on next page

Title	Date founded if before EMAP control	Date founded or acquired by EMAP	
Market Harborough Mail	1890	1944	
Newmarket Journal	1872	1955	
News-Echo		1974	merger of Wellingborough News and Rushden Echo: last issue 15.7.77
Northamptonshire Evening Telegraph	1897	1901	
Peterborough Advertiser	1854	1897	merged with Peterborough Citizen 1946; twice-weekly to 1975; once-weekly thereafter
Peterborough Citizen		1898	
Peterborough Evening Telegraph		1960	
Rushden Argus	1889	1901	merged with Rushden Echo 1930
Rushden Echo	1897	1930	see News-Echo
Spalding Free Press			see Lincs Free Press
Spalding Guardian	1880	1887	
Sports Telegraph (Pink 'Un: previously Football Telegraph)	1895	1901	discontinued 1974
Stamford Mercury	1712(?)	1951	
Suffolk Free Press	1855	1922	
Thrapston Journal	1888	1901	last issue 6.4.73
Wellingborough News	1861	1901	see News-Echo
Wisbech Advertiser	1845	1946	became Fenland Advertiser 1975

INDEX

224

231

232

234

pany, 71; *Stamford Mercury* director, 72; company management, 90, 155, 208, 214; 75th birthday, 93, 94, 133, 202; hopes for R. P. Winfrey, 59, 105; death, 97, 99; tributes, 60. See Belgian refugees, Castor House, Footpaths, League of Nations Union, National Education Association, PSA, Pharmaceutical Society, Admission of Press, Red Cross, Riot Act, Smallholdings, Workmen's Hall, World Brotherhood; also Mrs E. P. Willson, Mrs A. L. P. Eades, Mrs R. P. Agutter (daughters)

Winfrey, Lady (wife), 15, 16, 18, 34, 36, 37, 55, 56, 61, 90, 94, 95, 97, 98, 104, 106, 128, 149

Winfrey, Richard Finch (nephew), 33, 52

Winfrey, Richard Francis (father), 1, 2, 9, 12, 13, 26

Winfrey, Richard John (grandson), 90, 95, 98, 106, 110, 138, 150, 156, 157, 160, 161, 176, 177, 179, 181, 192, 193, 195, 198, 212, 213, 215

WINFREY, RICHARD PATTINSON (son): early days, 24, 44, 52, 69, 104, 105; relations with father, 93, 106; Parliamentary elections, 58, 59, 60, 71, 105; first directorship, 85; barrister, 95, 105, 111; marriage, 60, 95, 105; character, 108, 109, 110, 114, 132, 139, 153, 182, 190, 208;

company management, 90, 98, 99, 119, 121, 132, 133, 139, 143, 144, 149, 153, 158, 169, 204, 212; United States tour, 107, 108; American Medal of Freedom, 108; caravanning, 111; BBC, 113; European tour, 116; magistrate, 111, 113; Royal Commission on Betting etc, 111; Royal Commission on the Press, 121; relations with staff, 108, 133, 134, 139, 153, 169, 170, 171, 179; Africa tour, 63, 156, 175; health, 178, 191; view on national publications, 148; criticisms, 160, 208; 65th birthday, 202; portrait, 112, 203; view on permissiveness, 208; retirement, 112, 188, 194, 203, 213, 215. See East Midland Allied Press, Horses, Ministry of Information, Offset printing, Press Association, Prisoner-of-war parties, Rates, Rowing, Sir Halley Stewart and Trust

Winfrey, Mrs R. P. (daughter-in-law), 95, 96, 112, 113, 133, 192, 202

Wing, Tycho, 46

Wireless pictures, 81

Wisbech, 9

Wisbech Advertiser, Wisbech Advertiser & Pictorial, 118, 119, 123, 124, 125, 132, 135, 136, 164, 168, 179, 183, 209. See *Fenland Advertiser*

Wisbech Chronicle, 10, 30

Wood, Arthur, 212

Wood, Ian, 142, 199